LOBBYISTS FOR HIRE

To Muriel, Rachael and Paul

Lobbyists For Hire

KEVIN MOLONEY
Bournemouth University

Dartmouth

Aldershot • Brookfield USA • Singapore • Sydney

Published by
Dartmouth Publishing Company Limited
Gower House
Croft Road
Aldershot
Hants GU11 3HR
England

Dartmouth Publishing Company
Old Post Road
Brookfield
Vermont 05036
USA

British Library Cataloguing in Publication Data
Moloney, Kevin
Lobbyists for hire
1. Lobbyists 2. Lobbying
I. Title
324.4

Library of Congress Cataloging-in-Publication Data
Moloney, Kevin, 1943-
Lobbyists for hire / Kevin Moloney.
p. cm.
Includes bibliographical references.
ISBN 1-85521-794-5
1. Lobbying–Great Britain. 2. Lobbyists–Great Britain.
I. Title.
JN329.P7M65 1996
324'.4'0941–dc20 96-1352
CIP

ISBN 1 85521 794 5

Printed and bound in Great Britain by
Ipswich Book Co. Ltd., Ipswich, Suffolk

Contents

Preface .... **ix**

1 Lobbyists for hire: mercenary soldiers for the Anonymous Empire? **1**
Commercial lobbying - a 'naughty and nice' image? 2
Nomenclature 5
Relations with public relations: an illuminating dispute 6
Business aspects - size and activity levels. 8
Business apects - fees 10
European and Canadian aspects 11
Their Background 12
What do commercial lobbyists do? 13
Whom do commercial lobbyists lobby? 15
Lobbying styles 17
Are commercial lobbyists effective? 17
Conclusion 19
Note 20

2 Lobbyists for hire: public relations and group theoretical perspectives **21**
Introduction 21
Relationships with public relations perspectives - the pluralist, liberal model. 22
Relationships with public relations perspectives - critical theory. 25
Political studies perspectives on commercial lobbying 27
The classical pluralist 'fit' 28
'Fit' with other models 29
A neo-pluralistic perspective 31
A privileged interest? 32
Conclusion 34
Notes 34

3 Lobbyists for hire: the clients **36**
Introduction 36
Staff officers to the Board 36
Patterns of involvement 38
Document monitoring: is it lobbying? 38
The propensity to hire lobbyists 39

1. The light hirers: 'you don't launch unguided missiles' 39
2. The intermittent hirers: 'a project basis' 41
3. The heavy hirers: 'I use them as eyes and ears' 41
light hirers 41
intermittent hirers 42
heavy hirers 42
Background to positions on the propensity to hire scale 42
The light hirers 42
The intermittent hirers 44
The heavy hirers 45
Lobbyists as suppliers of access to decision-makers 46
Direct access by clients 49
Lobbyists as suppliers of representations to decision-makers 52
Lobbyists as suppliers of policy advice to clients 52
Lobbyists as suppliers of administrative support 55
Lobbyists as fee chargers 56
Lobbyists as sellers of services to clients 60
Lobbyists and client perception of confidentiality and of conflict of interest .. 60
Lobbyists and client perception of their reputation 62
Conclusion 63
Notes 64

4 Lobbyists for hire: a profile (part one) 65
Introduction 65
The lobbyists 65
Lobbyists and their clients by sector 67
The good client 70
'We're a distress purchase': the business of getting clients 72
Lobbyists and fees 75
Lobbyists: nomenclature and self-perceptions 79
Conclusion 82
Notes 83

5 Lobbyists for hire: a profile (part two) 84
Introduction 84
'The cerebral and the arms and legs' - a range of services 84
Backgrounder and foregrounder types 90
Gaining access to and making representations to decision-makers 91
Lobbyists, clients and policy 97
'Part of the machinery of government almost' - lobbyists' perceptions of relationships with decision-makers 99
'One of a great many voices in play' - lobbyists and their perceptions of value for money to clients 104

Conclusion 109
Note 110

6 Lobbyists for hire: the decision-makers 111
Introduction 111
A range of reactions: MPs 113
More positive than negative: '. . . they do oil the system' 113
More negative than positive: 'They're just paid hacks' 115
More neutral than for or against: 'They're a little help: they're no hindrance' 116
A range of reactions: civil servants and special advisers 117
'Good lobbying is best conducted if it's not so naked' - seeking contact 119
'They came in themselves but I think with a hire lobbyist in tow' - how the decision-makers are lobbied 121
Why decision-makers let themselves be lobbied: 'the art really lies in filtering out naked self interest' 125
Perceived influence and effectiveness 127
Concerns in the relationships 130
Conclusion 132
Notes. 134

7 Lobbyists for hire: corporate accessories 135
Focus on the hiring 135
Commercial lobbyists as corporate advisers 137
Hired lobbyists as political advocates 138
Commercial lobbyists are client-led 139
Varied relationships with decision-makers 140
1950 to 1994: a long perspective 141
The well connected hyphen 144
Hired lobbyists and effectiveness 145
Theoretical perspectives on commercial lobbying 148
The Nolan Committee and light 150
Nolan and the future 153
Notes 155

Appendix 1 A note on commercial lobbying and Parliamentary representation 157
Individual v functional representation? 157
A complex reconciliation 158
Lobbyists and constituencies 159

Appendix 2 Attributes of the 'perfect' lobbyist for hire 161
Introduction 161
Personableness 161
Policy knowledge 162
Recognition of mutuality 162
Timing 162
Contact with client 163

Annotated bibliography 164
Official publications 164
Books and monographs 164
Unpublished theses 174
Journal articles, papers and booklets 175
Newspapers, Magazines, Yearbooks and Directories 179

Preface

Observing public affairs as citizen, teacher and hobbyist makes you a great spotter of movements in the political undergrowth, that part of the political structure, supportive of the great functions, institutions and rituals of state, but overhung and obscured by them. Observation throughout the 1980s and 1990s suggests that lobbying is a distinguishing, widespread and growing feature of contemporary UK politics and in response to this supportive environment, the species *lobbyist* is becoming more varied.

Lobbyists thrive on change relationships - either furthering them or hindering them - and in that battle for the marginal advantage offered by change, permanent spokespersons for companies, trade associations, charities and non-governmental voluntary organisations are a well-observed feature. But from the early 1980s, a new breed of lobbyist was spotted: spokesmen and women who made a living hiring themselves out to different interests; speaking for a succession of big companies, often during contested take-over bids.

These lobbyists for hire are often disapproved of as one of the less attractive imports from American politics. They, on the other hand, justify their work in the solemn terms of the right to petition Government and the right to seek redress. Who are these new lobbyists? Why have they appeared in numbers now? What do they do behind the bland corporate-speak of large organisations? The push and pull of public criticism and self-defence has given them a 'naughty and nice image.' But do they enhance or endanger the public policy-making process? The research for this book (and its antecedent PhD) concludes that lobbyists for hire - commercial lobbyists - are a small, distinct, accepted but minor addition to the cast of role-players in UK public policy-making. Their differentiating feature, marking them off from other types of lobbyist, is that they are for hire and it is *the feature* which is the least previously written of. There is little explicit theory of commercial lobbying: it is best accounted for as an implication of neo-pluralism (Chapter Two).

They are mostly hired by large businesses and less so by public sector interests facing change (Chapters One and Three). These clients show varying propensities to hire and services hired in by clients can be grouped under four headings (Chapter Three). Commercial lobbyists are client-led and have no independent political influence (Chapters Four and Five). They are businesses seeking market share, offering only what hirers want. Their work can be viewed through the prism of two ideal types: backgrounder and foregrounder (Chapter Five). On balance, they work on the processes of policy-making rather than its contents; are less rather than more visible in the policy process; more reactive than proactive in their client relationships.

They have a range of negative and positive relationships with decision-makers (Chapter Six), who accept them principally because they are the access to information otherwise difficult to get.

There is no proven method for evaluating their contribution to UK public policy outcomes (Chapters One and Seven). The evidence suggests that the contribution is minor. But this 'minor' conclusion has to be qualified when looked at from the hirers' viewpoint, from the viewpoint of large companies: for them, the hiring may help yield competitive advantage.

Commercial lobbyists are corporate accessories (Chapter Seven) and the source of any concern about their practices and about asymmetrical access to decision-makers lies in the nature of their relationships with other more substantial players in the UK public policy process.

What is 'naughty' and what is 'nice' about hiring lobbyists will be better understood if this policy process is more transparent and accessible. The early 1995 hearings of the Nolan Committee and its first report on MPs, Ministers, outside interests and lobbying is a means to both better understanding and maybe to better practice. Nolan is a light shining into this undergrowth and the fundamental characteristic of its reform programme is that where hired lobbyists cause concern in public policy-making, the solution lies in the reform of MPs' and Ministers' behaviour and in the reform of the machinery of Government. Hired lobbyists relate to political structures and cultures largely as a consequence and not as a cause. They are agents, not principals.

My thanks to more expert observers for their help in spotting movement and growth in the political undergrowth, especially to Prof. Geoffrey Alderman, Dr. Julia Kiely, Dr. Jon White and Prof. Grant Jordan. And without the technical mastery of Sue Lindley of Bournemouth University's Electronic Publishing Unit, this text would not have been produced. Finally, thanks to all those clients, lobbyists and decision-makers who gave time and views on the new species *hired lobbyist* therein.

Kevin Moloney
October, 1995.

1 Lobbyists for hire: mercenary soldiers for the Anonymous Empire?

'You have to see lobbying as a battle.' *(The Government Report 35)*

Although lobbyists for hire (commercial lobbyists) came to public notice, if not notoriety, in the UK from the mid 1980s onwards, it was Finer (1966, 2nd ed.) who first noted their increase in the eight years between the first and second editions of his *Anonymous Empire.* By 1966, he had detected that the Empire was making more use of what could be described as an 'army of mercenaries' - professionals offering their services to interests which wanted to lobby public office holders and which were willing to pay for those services. He made clear that he was talking about lobbyists for hire, although he did not use that term.

He was explicitly not concerned with what can be called the 'regular army' of lobbyists, those who are employed full-time by an organisation. Instead he links the lobbyists for hire with the then 300 public relations firms in London which had a relationship 'something like that of an advocate' (Finer; 136) to their clients. He listed some of the issues with which these firms could have been involved: the aftermath of the Belgian withdrawal from the Congo; the public standing of the Portugese dictator, Dr. Salazar, in the UK, and the activities of the North Scotland Hydro-Electric Board.

He wrote that 'a number of PR agencies have begun to act as "contact men" with Members of Parliament' (138). He did not object intrinsically to 'this go-between role'. It was the failure to disclose it which irked him and he suggested the establishment of a body like the Press Council which would enforce an ethical code and register lobbyists, their clients, payments, methods of lobbying and the legislation targeted. Finer notes that the 'suggested Council by its nature would disclose MP advisers to PR firms who acted for a consideration' (139). Finer's major focus of criticism was the lack of transparency in British lobbying and he would not have been surprised that it took until 1992 for a Select Committee to recommend a register of these lobbyists. Nor would he have been surprised at the impassioned resistance shown by some MPs in Parliamentary debate and votes in the summer of 1995 to the Nolan Report's recommendation for disclosure of MPs' earnings from lobbyists.

Finer's work looked at interest group politics at the points of decision-making in Whitehall and Westminster: the focus here is a practice in support of those politics.

Clearly group politics are a necessary condition for the existence of commercial lobbying while commercial lobbying is not a sufficient condition for group politics. Because of the centrality of groups to UK politics, academic study of them is established (inter alia Stewart [1958]; Alderman [1984]; Wilson, G. K. [1985]; Grant [1989]; Jordan & Richardson [1987]; Rush (ed.) [1990]; Richardson [1993]).

But in this literature commercial lobbyists hardly figure, with little more than occasional walk-on parts in a larger play. Those parts are centre stage here and the other happenings and role players of groups are off centre - though always present, just outside the main frame and always providing the contextual linkages through which to understand 'for hire' lobbying.

Commercial lobbying - a 'naughty and nice' image?

There was a time in UK politics when hiring lobbyists was hardly known and what was known was not admired. Doig (1990; 49) reported that Attlee's Government set up a Select Committee in 1950 which did not 'see any future for the "the intermediary", the private middleman . . .'.

Doig also noted (50) that the Committee on Intermediaries was not prescient: 'What it did not, or could not anticipate, however, was the possibility of those from inside the "system" setting themselves up as intermediaries and selling their knowledge, access and contacts'. Today these lobbyists for hire are now a distinct, additional and quite visible feature of the British system of public policy-making. Indeed Finer can be credited in part with the term 'the lobby' coming into the mainstream of UK language: his obituarist (*The Times,* June 1993) noted that it had a 'rather too American ring' to win speedy widespread usage and that 'lobbyists' only became current in the 1980s.

These 'for hire' lobbyists have been described variously. Apart from 'contact men' (1966; 138), Finer also called them 'hired advocates' (139). Another term used is 'commercial lobbyists' (Jordan & Richardson 1987; 261) and 'parliamentary consultants' (Alderman 1984; 132) yet another. Alderman wrote that:

> Parliamentary consultants are brokers. They act as advocates for their clients in much the same way as solicitors and barristers present cases in court. They spend a great deal of time just meeting people, listening as well as talking. A pressure group could lobby on its own: many do so. Otners, particularily those immersed in the ways of the British government or not fortunate enough to have acquired the services of an MP or ex-MP or an 'honorary research assistant' to an MP, save themselves a great deal of time and probably money by employing professional assistance.

Grantham (1989) favoured the description 'political consultant' but noted also the titles 'public affairs', 'government relations', and 'political PR'. Later, 'political consultant' is again favoured by Grantham and Seymour-Ure (1990).

Turning to the three contexts in which lobbying is most discussed, (the political, the journalistic and the academic), the most common descriptor is also the oldest: lobbyist. It is the description used by the House of Commons' Select Committee on Members' Interest in their 1987-88 and 1990-91 reports. Bryce (1928; 928) used lobbyist when he wrote at the end of the 19th century and quoted an American source, Mr. Spofford, in an amusing listing of the different versions of the lobbyist's calling. Greer (1985; 19) used it when he wrote about the professional lobbyist and called for a register of such people.

Some practitioners, however, appear to be coy about the word lobbyist. Of the 129 members of the Public Relations Consultants' Association (PRCA) listed in its 1989 *Public Relations Year Book* less than 20 listed lobbying as a service offered but none used the word itself. Favoured instead were titles such as 'government relations', 'government affairs', 'issue management', 'parliamentary counselling', 'parliamentary relations', 'political counselling', 'political opinion forming' and 'public affairs' (the most common). This plurality of titles makes it difficult to accurately measure amounts of lobbying done by public relations firms (and by lawyers). In the case of PRCA members, measurement in the first instance would mean establishing that different titles are descriptions of the same or similar activities and secondly it would mean establishing that lobbying can be separated from public relations activity in general.

Why did PRCA members not use the word lobbying? This is perhaps an indication that its connotations are both negative and positive - and perhaps predominantly negative for practitioners vis-à-vis their own self-esteem and commercial advancement. Indeed many references to lobbying are pejorative. Wootton (1970; 17) described 'lobby' as 'derogatory an epithet as one can think of . . . ' in the US. In a foreword to deKieffer (1981), Congresswoman Pat Schroeder noted that in the 18th century, lobbyists were called 'lobbiers and were little more than merchants of greed' and that 'today . . . the greed factor has been diluted by the rise in citizen group lobbying'.

Alderman (123) referred to pressure groups (sometimes the clients of lobbyists for hire) as generating 'suspicion, mistrust and even fear' in British Government. He had already noted (5) that 19th century English writers described lobbying in a tone which suggested that it was 'foreign if not actually immoral'. Richardson and Jordan (261) quote Alderman as above and then target the 'for hire' lobbyist for a sceptical mention:

> For no very clearly articulated reasons, 'professional' lobbying seems to give rise to more unease than a cause or a company putting forward its own case (264).

Jordan picked up the same tone when he writes about 'naughty and nice' lobbying, (1989; 107-113) and the front cover of the first UK book entirely devoted to the subject (Jordan (ed.), 1991) shows a huddle of rather worn, raffish, middle-aged men talking over drinks and a cigar. The sub-title of the text is *Politics for Profit in Britain.* A practising lobbyist for hire, Ian Greer, reflected this air of being at the shadowy edge of the acceptable. He wrote (1985, acknowledgements):

> The Parliamentary lobbyist who emerges from the shadows to write a book about the intricacies of his art must, in the public perception, be a contradiction in terms. What has emerged is an attempt partly to dispel the mystique in which the media fondly shroud the work of the lobbyist.

Later he expands on the role of the press in this murky image creation (119) with the observation that the 'press at times likes to portray the lobbyist as a somewhat shadowy or sinister figure working furtively behind the scenes on behalf of equally shady clients . . .'. Greer would no doubt feel vindicated on reading one vitriolic attack on his 'art' by a journalist under the headline 'The Unsavoury Enemies of Democracy' (Howard, 1989).

Jordan perhaps best summed up this air of uncertain moral standing when he quotes an American lobbyist:

> My mother has never introduced me to her friends as 'My son, the Lobbyist'. 'My son, the Washington Representative', maybe. Or 'the Legislative Consultant'. Or 'the Government Relations Counsel'. But never as 'the Lobbyist'. I can't say I blame her (Jordan; 13).

Dubs went beyond social embarrassment and (1989; 193) mounted a critique of 'for hire' lobbyists: they can 'buy' influence because they have 'much greater resources than social lobbyists'; they have conflicts of interest, working sometimes for both Government departments and clients who relate to those departments; they claim 'success' fees (fees predicated on pre-stated outcomes) and they retain MPs.

Concern over 'buying' influence was also picked up by Rush (1990) who wrote about commercial lobbyists as a resource in what he called 'pressure politics', adding:

> . . . although it does not follow that the wealthier will always succeed, there is a danger that, however legitimately, money will be the key to success. (146)

But these lobbyists also have countervailing advantages for Dubs (195): they reduce overheads for their clients; they have computer databases for targeting groups; they know MPs and civil servants; they can do research, and can lobby Brussels. In the end, although he criticises the activity, he recommends it in some circumstances.

But the major thrust of his book was to develop another category of lobbying in contra-distinction - social lobbying which is defined (192) as 'lobbying by pressure groups, trade unions and concerned individuals done for non-commercial motives which are usually ideological or political'. In fact, his text can be seen as a DIY manual on how the politicised layperson can lobby: he de-professionalises lobbying, saying that much of his advice is common sense. The *Government Report* (1987) can also be seen as a training text but for the professional. It surveyed MPs, Ministers and officials and drew a picture of the operational circumstances facing lobbyists which could be the content of a staff development programme. Wolpe (1990) set himself this training task for the Washington DC professional lobbyist and deKeiffer (1981) for the citizen group lobbyist.

Nomenclature

This variety of descriptors raises the question of which title to use. In talking about the general process of groups influencing governmental decision-making, there is no reason for departing from the generic title of 'lobbyists' and 'lobbying'. A choice, however, is faced when we turn to lobbyists 'for hire'. The phrase 'for hire' lobbyist is attractive because of its Anglo-Saxon directness and its focus on the concept of switching among interests to be represented. 'Influence peddler' and 'corridor creep' are unacceptable, at least on ground of propriety.

Dropping the epithet leaves just the proper noun 'lobbyist' and that descriptor is the most common referent to the subject in political, journalistic and academic circles. (Davies [1985] noted that 'lobby' was used in Washington in 1832 and quotes *OED* that it entered British politics in 1856). But on its own, 'lobbyist' is not specific enough for it includes lobbyists who are the full-time employees or voluntary workers of an organisation. This work follows Thomas and Hrebenar in defining in-house lobbyists as lobbyists who lobby only for their employer (1990; 5).

Reluctance on the part of some lobbyists to use 'lobbyist' publicly about themselves has been noted eariier. Perhaps these recalcitrants are seeking the exclusiveness of a new title which will be attractive commercially because of its novelty. This is not a relevant concern here and it is argued that 'lobbyist' should be used but with an epithet which distinguishes the mobile freelance from the full-time employee. 'Professional' will not do as it implies that there is another category which falls below some standard of behaviour. 'Parliamentary' as the epithet would be misleading as much of the lobbying is not directed to Westminster, while 'political consultant' is too broad, not fully connecting with lobbying and suggestive of American image-makers operating in politics. 'Consultant' is another possible epithet but it carries two possible connotations which are in tension with each other. These connotations are: an air of functional superiority as implied by teams of medical doctors in a hierarchy headed by a clear chief; and secondly an expert available for hire to address a wide variety of situations, as in management consultant.

The first of these connotations carries an air of functional hierarchy and status superiority which is unwarranted here and the epithet should therefore be avoided. The second connotation is close to the 'for hire' sense which needs to be expressed but the mixing of the two senses above makes the use of 'consultant' confusing.

'Commercial' has a market place connotation which is relevant and suggests movement between clients without being mercenary. 'Commercial lobbyist' is therefore perhaps the least unsatisfactory descriptor to use about individuals. It is noted that Jordan and Richardson (1987) used this title as a generic descriptor in their book and that *The Independent* newspaper (31 December, 1991; 1) also employed 'commercial lobbying' in a report on a Commons' register for lobbyists. *The Commercial lobbyists* was the title of the first complete UK text (Jordan) devoted to lobbyists for hire.

Usage here will therefore be 'commercial lobbyist' as the major descriptor. But the phrase will not be used in the sense of lobbyists working only for commercial interests, for such usage would be inaccurate. For variety and ease of reading, the terms 'lobbyist for hire' and 'hired lobbyist' will be used as alternative descriptors. (Jordan [65] pointed out that the descriptor 'contract lobbyist' is largely an American usage). When writing about a group of commercial lobbyists organised together in a business, the term 'lobbying firm' will be used.

Relations with public relations: an illuminating dispute

The review of what commercial lobbyists call themselves reveals a debate (reflected later in the views of lobbyists in Chapter Four) as to whether they are in public relations or not. Some are emphatic that they are not and behind this self-defined act of exclusion is apparently a perception by them that public relations has a lightweight, non-respectable, gimmicky reputation which some lobbyists, who perceive themselves to be participants in public policy making, do not want to be associated with.

It can be argued that this judgement is behind the views of two lobbyists who have spoken publicly about the relationship. Jenny Jeger, who was a founder member of the lobbying firm GJW Government Relations, is quoted by *Marketing* magazine (1984), as saying: 'We do not consider ourselves to be PR people - in fact we dis-associate ourselves strongly from PR agencies.'

This was a long held view for she repeated it in the public relations weekly trade magazine *PR Week* (1989) under the headline 'Lobby falls foul of its 'booze and bribes' image', adding the charge of incompetence.

The latter charge is repeated by Greer (1985; 121) who says that 'a great deal of damage' has been done to the reputation of commercial lobbyists because public relations companies have lobbied without the 'necessary knowledge and skills to support a client's case'. Hull (1991; 8) takes up a similar allegation when he writes about lobbying in Brussels from his vantage point of adviser to the EU Environment Commission:

> Public relations firms on the whole are not well regarded. They tend to be perceived as glib purveyors of a tale which they have prepared for a particular meeting and unable normally to get involved in any kind of detailed discussion of an issue because they do not understand it fully once the discussion strays outside their brief.

The Government Report also asked its sample of MPs, Ministers and officials about whether lobbying is part of 'PR'. There were critical remarks about public relations with over 70% of the sample not wanting to be 'PR targets' (21), and with PR personnel picked out for a general broadside against inappropriate, lightweight lobbying.

But *The Government Report* assumed definitions of public relations and did not explicate them. Lack of research, one-sidedness and overselling (12-13) were castigated as lobbying failures and lobbying success was found to lie in large part in 'quality of the argument' (4) and in 'advocacy' of a case delivered with 'professionalism' (4). There is a tendentious quality to the report in this respect because the implication is that these points of good lobbying practice cluster around a non-public relations pole which could be described as lawyer-like issue advocacy. Behind this may be the usage of the words 'public relations' as a ritualised term of disapproval.

This dis-association theme is developed by lobbyist Charles Miller (1987; x) who wrote that he wanted to take the 'science and art' of dealing with the UK Government out of the 'often lightweight province of an exercise in PR and put it in its proper perspective'. He added that working with Government borrows technical knowledge from the legal profession and contacts from public relations. Lobbying is an extension of public relations when image building and mobilization of opinion is required but parts company from the latter when advocacy and knowledge of public policy is required.

He makes public relations a strong peripheral device aiding lobbying but outside the core activity of case advocacy to public policy makers. He concluded that the two disciplines work well side by side and that both must be learnt by those seeking to influence Government. (Hennessy [1989; 342] writes of Miller's book as the 'equivalent of Questions of Procedures for Ministers for those who would influence the mighty').

All this positioning - polite and impolite - has business consequences in the market place for hired lobbyists. The manoeuvring continued when *PR Week* (1989) reported that many commercial lobbyists were not members of the Public Relations Consultants Association (PRCA) while another director of GJW, Wilf Meeks, is quoted as saying that his company supports the introduction of a Parliamentary register of lobbyists but does not want it to be policed by the PRCA - 'a self-important trade association'. Again the thrust is dis-association from public relations. On the other side, the PRCA believes that most of its members are engaged in lobbying and that there had been a substantial increase in fee income from the activity.

It is clearly not in the interests of public relations consultancies to let themselves be excluded by job demarcation from a growing activity - especially if the boundaries are drawn up by competitors. Equally, it is not in the interests of lobbyists who have no financial or organisational link with public relations firms to welcome newcomers into their market. These lobbyists are a business. The business development perspective should always be in mind when relations between independent lobbying firms and public relations consultancies are discussed.

This public argument about the lobbying/public relations connection is important because it is a reminder that commercial lobbying is a competitive business with matters of perceived status surrounding it. The connection also illuminates what hired lobbyists do.

Business aspects - size and activity levels

A 1986 estimate, (Norton & Grantham,1986; 4-8), put the number of lobbying firms at between 30 and 40 while there was another 40 to 100 individuals who operated alone as lobbyists. On top of these categories, there were the 40 to 200 public relations companies which offer lobbying as one service among many. *Dod's Parliamentary Companion* in 1987 (716) included for the first time a list of 'parliamentary consultants' (commercial lobbyists) and by 1989 the list had nearly trebled to 36 (504) and to 45 (797) by 1993. The 1991/92 *Directory of Public Affairs and Government Relations* (Lloyd & Atack) had 35 entries (but publication was discontinued). Hennessy (1989; 340) judged them to be a necessary inclusion on another list - that of 'pressures pushing through the walls of Whitehall and onto the ministers' and officials' desks'. Grantham (1989; 503-518) describes it as 'one of the major growth industries'. There is some evidence that demand for lobbying continues to grow in the 1990s: PR Week (1994, May 26) reports that lobbying accounts for a third of the reasons given by companies for hiring PR agencies.

Doig (1986a; 518-519) wrote that there are 'two main reasons for the upsurge - or the awareness of the upsurge - in the use of professional parliamentary lobbyists or consultants'. He listed the lobbyists as being more sophisticated in their techniques of persuasion and secondly 'an increasing number of MPs for whom the world of lobbying and consultancy work is a lucrative activity that they can handle together with their Parliamentary duties, thus complementing adequate but not excessive parliamentary incomes'. Grantham and Seymour-Ure (Rush, 1990; 46-47) are more systemic in their analysis of growth. They write of groups pushed out of the policy process by Thatcherite dismantling of corporatism seeking ways back to decision-makers and of the impact of 'radical policies' such as privatisation and deregulation on 'previously dormant groups'. Willis and Grant (1987) have written about the paradox of the 1980s anti-intervention administrations making for the increased politicisation of business as Government seeks to make it responsible for economic management.

There is no current, comparative data on commercial and in-house lobbyists in terms of numbers employed; budgets; issues lobbied on, and contacts with decision-makers. Other dimensions of commercial lobbying are as ill-defined. For example, client identities, their numbers and their public or private status are not clear. What are fee levels and how are they constructed? How is value for money determined by clients? How do decision-makers view hired lobbyists? Are they seen positively or negatively? The literature is largely silent on these matters.

A start to profiling has been made by Moore (1991) who has done in the UK the only previous work which focuses on the business and organisational aspects of commercial lobbying. He looked at GJW, one of the oldest lobbying firms in the UK, and found that 126 organisations were on GJW books over the financial year 1991-2. Companies accounted for 66% of the total and trade associations for another 14%. Public bodies were 12% and the remaining eight per cent were charities and pressure groups. Moore noted the 'overwhelming' predominance of the private sector, listing companies such as property developer Olympia & York, British Sugar and the shipbuilding and armaments manufacturer VSEL (27). Grant (Jordan (ed.), 1991; 100) also noted that 'a large company will probably make use of outside consultants' while earlier Willis and Grant (1987; 170) had listed hiring lobbyists as one of five routes through which companies try to influence public policy.

Balance sheet and profit and loss figures are not given by Moore. But journalism has reported some other important financial indicators. In 1980 three partners formed GJW as a private company but they sold out to the advertising group Lowe Howard-Spink and Bell in 1987 for an estimated £5m; bought it back in 1993 for £1m, and then achieved an audited fee income of £2, 739, 000 (*PR Week*, April, 1993). This placed them in 14th position in the *PR Week* Top 150 consultancies for 1993.

Commercial lobbyist Charles Miller, of the Public Policy Unit, has been the most forthcoming in public about the business aspects of his work (*Financial Times Weekend*, Feb. 29/March 1, 1992, p. X). He reported a turnover of £770,000 with a pre-tax profit of £115,000 in 1991 from some 30 clients. He had a £38,000 salary. Another lobbyist, Douglas Smith, was also forthcoming about the financial aspect of establishing a new lobbying firm (*PR Week*, May, 1993) when he stated that his firm Westminister Advisers moved from £16,000 fees to £166, 000 in 12 months.

Even if there was better knowledge about the size of UK activity, it would not be a big business by the standards of Washington DC. In Jordan (1991), Graham Wilson (65) explained why hired lobbyists have flourished there to the extent of a registered total of 23,011. Moore (54) estimated that they generate the equivalent of £10 billion income, this suggesting that American hired lobbyists are more numerous and productive than the British coalmining industry. The latest US figures are in Heinz et al. (1993; 11) who reported a lower total: in the decade up to 1975, there were between 3,000 and 4,000 lobbyists in Washington and that by 1988, the figures were between 15,000 and 20,000.

Business apects - fees

Apart from journalistic and self-interested estimates, there is no accurate estimate of total fees of commercial lobbyists in the UK. This section brings the published references together for the first time. In 1984 the Select Committee on Members' Interests noted an increase in lobbying generally in its final report but did not quantify (House of Commons 1984-85, 2). A problem here is separating lobbying from other public relations activities. Willis and Grant (172) noted large growth in the latter in the 1980s but the figures quoted do not distinguish lobbying from marketing support work. The PRCA estimated that in 1983 income from commercial lobbying for its members was 'very small' but that by 1988 it had increased to £7m and was some 6% of the membership's total income. The 1989/90 edition of the *PRCA Public Relations Year Book* showed the latter was £142m. Assuming a 6% share again, this gives commercial lobbying an £8.5m turnover by 1990.

Grantham (1989; 505) said that '. . . the industry as a whole is now believed to be worth in excess of £10m a year, up from an estimated £3.25m in 1983/4'. He also quoted a 1985 survey of 180 sizeable UK companies which found that four out of every ten hired lobbyists. Hollingsworth (1991; 111) wrote that political lobbying had 50 firms in the field and a estimated total turnover of £10m. *PR Week* reported (October, 1993) that turnover has risen to an estimated £20-25m. Hollingworth quoted the 1985 survey mentioned above, suggesting that there is no up-to-date monitoring of the field.

Hollingsworth also reported that fees per client range from £2,500 to £5,000 a month and the average annual rate is about £30,000. *PR Week* reported (October, 1990) Westminster Strategy, a large lobbying firm, charging its 30 clients average retainer fees of between £1,500 and £15,000 a month with the average company paying £4,000. Berry (1992; 221-222) set out some fee bands. He noted that for monitoring and information service work, hired lobbyists charged fees between £500 and £1,500 a month and that for direct lobbying work in contact with Ministers and civil servants and for high profile media campaigns, the fee of £5,000 per week was not uncommon. He noted that lobbying companies were professional in the sense that they are in the business of making money and that most lobbyists worked for the highest bidder. Miller (1992) reported individual fees between £1,000 and £15,000 a month. At the other end of the scale, Berry noted that lobbyists will 'in exceptional cases . . . work for nothing' for charities. Moore supported this (27), noting that some clients of GJW in the charity/pressure group sector were non-fee paying.

Fees are also paid out by lobbyists for hire to those who supply services to them and Berry, Doig and Hollingsworth have looked at these payments. Berry said (225) that 'on one level, the relationship is clearly about making money' and that MPs retained by commercial lobbyists were 'likely' to receive annual payments of around £5,000 and £10,000. He noted (226) that some lobbying companies refuse to make such payments on the grounds that it is possible to have access to the policy-making without payment and that such a 'practice is ultimately counter-productive and even potentially damaging'. He calculated that at least 29 PR and lobbying companies are making such payments.

Doig (1986a; 524) calculated from the Register of Members' Interests that 150 MPs held 280 consultancies between them and that 99 are 'consultants on parliamentary matters'. Hollingsworth estimated much higher figures (1) of 382 MPs in January 1991 with commercial interests, holding 522 directorships and 452 consultancies. But these figures appear to be the totality of all MPs' commercial relationships outside the Commons. Links with lobbying firms would be a sub-set of that total. Hollingsworth calculated (119) that there were 35 MPs who were paid advisers or directors to lobbying firms, a figure based on the Register of Members' Interests. His estimates were perhaps accurate for *PR Week* (April, 1993) calculated 'at least 38 MPs linked to agencies'. Doig's figure was 39 MPs who are involved in 'ownership of or employment by consultancy or public relations firms'. He is the most persistent academic critic of the current lobbyist-MP relationship and he has focused on the money linking MPs and lobbying firms (534):

> Support of interests as a result of a personal or ideological interest is one thing: support of interests in return for payment is another.

The latest figures on totals of outside interests of MPs came from the Nolan Committee's first report of May 1995. They are in line with Hollingworth's, namely that 389 of 566 eligible MPs - almost 70% - have financial interests with outside bodies while its estimate of 26 Members with links to hired lobbyists is lower than Doig's or Hollingworth's.

By American standards, UK commercial lobbying is under-developed but it would appear to have doubled or trebled in size during the 1980s. One journalist believed that the political climate in which it operates has become more propitious. In the *Independent*, Marr noted (1992), in a commentary on public expenditure, that 'the days of listening to lobbies are back'. Such times are salad days for hired lobbyists, as is indicated poignantly by the reported loss of £2m in fees for the lobbying firm Ian Greer Associates following allegations in the *Guardian* newspaper that it was involved with payments to two MPs to ask Parliamentary Questions on behalf of Harrods, a client (1n).

European and Canadian aspects

Growth in lobbying has also been noted at EU institutions by Hull (1991), Galle (1992) and Mazey & Richardson (1993) and is analysed here as a comparator of the UK experience. M. Galle, a Euro-MP, has been asked by the European Parliament to devise a scheme of regulation for the 3,000 lobbyists he quoted as operating there. At the same time and perhaps not by coincidence, the European public relations industry has showed an interest in the control of lobbying and and in what may be a defensive move, their trade association CERP (Confederation Européenne des Relations Publiques) is reported by *PR Week* (February, 1993) to be circulating a proposal for a register of lobbyists.

But the Galle figure above may understate activity, for Van Schendelen (1993; 6) reported 10,000 such persons and puts the rapid growth in numbers down to the implementation of the 1986 Single European Act. UK lobbyists were represented in Europe in some force for Lloyd & Atack (viii) reported 15 London lobbyists with European offices. An example of their attention to matters European is the background briefing on EU institutions produced by Laptev (1993) for lobbying firm Charles Barker.

Mazey & Richardson (8) repeated the 3,000 estimate of Galle. They note that one of the 'most striking developments since the mid-1980s has been the rapid increase in the number of professional lobbyists, financial consultants and law firms locating in Europe'. They quoted the magazine *Fortune* as reporting that the PR firm Hill and Knowlton had 21 consultants in Brussels in 1990 and gave the magazine as a source of the 3,000 figure - a figure which was three times higher than in 1987/88. They suggested that saturation had been reached and may be followed by a 'shake-out' as clients 'become more sophisticated in their understanding of the EC (sic) and demand more than mere information-gathering'.

Commercial lobbyists are registered by law in Canada and Rush (1993) has reported that the Canadian Lobbyists' Registration Act of 1989 requires an up-to-date, computerised record open to the public. Hired lobbyists must register and give the names of clients and the subject matter lobbied on but, after themselves lobbying, they fought off a proposal that fees be disclosed. Despite their opposition to registration, Rush (15) showed how some lobbyists have used the register for business intelligence, revealing competitors' accounts and suggesting sources of new work. By extension, a more informed profile of the UK commercial lobbying business would be a by-product of the proposed Commons' register of paid lobbyists (House of Commons 1990-91; 81).

The paragraphs above focus on commercial lobbying in the national contexts of Europe and Canada. But Helm (1991) in *The Independent* touched on - and for the first time in the literature - a new, international context for commercial lobbying. She noted a trend of 'privatising diplomacy' where foreign governments can be represented in the UK by lobbyists; what was new was not the overseas provenence of the client but that the clients were governments.

Their Background

Grantham, (1989; 507-509), noted the 'disparity' of occupational backgrounds and listed fifteen lobbyists by name, summarising their pasts. But what stood out, rather, was the common background of previous involvement with Government as either MP, research assistant, party worker or civil servant. Grantham and Seymour-Ure (1990; 50-56) have drawn up a table of seventeen of the biggest lobbying firms and given short details of their chief personnel: it was in essence a list of people who have changed roles inside the public decision-making process, not a collection of people drawn from a range of significantly different backgrounds. The implication is that hired lobbyists are likely to be political insiders and that they are hired because they possess detailed knowledge of the processes and personalities in the public decision-making process. This insider status may be a major supply side factor affecting their fee levels.

Jordan and Moloney (1993) reviewed the literature on the background of hired lobbyists and noted their 'insider' status: they concluded that the UK literature repeatedly makes the point that lobbyists should first know the political system well from the advantage point of cognate careers. These are usually identified as political, civil service or party apparatachik careers and there is, they argue, an implication that good lobbying can only be done with such backgrounds.

What do commercial lobbyists do?

Hollingsworth (112) wrote that their role is 'to act as a conduit between commercial and consumer outfits and the government' because both parties needed an introduction to each other. Greatorex (1989; 9) elaborated with:

> Clients are offered three main services by lobbyists: monitoring (a daily summary of what goes on at Westminster); mine-detecting (looking for legislation which may affect a client's interests), and fire-fighting (last-ditch aid for a client under threat from new laws or needing political support in a crisis).

In more formal language, Charles Miller told the Commons' Select Committee on Members' Interests (House of Commons 1987-88, 6 ; 416) that lobbying was:

> the business of advising organisations on understanding, monitoring and dealing with the system of government effectively.

He added that the essential characteristic was a combination of research, intelligence gathering and advocacy to targeted individuals in Whitehall and the Commons and that his workplace was organised like a barrister's chambers to achieve this (417).

Wolpe (1990), however, entered the debate about lobbyist/advocate similarity with a strong assertion about the political nature of the lobbying act:

> It is also a myth that only lawyers are capable of providing the most effective lobbying material, or that a lawyer is essential to drafting a bill or amendment. Lawyers hardly have a monopoly on the lobbying process which is based on

> political and substantive expertise. In lobbying, their legal skills are secondary to their persuasive and rhetorical abilities. . . If anything lawyers tend to be verbose: on the Hill, the premium is on brevity and punch. . . As with anyone else, lawyers make good lobbyists when they exhibit political skill (28).

The lobbying firm GJW told the Select Committee (House of Commons 1987-88, 6; 439) of three lobbying functions - monitoring; explanation and education; and influencing legislation (a process Wolpe [3] has called the 'dance of legislation').

Grantham and Seymour-Ure (1990; 66-67) have described monitoring as the daily scrutiny of the Order Paper and Hansard for both Houses; of Green and White Papers; of Early-Day Motions; of Select and Standing Committees meetings; of departmental press notices; of Government and other official reports, and of the output of bodies such as think-tanks and political parties. They then list a more active and substantial task which is to identify those actors in the political process who influence decisions important to their clients. They add that the principal aim is:

> to build up a body of relevant parliamentarians and officials (and anyone else involved with a policy) who are well informed and well-disposed towards a client's case.

But well-informed and well-disposed people are not enough for lobbyists seeking to influence behaviour because:

> . . . it is not passive support that is sought. MPs (and where appropriate, peers) will be urged to table Questions and Early-Day Motions and, where relevant, amendments to bills and advance the case in debate and through meetings and correspondence with the minister.

What these definitions share is a description of lobbying as a continuum of activity which is passive at one end and active towards decision-makers at the other end. It is the difference between collecting data and arguing a case.

This continuum was more fully described by commercial lobbyist David Wedgewood (1987) who delineated his work into an intelligence role and an operational one, each of which can be divided into three sub-areas. Thus monitoring, interpretation and research comprise the intelligence role while the operational role is planning, passive representation and active representation. Wedgewood notes that this latter is popularly known as lobbying and consists of contact with decision-makers to start, stop, or amend legislation; initiate or respond to debate; or have a question asked or countered. He concluded that without the previous five stages, this sixth is unlikely to be successful. For Smith (1992), who is also a commercial lobbyist, lobbying again has several ingredients: communication and pressure. Its objectives range from seeking information, agenda-setting to redressing grievances. Green (1992) also made a distinction between monitoring and lobbying but apparently as distinct and unrelated categories.

Whom do commercial lobbyists lobby?

Much has been written about the targets of lobbying (Westminster and Whitehall) but the nature of the issues lobbied about gets little attention.

About location, Grantham noted (1989; 503) that the title 'Parliamentary consultancy' tends not to be used because it over-emphasises the importance of Westminster. *The Government Report* (23) also picked up on the role of Westminster and half the report's sample of decision-makers thought that lobbyists suffered from 'a failure to appreciate the difference between appearance and reality in the power of MPs . . .'. A junior Whip is quoted:

> There is a major difference between an MP being involved and committed to an issue and mechanically passing representation to a Minister. The MP as a post box is a greatly over-valued asset. Organisations think they are accessing power when in reality their representations either reach the right people via a longer route or they pass through the system unnoticed.

Over 70% of the survey believed that failure to deal effectively with Government stemmed from:

> inadequate understanding of the workings of Government and particularly of the way in which decisions are made on policy and legislative issues (13).

One former Minister said:

> Much lobbying forgets the real art of Government-related advocacy: knowing where decisions gel in the system. Success usually lies in putting your arguments well to officials. You can take MPs to lunch at the Horseguard's Hotel and often see across the room the officials you ought to be lobbying (17).

Casey has called the focus on the legislature a 'very narrow definition' (1991;1) and he preferred 'to solicit the support of influential people': perhaps unsurprising in his case given that he was an Under-Secretary at the DTI before practising as a commercial lobbyist. Miller (1988;13) graphically makes the same point when he says that 'the real lobbying work is still carried on in those dull [Whitehall] offices'. But this does not appear to be a point taken by lobbyists generally for *The Government Report* found that current and former civil servants reported that they were neglected by lobbyists.

But the case for Parliament as a significant, continuing target for lobbying is made by Judge (1990;19-31). He is critical of pluralist writers such as Richardson and Jordan who characterise policy-making as 'bureaucratic accommodation' between Government departments and pressure groups arranged in 'policy sectors' and 'policy communities'. This leads to the sectorisation of Government into 'sub-governments'.

Judge counter-argued with a restatement (28-29) of the views of classical pluralists like Dahl and Truman that pluralism operates in a climate of shared values which are expressed in elections and representative institutions. In this way, lobbyists (in-house or hired) have to heed Parliament as its consent to 'bureaucratic accommodation' is needed in the 'last instance' (39).

Jordan and Moloney (13) have argued that good lobbying practice about where (and how) to lobby must be predicated on assumptions about the case being made. They noted criticism about the lack of access to official channels in Britain and the EU but they suspected that groups with access difficulties are making demands too major to be handled in such channels. The lobbyist who is using official rather than political channels (Whitehall rather than Westminster) was likely to want something specific and congruent with established values and policy. Here the lobbyist was in a position to argue that in the light of existing understandings, a minor sounding change would be sensible. The lobbyist was not usually in the business of asking for things that appear to be controversial.

About the nature of issues lobbied on, technical policy can hide the politically controversial and how the technical and the political aspects of an issue are presented is a major lobbying skill. For example, by getting lightweight trucks reclassified as cars in 1989, Japanese industry was able to save $500m in US taxation per year (Choate, 1990; 4).

The technical competence of civil servants can also influence where lobbyists lobby. The relatively high UK level of official competence means that Whitehall is a very substantial target but, ironically, lobbyists in Brussels can sometimes find underdeveloped competence an advantage. Gardner (1991; 66) noted:

> The low ranking Eurocrat working on a technical proposal frequently suffers from a 'European information deficit' all his own. He may be the only government official assigned to develop a proposal in a highly technical area.

Hull (1991; 4) also painted a picture of isolated Brussels officialdom:

> the early thinking about any proposal takes place usually in the office of one person who will have the responsibility of drafting legislation . . . At the beginning he is a very lonely man with a blank piece of paper in front of him, wondering what to put on it.

Berry (1984; 120) also took up the competency point when he argued that successful intervention at the technical level requires mastery of the brief by the American lobbyist:

> Lobbyists who have mastered the complexities of their policy area enter a select group of experts who talk the same language. Washington representatives with a high level of policy expertise are more valuable to those in government because policy makers can draw upon their knowledge of efforts to solve difficult issues.

Miller makes a similar point when (1987; 135) he analysed the roles of advocacy and public relations in UK lobbying.

Lobbying styles

In an analysis of lobbying styles, Jordan and Moloney (9) argued that a too high profile style and a too long request list adopted by some American lobbyists were inappropriate in the UK and Europe. As a member of the European Parliament put it, 'hard sell' and 'instant' lobbying are out of tune and even seen as offensive (quoted in Gardner; 63). Lobbying over the fine point of policy was more likely to succeed than frontal assaults on principles.

Scholzman and Tierney (1986; 369) made this point about American lobbying:

> The probability of success appears to vary inversely with the scope of the demand. Organisations whose political ends are narrow and technical are more likely to be influential than those whose goals are more encompassing. In general, it is easier to affect the details of policy than its broad outlines: and . . . this is not a negligible form of influence.

Berry (1984) noted that no US interest group ever gets all it wants. So the lobbyist is engaged in indentifying the workable compromise. Wittenberg and Wittenberg (1989; 105) agreed:

> Lobbying is often the art of compromise, so the guy you represent must agree in advance on what would be an acceptable result. And you need some flexibility to make a deal.

Smith (1988; 323) gave the example of Congressional staff going out to lobbyists to get expert views on proposals: 'Does that work? Does that solve your problem? And, if not, how can we correct it?' The views of decision-makers in Chapter Six puts the above behaviour into a UK context.

Are commercial lobbyists effective?

According to Grant (1989; 113-115), methodological problems prevented a clear answer to the larger question of evaluating interest group effectiveness. Wootton called it (1970; 73) 'a real Irish bog of a subject that has claimed many victims': Wilson (1990; 34) concluded that it was impossible to measure. And it is argued here that by extension the same problems prevent a clear answer to the narrower and dependent question of evaluating the effectiveness of hired lobbyists. Miller (Jordan 1991; 63) and Grantham and Seymour-Ure (Rush 1990; 72) made similar points. Noting Richardson's (1993; 7) view that policy-making is becoming more complex and unpredictable because of 'the increased mobilisation of interests in society', the chances of developing a methodology decrease.

Grant (1989) listed the difficulties of evaluating group effectiveness. They were the problems of secret government; the simplicity or complexity of objectives sought through lobbying; difficulties of identifying whether lobbying action or some other behaviour brought about success; internal politics of the group influencing which and how issues are lobbied, and finally government tactics of initially appearing obdurate in order to concede later.

Commercial lobbyists, as the agents of interests and an intervening variable between interests and Government, are another difficulty. Interests groups (usually in the form of sectional groups) are their clients. Hired lobbyists are therefore constrained in their actions by the institutional and environmental factors which influence groups - their clients. They have to act in the context given by their principals and this constraining context makes evaluation of their effectiveness problematical. None of the UK literature offers a methodology for evaluating the effectiveness of hired lobbying but there are *post hoc* and often self-interested claims in the literature that particular lobbies were effective (Rush (ed.), 213-231; Jordan (ed.), 120-135; Grantham, 509-511). The interviews with lobbyists in Chapter Five indicate that they do not claim any evaluation methodology: furthermore they hesitate to claim that their lobbying was the single cause of effectiveness in any particular case.

In the US literature, Heinz et al (1993) showed similar reticence in their study of Washington lobbying but Thomas and Hrebenar in their analsysis of lobbying at state level (1990) offered a model for evaluating effectiveness. (See Grant [1989; 117] for a typology of factors affecting group effectiveness). They surveyed (25-27) 'policy-makers and political observers' in US states and combined ten factors into their model. These included how well the public official knows the commercial lobbyist; perceived levels of lobbyist credibility; nature of the specific issue lobbied on, and overall political influence of the group. But their model has a millenarian air about it in that conditions 'must all be present to produce the ideal situation of maximising the influence of a lobbyist . . . ' Secondly it is not clear whether the model is about the effectiveness of groups or of hired lobbyists: one of the factors is 'potential for the lobbyist's group to enter into coalitions and to compromise'. The model also has a low predictive quality in that most of the conditions have high degrees of non-measurability (e.g. 'political cohesiveness of the lobbyist's group membership'). Secondly it is not clear how to relate degrees of effectiveness to various factors.

On balance the measurement difficulties remain. Grant (73) summed up:

> . . . it must be noted that although many consultancy firms are very politically sophisticated and display a high level of professional skill, there is always an element of the 'emperor's clothes' about the work of professional lobbyists. There is never a tangible end product which can be attributed to the efforts of the lobbyist: if the campaign is successful, it may have nothing to with the lobbyist's efforts.

Grant (116) suggested, after Whiteley and Winyard (1987), that interviewing participants and getting their subjective assessment (the method used here) may be the best available method for measuring lobbying effectiveness if the direct observation of policy-making was not possible.

Alongside the effectiveness debate about the activity of lobbying, there is a literature (mostly US) on the perceived behaviour of the individual lobbyist. It lists personal attributes. Thomas and Hrebenar did this when they made perceived levels of lobbyist 'credibility, reliability and knowledge' one of their factors. The American literature has several other examples of attribute-listing: Milbrath (1963); Dexter (1969); Berry (1984); Drew (1985) and Cates (1988). Jordan and Moloney (1993) have shown that there is a remarkable agreement among them as to which one single attribute makes for a 'good' lobbyist - high ethical standards of personal behaviour.

Hull (10) set out another list of (seven) personal attributes for the 'good' lobbyist at the EU Commission where he worked for 14 years. The list was a distillation of his personal experience and as such is marked off from the Thomas-Hrebenar list which was distilled from a survey. The Hull list included: research the case; tailor the case to the official involved, be brief. But it is important to note that what is being described in attribute-listing is the perceived 'good' *behaviour* of individual lobbyists - not a methodology for evaluating lobbying *outcomes* by groups or by lobbyists. The distinction is similar to that between the behaviour of the 'good' soldier in battle and why a battle is won.

Conclusion

The analysis above shows commercial lobbyists as a small, distinct addition to the *dramatis personae* of UK public policy- making: an addition which grew in size and influence in the 1980s and early 1990s. The literature mostly sees them as part of the interest/sectional group picture. But in the focus here, they are businesses offering services to clients in order to get client interests treated favourably in the public policy process. They trade under various titles and some declare themselves to be in public relations. Their public image is a mixed one.

By occupational background, hired lobbyists are mostly men from political and public administrative areas. They sell their services generally to the highest bidder and work mostly for big business. (Bruce [1994] reported a survey that medium-sized businesses use trade associations, their own directors and MPs for lobbying before hiring someone). They are mostly discreet about their clients' identities, what they do for clients and the issues lobbied. But there is no or little evidence that the lobbying methods they employ are different from the methods of in-house lobbyists. Good practice on when to lobby on policy formation, on what aspects and to whom appears common with in-house lobbyists. Evaluating their effectiveness is mostly difficult, if not impossible.

It appears therefore that there is a significant knowledge gap about commercial lobbyists in relation to their 'for hire' characteristic - their differentiating feature and one which puts them into a competitive battle for clients. The task is to investigate questions generated by this characteristic. Questions such as: what do clients hire them for and why; how are they used; how do clients judge value for money; how do hired lobbyists find clients and how do they describe their work; how do MPs, Ministers and civil servants view lobbyists for hire; why do decision-makers interact with them, and what can be said about effectiveness.

The next Chapter sets out theoretical perspectives through which commercial lobbying can be analysed.

Note

1. The trade magazine *PR Week* reports (July 28, 1995; p. 9) that Ian Greer Associates is having to 'rethink its strategy' following the allegation and the consequences for its reputation with clients.

2 Lobbyists for hire: public relations and group theoretical perspectives

Introduction

The preceding Chapter found that most of what has been written about commercial lobbying dealt with the concrete, observable and measurable aspects of the topic. There is no theory of commercial lobbying, explaining and predicting its role in public policy-making processes or in interest group activity. There is not even a less rigorous attempt to build a perspective relating hired lobbying to more theoretically developed areas.

The start here is with a basic empirical observation and its relationship to various theoretical perspectives. The observation (explored by Moore 1991) is that commercial lobbyists hire themselves out principally to business interest groups (1n) and that it is only their hiring which makes them players in the public policy process.

This Chapter explores whether commercial lobbying can be explained in terms of theoretical perspectives drawn from public relations and interest group activity. It is argued here that conceptually, commercial lobbying can be viewed either as public relations activity or as that political behaviour known as interest group activity.

By way of general characteristic, commercial lobbying is an adjunct, an embellishment to group activity and it can only be analysed and understood as a linked activity. Without linkages to groups, commercial lobbyists have no meaningful role. Norton and Grantham (1986) have developed further this linkage concept with groups and have usefully described commercial lobbying as a hyphen, bringing together interest groups and government. Commercial lobbying is a parasitic activity in that it relies on group activity and could not happen without it. (It could also be portrayed as doubly parasitic in that it also needs government activity). Therefore the question explored in this Chapter becomes: is there a theoretical perspective on public relations and on group activity which accounts for business lobbying in such a way as to explain, at least implicitly, the hiring of lobbyists?

Although commercial lobbying will be viewed as public relations activity in this Chapter, it should be remembered that - as noted in the preceding Chapter - this claim is disputed by some commercial lobbyists. As public relations, it can be explained in the terms of competing perspectives.

It is not disputed in the literature that group activity, and commercial lobbying as an extension of such activity, is an act of politics. The title of Truman's text (1951) on groups is *The Governmental Process*; Holtzman (1966; 1) and Hague and Harrop (1989; 114) assert that politics and interests are inseparable; and the sub-title of Jordan's *Commercial Lobbyists* (1991) is *Politics for Profit in Britain.* This Chapter looks at pluralist and more hegemonic models of public relations and group activity.

Commercial lobbying may raise some new questions about the nature of the representation by MPs, given that the latter say they are now the objects of much more lobbying by commercial lobbyists and that most of that lobbying is not constituency-based. These questions are treated in Appendix One.

Evaluating the outcomes of commercial lobbying is not dealt with here for it has been reviewed in Chapter One. Also decision-makers discussed it extensively in their interviews and it is analysed in the concluding Chapter.

Relationships with public relations perspectives - the pluralist, liberal model

While the first Chapter described the relationships between commercial lobbyists and public relations people largely from the position of practice, there is a set of interesting possible relationships to be explored from the vantage point of public relations theoretical perspectives.

Commercial lobbying can be related to either of two competing perspectives about public relations. These perspectives are the application of concepts developed in political studies. The linkages between public relations practice, theoretical perspectives and their philosopical underpinning have been analysed by Grunig and White (1992).

Public relations perspectives are the product of a small, applied but developing academic discipline, largely led by Americans, which attempts to theorise the activity of public relations in relation to management, political and communication studies. The emerging results are three perspectives (the systems, the critical and the rhetorical) with the dominant one in the US and the UK being the systems perspective, first fully stated by Grunig & Hunt (1984). The systems perspective regards lobbying as a public relations function (it is usually labelled the public affairs component of public relations: see Mackey [1994] for an introduction to paradigmatic thinking about the latter) and it is seen as one-way or two-way communication between organisations and external public groups. Indeed the preferred form of public relations is two-way symmetrical communication and Grunig wrote (1989; 29) that organisations employing this form:

> use bargaining, negotiating, and strategies of conflict resolution to bring about symbiotic changes in the ideas, attitudes, and behaviours of both the organisation and its publics.

The group environment in which this activity unfolds is, in other words, pluralistic and Grunig (38) identified 'interest group liberalism', complete with open competition among groups, as a pre-supposition for this preferred form. For Grunig, lobbying and his favoured (two-way communications) form of public relations are largely synonymous.

Pearson (1992; 114) developed this public relations - as - pluralism theme in a review of public relations histories. He quoted Hiebert (1966) who wrote in a biography of Ivy Lee, one of the founders of modern American public relations, that:

> Ivy Lee and public relations played a significant role in preserving the pluralism of American society by opening channels of communication and allowing opposing groups to understand each other.

Hiebert is also referenced with: 'Without public relations, democracy could not succeed in a mass society.' This liberal, pluralist perspective is reflected in American textbooks on public relations. For example, Baskin and Aronoff (1988; 338) wrote about lobbying:

> Although the term has acquired an unsavory connotation of graft and influence peddling, lobbying has long been recognised as a legitimate activity. James Madison, writing in 1788, held that an essential characteristic of a representative society is that the various interest groups in society are permitted to compete for the attention of government officials.

Cutlip, Center & Broom (1985; 15) wrote that 'lobbying is an outgrowth of . . . a democratic system functioning in a pluralistic society' and later (451) that 'It is a basic democratic right that every idea, individual and institution shall have a full and fair hearing in the public forum . . . ' while Wittenberg and Lesly (Lesly, 1991; 75) called attention to '. . . the many years of punching, pushing, tugging and shoving by the multiple interests that demand to be heard and attended to in the American democracy. . . ' Canfield and Moore (1973; 305) and Ross (1977; 166) take similiar positions.

Crable & Vibbert (1986; 36) wrote that:

> Instead of waiting until an issue of critical importance arises, organisations can engage in a more or less continual dialogue with citizens' groups, public officials, and special interest groups in their environment.

In the UK, commercial lobbyist Ian Greer (1985) develops the liberal, pluralist theme. He writes, inter alia, about 'how the law-maker is only as good as the information he is given'. His choice of title is indicative - *Right To Be Heard* - and he says (9):

> In a democratic society, we have not only the right but also the duty to inform our political representatives of our views on matters that affect us.

From the viewpoint of this liberal public relations perspective, lobbying is pluralism in progress. It is pluralism happening. It is the activity of the interests competing with each other and pressing their cases on public policy. And it is arguable that there is public benefit in these representations because often legislation is 'better' as a result. Jenny Jeger, one of the founding directors of lobbying firm GJW (2n), shared this view of democratic benefit, when she rejected the view that lobbying is anti-democratic:

> What the question says is nobody should ever criticise any element of any piece of legislation; legslation is beautifully drafted; there are no flaws in it; people should be un-informed about legislation in front of them; members of the Shadow Cabinet who have no resources to find things out except by those who volunteer should not be informed about arguments; should not be meeting people who are against legislation or who want a point put they can't find accepted by the Government; that civil servants should not talk to outsiders about how to draft legislation; should not seek advice; that everybody has so much time to do all this properly and thoroughly and carefully.

From this perspective, therefore, lobbying - in both its commercial and in-house versions - is legitimated and is so from two aspects. There is the functionalist legitimation that it is a communications system which negotiates, bargains and resolves conflict (Grunig and Hiebert). Secondly there is the constitutionalist endorsement that it enhances American and British politics. Greer suggested that it is a 'right'; Jeger argued that it leads to more effective legislation.

The constitutionalist argument can be expanded into the above-mentioned 'hyphen effect' where lobbying is a smoothing interface between Government which needs information about the effects of its actions, and outside interests which need access to public policy-making in order to protect their interests. Norton and Grantham (1986; 7) wrote:

> While the activities of some lobbyists constitute a problem, professional consultancy firms can and often do help provide a link between Whitehall/ Westminister and outside bodies. They constitute something of a hyphen in the relationship. The benefit is a two-way one.

Broadly the evidence of the literature review supports the explanatory power of the liberal, pluralist perspective of public relations. From this perspective, it is clear that commercial lobbying, as a sub-set of lobbying, is an activity which undertakes the 'hyphen effect' between groups and government. It is also clear from this perspective that lobbying as public relations is essentially a liberal, pluralist activity in the political studies sense. Here the liberal, pluralist perspective of public relations and the liberal, pluralist perspective of group activity are one and the same and are describing the same benign activity in the same language but from different disciplinary stances.

From these two perspectives, any critique of commercial lobbying:

> lies not so much in what they do (which can be beneficial to the making of public policy) but rather in the manner in which they - or at least some of them - do it and in those who undertake it (Norton & Grantham, 7).

What can a liberal, pluralist perspective of public relations offer to this analysis? Its major effect will be to divert the spotlight away from questions of legitimacy, either functional or political/consititutional, and to focus instead on questions of effectiveness and efficiency. The spotlight will be turned away from the following categories of question. Is the hyphen an accessible and open bridge for all groups? Or is the bridge closed to all but the wealthy and the powerful? Is this good, bad or immaterial to the society in which it happens.

Olasky (1987) has given an answer to these questions and it is negative. He declared that he wrote for 'political conservatives and libertarians'. He argued that contact between the business interest and government is inimical to free enterprise and to political freedom and that public relations practitioners should stop making that contact. For him, the hyphen makes for a degraded society:

> For over a century, many major corporate public relations leaders have worked diligently to kill free enterprise by promoting government-big business collaboration. Over and over again, many corporate public relations executives have supported economic regulations with the goal of eliminating smaller competition and ensuring their own profits. They have sold such restrictions on freedom by promising better service, but their frequent inability to deliver has left residue of public disbelief in the promises of corporate America (2).

For Olasky, the hyphen is a negative, part of the machinery of 'corporate collaborationism' which he defines as alliances of large corporations with each other and with the Federal Government.

Relationships with public relations perspectives - critical theory

A competing perspective to the liberal, pluralist one is that of critical public relations theory as exemplified by Smythe (1981), Gandy (1982 and 1992) and again it is argued that it is closely derived from a broader political studies perspective. In this case, the basic paradigm is neo-Marxist in its ideological form. Smythe argued (71) that public relations is part of a 'Consciousness Industry' creating acquiesence to monopoly capitalism. Gandy (1982) developed an explicit theory of how this acquiesence was achieved - his concept of 'information subsidy'. He sought to explain how the mass media agenda is set and for what purposes, and how this affects the distribution of power and values in society. He argued (8) that there is a market for information in society 'characterised by both shortage and supply'. Because information is 'at the heart of individual and collective decision-making, control of information implies control of decision-making'. The exchange of information is determined largely on an economic basis and 'mal-distribution in economic resources will be reflected in mal-distribution of information'. This mal-distribution is aided - if not caused - by 'information subsidies' which reduce the price of information creation and distribution. He concluded:

> It is through the provision of information subsidies to and through the mass media that those with economic power are able to maintain their control over a capitalist society (8).

He described the role of public relations, which includes the lobbying function, in the production of information subsidies (64):

> It is the modern public relations firm that plays the central role in the design and implementation of information subsidy efforts by the major policy actors. Unlike the advertising agency, it is the responsibility and general practice of public relations specialists to generate unpaid publicity. It is, in fact, the public relations specialist who is most often relied upon to deliver the undercover subsidy where the source and the source's self-interest is skilfully hidden.

Gandy (1992) has updated these views in the light of the 'Information Age' which is characterised by work changes 'where increasingly larger shares of the workforce are engaged in the production of information goods and services' (158). He argued that public relations will play a part, via information subsidies, in the US's international role of spreading the messages of deregulation and privatisation.

Firstly it should be noted that this public relations model shares one characteristic with the previous liberal, pluralist model: it is largely the micro development of a larger macro view. Secondly, it has developed a theoretical concept in 'information subsidy' which parallels, in communication studies, the economic concept of cost subsidy and which at the level of conceptual tool has considerable explanatory power.

But there are methodological problems about demonstrating empirical support for this perspective. These are the same obstacles as those facing the larger critical theory and neo-Marxist projects. The first relates to the general difficulty facing all Marxist statements about dominant group activity producing 'false consciousness'. Does the 'modern public relations firm' of Gandy (or the hired lobbyist) recognise what they do in the same terms as Gandy? Are they conscious of operating a subsidy for the purposes attributed to them: and if not, how is Gandy's case demonstrated, as opposed to asserted?

The argument here is that it is unlikely that the public relations firm (or hired lobbyist) will reject the conventional, self-enhancing values associated with the liberal perspective of public relations and see themselves from the critical theory stance. There is no data so far showing that they do reject the liberal perspective and Gandy (1982) offered little empirical evidence: he listed (69) some public relations techniques in an implied critical way but he did not offer case studies or interview data of information subsidies being constructed. Gandy (1992) is largely theoretical assertion. An analysis by Turk (1985) of the effect of information subsidies operated by state agencies to get their material into Louisiana newspapers was inconclusive in that only about half of the coverage came from subsidised sources. The claim of validity for a critical theory perspective on public relations and on commercial lobbying has yet to be demonstrated and whether it can be done through empirical evidence is an open question.

A demonstration of theoretical validity, as opposed to empirically based validity, could be argued through critical theory in the manner of the Frankfurt School (Bottomore, 1984). Such an argument is essentially non-empirical, if not anti-positivist, and could be set out as follows. Commercial lobbying is an information subsidy in operation in that it furthers a powerful organisation's interests vis-à-vis public policy. The subsidy is paid to a lobbying firm to construct an information good, in the economist's sense, on behalf of the commissioning organisation and that organisation is likely to be a large business. The creation and presentation of the good and the persuasion employed to get it accepted is often done in a confidential way through private meetings with Ministers, civil servants and MPs. The characteristics of this process are control of economic resources by powerful business interests and privileged access to decision-makers.

However, any notion of validity claimed through critical theory is rejected here as too metaphysical. But the critical model of public relations does offer an alternative model to the liberal, pluralist one and it therefore has the value of creating an opposing and challenging theoretical pole: the theoretical tension between the two may be fruitful in generating new analysis. The concept of 'information subsidy' is useful in creating this tension.

Overall, the liberal pluralist perspective on public relations developed by Grunig and Hunt accounts for the observation that much of the public relations of business is competitive against other groups. But it makes no explicit elaboration of a public relations practice called commercial lobbying.

Political studies perspectives on commercial lobbying

The above section looked at competing public relations perspectives as explanatory models of commercial lobbying. It also concluded that the perspectives are largely, if not exclusively, re-expressions of broader, political studies perspectives on group behaviour. This re-emphasises the derived and applied nature of public relations theory and raises a question about its theoretical under-development.

It is appropriate, therefore, to apply a broader perspective here. Can political studies perspectives on groups explain commercial lobbying, even implicitly? A literature review undertaken for this section has shown that the broader political studies literature is not explicit about hired lobbying where it theorises about lobbying by groups. The task of this section is to examine whether these perspectives have the implicit capacity to account for commercial lobbying.

A starting point is to relate commercial lobbying to a typology of groups. Hired lobbyists are in contact with the protective and promotional type of interest groups developed in Hague and Harrop's typology (1989; 121-125) rather than with the customary and institutional types of groups. Hague and Harrop (115) also noted about pluralistic models that they compete for the attentions of government.

The classical pluralist 'fit'

The literature review suggests that commercial lobbying (lobbying capacity hired by an interest) will 'fit' with pluralist models of politics associated with Truman, Dahl (3n) and Lindblom (and, it will be argued, particularly with the latter). This is because lobbying, persuasive contact with government, is a consequence of competitive group activity.

Truman's model of pluralism raises fruitful questions of 'fit', particularly when relations with business interests are explored. Truman (37) noted that any group in society may function as a political group making a claim on government. Thus 'An economic group, such as a corporation, that seeks a special tax ruling in that respect functions as a political interest group'. Groups compete for access to decision-makers and access is influenced by the social standing and the internal organisation of a group, and also by the nature of the governmental institutions.

His model identifies business - which is the majority client of hired lobbyists - as a powerful interest. He said (265): 'Perhaps the most basic factor influencing access is the position of the group or its spokesmen in the social structure.' He added with specific references to business interests:

> The deference accorded a high-status group not only facilitates the acceptance of its propaganda but also eases its approach to government.

In contrast, he gave the examples of 'labour organisations' which had difficulties of access owing to 'handicaps in status'. Dahl also identified business people as economic notables: 'their authority is particularly great when policies impinge directly on business costs, earnings, investments and profits . . .' (1961; 76).

But it should be noted that while Truman's model attributes high-status to business interests and therefore much lobbying influence, it does not offer any very specific or elaborated theoretical explanation of why business needs to lobby, let alone hire lobbyists. He also noted that not all interests in the US are organised (511) but argued that associations of people with shared attitudes will organise into a political interest group if there is sufficient disturbance in the behaviour or expectations of those associated people. Here Truman has made observations with some power to explain commercial lobbying. Firstly disturbance to the behaviour or expectations of an interest, such as business, leads it to organise lobbying which could include hiring in capacity. Secondly there is actual or potential countervailing power opposing high-status business interests. Heinz et al. (1993) also remarked on the countervailing power concept in their study of American interest representation. Where there is countervailing power, it is argued here that business *may* use an extra resource to help it lobby.

Holtzman (1966; 8) has developed this disturbance-in-relationships concept as a disequilibrium theory of why interest groups are active in society: when their stable patterns of interaction are upset or threatened and - critically - the resort to private action fails to reproduce a favourable stability, they turn to the state to re-establish those patterns. What is useful here for the commercial lobbying phenomenon is that interests will only resort to a hyphen function such as lobbying government after inter-group mediation has failed.

'Fit' with other models

But other authors would doubt that group/commercial lobbying activity supports a classical pluralist model such as Truman's. Rather they would say that it reinforces a hegemony of powerful interests. Domhoff (1978) described himself as holding a 'class-hegemony paradigm'. He identified 'the special interest process' as one of the four ways in which the American dominant class maintained its position and has a place for lobbying. He wrote (25):

> Ruling class domination of government can be seen most directly in the workings of lobbyists, backroom superlawyers, trade associations, and advisory committees to governmental departments and agencies.

He noted that the people in the above groups who operated this special interest process were neither well known nor prominent members of the ruling class. They did not have to be: the process was structural.

The position of McConnell (1966) is less hegemonic than Domhoff but still concerned about the primacy of interest groups over broader interests. Writing before Lindblom (1977), the powerful position of private business interests concerned McConnell because he argued - with case studies of business, labour, land use and reclamation - that group politics were in conflict with a national politics in the USA. While he described, along with Lindblom, a scenario of advantage or privilege for some groups, he went further and expressed a Madisonian concern over a threat to the public interest from private interests. He wrote, shortly after Olson (1965) that 'relatively homogeneous groups have been effectively organised and have assumed a strong degree of power over particular areas of public policy through close collaboration with segments of government . . . (338). A British critique which is concerned with overweening interests is by Rivers (1974; 8) who warns about groups 'manipulating society to accord with their own interests'. Neither McConnell nor Rivers were explicit about hired lobbying.

Olson's thesis (1965) that interests large in numbers are less likely to organise than small interests is relevant to the differential power of groups. It provides an explanation of why numerically few producer groups such as businesses can be more effectively organised as groups than their customers, much more populous groups. (Mazey and Richardson [1992; 105] noted that producer groups are 'usually the most effective lobbyists' in EU institutions). His application of this differential to the UK's relative economic decline led him (1982) to attribute that decline to organised producer groups. McFarland (1976) predated the latter Olson thesis with an analysis which married Michels's law of oligarchy to group lobbying - ' organised, narrowly based elites tend to defeat unorganised majority interests' (28).

Downs (1957) took the market as a model for democratic politics: 'our main thesis is that parties in democratic politics are analogous to entrepreneurs in a profit seeking economy . . . they formulate whatever policies they believe will gain the most votes' (295). He introduced lobbyists into the model as a non-governmental intermediary between voters, parties and government who, as influencers, provide information on policy decisons.

Those most affected by a decision are those likely to bear the cost of providing information on policy and therefore to be the most well informed and the most listened to by government. A small producer group is more likely to incur lower costs in providing information than a large dispersed group such as consumers. Downs illustrated this with an example on tariff legislation where the cost to consumers of collating data, making informed judgements and supplying relevant information is much higher than for producers. Producers are therefore more likely to supply the information. (There is similarity between this model and Gandy's information subsidy [1982]). 'Under these conditions, government is bound to be more attentive to producers than consumers when it creates policy' (255). He added (256): 'Economically speaking, government in a democracy almost always exhibits an anti-consumer, pro-producer bias.'

It is possible to relate lobbying generally - whether in-house or hired - to Downs's thesis in the following way. Lobbying is a cost to the public policy-making system which can be transformed into a benefit by the process set out below. Government has to take into account the information provided by lobbyists about the effects of its decision-making. Voters do not express views on most of government's decisions outside of elections but government wants an estimate of the effects of their decisions. Lobbyists are non-governmental intermediaries who claim representativeness and who have information about policy effects. If Government takes the lobbyist's information into account and the outcome is a representative decision (i. e. one in line with what voters want), then the cost of lobbying has been transformed into the benefit of a governmental action which voters would approve of in an election.

But can commercial lobbying, as a sub-set of the general lobbying category, be related to this market analogue of political decision-making and so add to the descriptive power of Down's model? It could be argued that it adds to the costs and benefits of the policy-making system by increasing the supply of accurate information about policy consequences from a bigger number of interests. This would increase the representativeness of decision-making and increase the appeal to voters of governmental decisions. Demonstration of this argument is another matter.

What Olson and others above offer by way of inferred explanation about hired lobbyists is that their majority clients - businesses - are producers likely to be better organised than more populous groups; better resourced to pursue their interests, and therefore they may hire lobbyists as an extra resource.

But none of these authors was explicit about hired lobbyists. There is also the larger problem of any hegemonic group model (like producer group ones) bringing forth convincing empirical support. It is needed for it is manifest that business/businesses have varying experiences of advantage and disadvantage in liberal, market societies and that some businesses fail altogether. The neo-pluralist model can account for such negative business experiences.

A neo-pluralistic perspective

The classical pluralist model is not developed enough in its analysis of the business interest to explain why large businesses hire lobbyists. It cannot take the argument much beyond the implication that Truman's high status groups such as business do lobby. It does not have much power to explain why individual businesses lobby against other businesses; why some lobbying fails.

Marsh and Locksley (1983; 1-21) noted that the power of capital was 'qualitatively as well as quantitatively different' from other groups. Dunleavy and O'Leary (1987; 293-297) noted that for neo-pluralists 'business interests occupy a position of special importance compared with other social interests when it comes to influencing public policy-making'. Smith (1990) further developed the classical, reformed and neo-pluralist typology by identifing the amounts of influence attributed to the business interest as the distinguishing feature between the categories. He described the key feature of neo-pluralism as the assumption that the business interest in the modern Western state is privileged as opposed to advantaged (316) and that the distinction springs from structural power. He was following Lindblom (1977) who argued that the state needs the economy to be successful and that it therefore has to give to business inducements to ensure that end. The neo-pluralist argument of Smith/Lindblom is that the market economy gives business the power to make many decisions and that these many decisions are outside of government control. These decisions are in the hands of business with whom government must collaborate to make the economy prosperous. (See Wilson, G. K. [1985; 6] for an elaboration of Lindblom that business incurs opportunity costs in the form of lost profits when the state does not co-operate with it and that business needs state involvement).

Wilson in Jordan (1991) asserted the structural power of business, writing about the American experience of commercial lobbying (75) that:

> American politics has often been criticised as being even more biased to the wealthy than politics in other democracies. The rise of contract lobbying [commercial lobbying] strengthens this criticism as contract lobbyists are necessarily more available to those with money to pay them.

Alderman, one of the first UK academics to identify commercial lobbying as an area needing more analysis, made a similar point (1984;133) in the UK context that the cost of hiring lobbyists makes them available only for wealthy interests.

A privileged interest?

Smith's distinction is based on the assumption that there is a significant difference between advantage which is variable according to circumstance and privilege which is entrenched. Grant (1994; 41) noted that privilege can mean both an observable quantity of extra advantage and a value judgement about worthiness.

But if business is privileged in Grant's first sense, why does business lobby in a general sense and hire lobbyists in particular? If the business interest is strong, why hire: if lobbyists are hired, is business weak? The response to this apparent paradox starts with the recognition that the category 'business' is a complex entity in a Western, liberal, market economy. To accord it a privileged position in one or both of the senses above would not necessarily deny that business has strong and weak characteristics in different political circumstances; different sectors; in different sized units (Grant, 41) and, as Vogel has argued (1989), in different historical periods.

The elaboration of the neo-pluralist perspective by Lindblom offers a way of handling this complexity. So far, the argument has used the undifferentiated category 'business' and it may be an adequate term at the level of macro theory which Lindblom sought to develop in *Politics and Markets.* He was describing (132 footnote) Western nations which demonstrated polyarchy (defined by Dahl [1971; 202]) as a regime where the opportunities for public contestation are available to the bulk of the population) and he was relating the two categories 'business' and 'government' to that concept.

He noted unequal resources among groups and how the inequality was maintained in ways which include commercial lobbying (141):

> The second characteristic [of polyarchy] is that participants in polyarchical politics remain grossly unequal in wealth. Some can hire a supporting organisation; others cannot. Some can hire public relations consultants, broadcast time, newspaper space and other public platforms; others cannot.

Lindblom also noted (179) that there is conflict between government and business and (187):

> businessmen do not get everything they want. But they get a great deal. And when they do not get enough, recession or stagnation is a consequence.

So at the level of macro categories, business (what Grant [1987; 3] called the aggregate of businesses) has to compete for power and influence with government in some circumstances. Seeking extra resource such as hiring lobbyists may be an indicator of this competition.

But Lindblom went on to deconstruct the category 'business' and argued that there is conflict between different business sectors and disagreement over the benefits they seek. He stated (178):

> On some issues, of course, privilege granted to one segment of the business community represents the withdrawal of a privilege from another.

Thus at this micro level of the category 'business' (the level of business sectors and of individual firms) as well as at the macro level, businesses have unsatisfied demands. Grant (1993) illustrated this double layering of dissatisfaction in his review of interest groups in the EU (4n).

Lindblom's elaboration of neo-pluralism allows a fuller explanation of the business/commercial lobbyist link than is available from other pluralist perspectives. It offers the following implicit response to the question: why do businesses lobby, including using hired lobbyists? Business is the most powerful and best resourced group in a liberal, market economy but it is more or less susceptible at different times to influence against its interest by government and by a few powerful groups. Business lobbies, therefore, as a bloc because it wants benign government policies towards the market. Businesses lobby as sectors or as single units because they want competitive advantage over peers in markets. They add to their existing lobbying capacity by hiring in more capacity where extra resource could gain advantage.

But the Lindblom position still has a weakness in that it offers *no specific explanation* of why business(es) hire in lobbying capacity. It takes the argument to the point of positing a generally strong business lobby but not specifically lobbying by hired lobbyists. The implication is that business will lobby using any lobbying type appropriate and that there is nothing so salient in the lobbying type known as commercial lobbying for it to be worth a distinct theoretical account.

Conclusion

There is no specific theory of, or perspective on, commercial lobbying and why business uses it. Can it be explained indirectly by theoretical perspectives from public relations and from interest group activity, offering inferred explanations?

The liberal, pluralist perspective on public relations is a better 'fit' explanation of what is known than the critical theory one, at least from the viewpoint of empirical demonstration. The former posited that all types of lobbying (of which commercial lobbying is but one) are acts of two-way communication between bargaining groups. But the liberal perspective offers no very powerful explanation for asymmetrical distribution of power between groups. On the other hand, the concept of information subsidy from the critical public relations perspective was a good conceptual tool for explaining this asymmetry. Demonstrating it is another matter.

The classical pluralist perspective of group activity, liberated from the narrow confines of public relations, offers only a generalised explanation of why business/businesses lobby. The elaboration of neo-pluralism by Lindblom is a better 'fit' explanation. It is able to account more explicitly for business/government lobbying (they need each other) and for individual, usually big, businesses lobbying (they are in competition). Because this perspective makes business *the privileged but challenged and fractured* interest in a market economy with many resources at its disposal, it infers that hired lobbyists will be used (and Lindblom specifies public relations consultants) as one lobbying type amongst others.

Notes

1. This text follows Truman (37) in not using the term 'pressure group' on the grounds that it emphasises a stage in group political acitivity and instead uses 'interest group' on the grounds that it is a 'more inclusive and more nearly neutral term'. 'Interest group' is defined, after Wilson (1990), as a collection of people who are organised; who are distinct from government and political party, and who want to influence public policy.
2. Said in a recorded and transcribed interview with Jenny Jeger at GJW's offices at Clapham Rd., London on 21 June, 1993.
3. Dahl's definition of 'Madisonian' democracy (1956) is, in part, an outcome of group competition: '. . . an effort to bring about a compromise between the power of majorities and the power of minorities. . . ' (4). What he calls the Madisonian axiom of a non-tyrannical republic is conditional on his paraphrase of Madison, namely that 'Factions must be so controlled that they do not succeed in acting adversely to the rights of other citizens or to the permanent and aggregate interests of the community' (11).

4. Grant writes in *Lobbying in the European Community* :

> Although business interests are likely to remain the most important category of interests organised at the Community level, this is not the same thing as saying that business generally gets what it wants at the Community level. The Member States remain highly influential, and they have political objectives of their own which are often not the same as business. The Commission also has its own agenda which often does not coincide with that of business. Business itself is, of course, divided. Some firms (e.g. firms in industries threatened by international competition such as consumer electronics and motor vehicles) may welcome a relatively interventionist 'European Champion' industrial strategy by the Community. Others (e. g. international chemical firms) would prefer the Community to concentrate on removing those remaining barriers which obstruct the free flow of capital between Member States, and those regulations which impair the operation of the market mechanism on a Community-wide basis (44).

3 Lobbyists for hire: the clients

Introduction

This Chapter is the first of four which analyse the behaviour of the major players involved in commercial lobbying. The subject here is the client, represented by a frequent employer of commercial lobbyists - the government relations and public affairs managers of large companies. It is thought that this is the first time their views on hiring lobbyists have been published extensively in a UK work.

Moore (1991, 27) found individual firms to be of 'overwhelming importance' as clients in his monograph of the lobbying firm GJW and Grant (1987; 109) has commented on large companies hiring lobbyists. The following were interviewed between 1993 and 1994: the former government relations manager of an unnamed UK based energy company (unattributable interview); Charles Lewis of British Steel; Frances Elliott of Thorn-EMI; Martin Knight of IBM UK; David Ramsden of Kingfisher; Anthony Weale of ICI; Keith Lockwood of Vauxhall and General Motors in the UK; Brian Millner of Pilkington; Christopher Leaver of J. Sainsbury; Tessa Marston of Grand Metropolitan, and Chrissie Kimmons of Glaxo Pharmaceuticals UK.

Staff officers to the Board

The most striking observation common about all these functionnaires was the sense of closeness to the centres of business corporate power. These managers were attending the inner sanctum of that power. Anthony Weale was late for the interview because he was briefing the Chairman of ICI about the political consequences of the death of Christchurch MP Robert Adley. For the ICI man and for the anonymous manager from the energy group, their function was board support: staff officers working for the controllers of two of Britain's largest companies. Lunch with Charles Lewis was in the dining annexe to the British Steel boardroom from where came applause for a retiring chairman. Lewis worked with a director who was a sitting MP and a former Minister and who could telephone direct to colleagues in the Government.

Martin Knight talked about IBM being a fundamental part of the UK economy and therefore Government listened. Chrissie Kimmons for Glaxo talked of her industry having daily contact with several Government departments. Keith Lockwood of Vauxhall was contactable at the Reform Club while at the other end of Pall Mall, tea was served by Pilkington in their office next to St. James's Palace. In nearby St. James's Square, Tessa Marston wanted to know the policy thinking of London, Brussels and Strasbourg policy-makers in half-a-dozen areas. As with several of her peers, matters European, especially regulation, were very much on the corporate agenda. The Sainsbury respondent confirmed that they had a general policy of lobbying directly themselves: two members of the Sainsbury family were in the House of Lords. All the companies visited were among the 100 largest UK companies listed in *The Times Top 1000 1991-2.*

Issues lobbied on included energy policy in the 1970s; out-of-town supermarket development in the late 1980s and TV franchises in 1991. More recently there was copyright policy; building regulations for steel and concrete; computer equipment in defence helicopters; European policy on computer software; electricity pricing; competition policy; integrated pollution control; European work councils; taxes on the emission of noxious gases; the level of regulation concerning building materials; the food chain; transport and employment policy; taxation policy; public health issues; monopoly and mergers policy; changes in accountancy conventions; the packaging of goods; science and technology policy and drug prices. The anonymous public affairs manager and those for IBM, ICI, Vauxhall, Pilkington and Grand Metropolitan talked of lobbying Brussels as well as London.

All except one manager were ready to talk on an attributed basis and only two - Sainsbury and Glaxo - showed hesitancy on using the word 'lobby': the former preferring 'communicate' and the latter finding 'lobbying' an inadequate descriptor for a day-to-day functional relationship with Government. The Glaxo informant did not use an alternative generic but in reply to the question 'Do you influence Government?', the reply was: 'I very much hope so. We're partners with Government . . . It's not a question of lobbying: it's a question of we are providing a public service to the public sector . . . '

It was clear that these corporate staff officers were used to political and public discourse in both the party political/ Governmental sense, and also in the organisational culture sense. They were always courteous, cautious at the start and as they warmed to the theme - which in part involved them in assessing their own role - they mostly appeared to be candid. But it was the restrained candour offered to the interested and attentive outsider, a candour that revealed no impurities in the inner sanctum they served: it was impersonal, rarely criticising named individuals or institutions and never offering a critique of their own organisations.

Patterns of involvement

In response to similar questions, patterns of converging and diverging opinion and behaviour appeared amongst the sample. By the fourth and fifth interviews, these patterns were suggesting confirmation that the group was a homogeneous one.

The first question was whether to hire or not. Others were: how is access to decision-makers gained; do intermediaries represent clients to decision-makers; do lobbyists advise on client policy; do they give administrative support? The analysis also examined lobbyists' fees; value for money; lobbyists as salespeople for themselves, and their reputation. What were the arguments for hiring or not hiring? Clients could see both sides. None argued that hiring was essential or not-essential under all circumstances: rather it was internal and external circumstance which decided whether or not to hire. Circumstance then influenced the use to which commercial lobbyists were put.

No client absolutely ruled out hiring. Four of them (anon, Thorn-EMI, ICI, Pilkington) had a policy of not hiring a commercial lobbyist, except for document monitoring (the scrutiny of official, media and research texts for company references). That was also the general policy of Sainsbury but exceptionally they were hiring the lobbying firm GJW to arrange receptions for MPs over the Sunday trading issue, while they did their document monitoring in-house. Two clients (British Steel, IBM) hired lobbyists on a project-by-project basis. (The British Steel informant had hired lobbyists previously on the same basis at Tesco and HTV). Four (Vauxhall, Kingfisher, Grand Metropolitan and Glaxo) had on-going, multiple relationships.

Document monitoring: is it lobbying?

Nine out of eleven clients (unnamed; British Steel; Thorn-EMI; IBM; Kingfisher; ICI; Vauxhall; Pilkington; Glaxo) used outside firms for document monitoring. Sainsbury and Grand Metropolitan used internal services.

One did not regard such monitoring as lobbying. Thorn-EMI used two agencies:

> who provide us with information . . . on issues which we watch . .. we chose them because they are very definitely not lobbyists . . . to me lobbying means using information towards a particular end. Providing basic information isn't lobbying: it's monitoring.

Others saw document monitoring as the minimal lobbying act. ICI had a general policy of self-reliance in lobbying but the respondent did 'qualify that very slightly by having a monitoring company for document search and early warning on Parliamentary Questions'. Pilkington also followed a self-reliant policy but used a lobbying firm for what the respondent called 'a sort of mechanistic side of things, that is to say they scan Hansard for me every day... ' The anonymous respondent used an external document monitor and said ' . . . it was very much if you like a minimal basis for employing lobbyists, merely as an arm, a convenience . . .'. For IBM, its use of an external monitor did not 'add any value to the information; so it is really just information coming from them to us to interpret'. For the Glaxo respondent, her monitors 'can literally get a speech or a press notice or . . . an announcement in the House and fax it through to me within . . . fifteen, twenty minutes'.

The argument set out by Wedgewood (1987) that lobbying can be divided into an intelligence role (including monitoring) and an operational role is accepted here. Casey, too, has included (1991; 2) monitoring as one of a 'range of services' offered to clients. For definitional purposes in this research, hiring a monitoring service or doing the work internally is therefore an act of lobbying, albeit a first, minimal step on the lobbying ladder.

The propensity to hire lobbyists

On the basis above, all the clients seen hired lobbyists and showed a range of engagement with them: whether in a minimal or light way or in a more involved or heavy way; whether by hiring in more or less of the services on offer; whether continuously or intermittently. The data can therefore be represented as a propensity to hire scale with three graduations. It is a quantitative scale about client behaviour rather than a qualitative one for it would be highly problematic to rank their intensity of need for lobbyists' services. Nevertheless, the data suggests that there is generally a positive correlation between amounts of services hired and intensity of need for them by the client.

1. The light hirers: 'you don't launch unguided missiles'

The anonymous international energy company did not hire a lobbyist for more than document monitoring 'because we could do it ourselves'. He said that his former company was, because of its size, 'in a way unfairly privileged' with access to decision-makers and was staffed up to lobby on its own. This self-reliant policy was reinforced by a negative experience when the company was once represented by a lobbyist to a Select Committee Chairman and:

> he [the Chairman] got very cross that he'd been approached by an intermediary and not by [name of the company] - too proud to speak to me that was what he said and he tooks us and our lobbyist to the cleaners through two columns of Hansard under Parliamentary privilege . . .

He added:

> This is the sort of situation that arises and that taught me . . . you don't launch unguided missiles through third parties without knowing exactly what is happening and you do try to remember always that people want to hear from the most relevant person.

The Thorn-EMI respondent said:

> . . . I myself wouldn't employ a third party to speak about anything which is important to this company.

ICI was also generally self-reliant:

> . . . it's our constant belief that a consultant can do nothing for us because we believe that if we've got a message to get across to Government ... we have to be capable of giving it ourselves. So it's up to us to understand what they want and to know who to give it to and have the relationships in place to do it.

Pilkington had the same policy:

> I don't use them [commercial lobbyists], never have and whereas never is a long time, I can't think that I would particularly use them to put Pilkington's views over . . .

For Sainsbury the same policy applied but with some flexibility:

> . . . we have traditionally taken direct access to Government, both at Minister level and at civil servants. Just recently, we have involved GJW as part of the Sunday shopping campaign, but that's the only intermediary we've used before.

This was said in the context of a review of its communications needs for the next five years and of two members of the Sainsbury family sitting in the House of Lords.

The use of lobbyists by Glaxo has to be seen against the pharmaceutical industry's relationship with Government. This was described by the informant as: 'The whole industry . . . is legally required to have a day-to-day relationship with Government.' Against this background, she hired in lobbyists for document monitoring, presentational advice and contact advice. Otherwise, Glaxo was self-reliant:

> Glaxo speaks to Government from Glaxo by fully employed, paid Glaxo executives at all times and exclusively. How can any commercial lobbyist, political lobbyist tell Glaxo or a pharmaceutical company its business . . . when we're in day-to-day functional contact with officials across the full spectrum of our business? How can a commercial lobbyist tells us about policy developments? We've got the information; we're got the knowledge about our business; we've got the skills; we've got the expertise.

2. The intermittent hirers: 'a project basis'

IBM UK and British Steel were in this category. The IBM said:

> Where . . . we use lobbyists in an overall term [other than for monitoring] is on a project basis where there's a specific objective in mind and it tends therefore to have a start and a finish date to something we want to achieve with Government and most recently we have used lobbyists to support particular marketing campaigns which we have sensed potentially becoming very political . . .

British Steel gave the example of its tinplate business (steel for food and drink packaging) taking the project approach; its strip products for buildings taking both the project and on-going approach while British Steel plc hired a lobbyist on an on-going basis for Parliamentary contact. (1n)

3. The heavy hirers: 'I use them as eyes and ears'

Those with on-going relationships were Vauxhall, Kingfisher and Grand Metropolitan.

The Vauxhall respondent said:

> I employ a company which is a public affairs company. I use them as eyes and ears. I use them - I can only be in one place at once - if I need to contact someone.

Kingfisher had an on-going relationship with Ian Greer Associates (IGA) to 'provide us with a strategy for political contact'. The same informant was also executive vice-chairman of the Shopping Hours Reform Council and had a similar relationship with lobbying firm GJW in that they were used by the Council in a 'strategic role'. He saw commercial lobbyists as essential, not wanting to 'head up a political unit in any corporation without the help, support and advice of the Parliamentary lobbyist'.

The Grand Metropolitan respondent made the most hirings. She employed five lobbyists, one from a large firm and four from smaller ones. (The Glaxo respondent hired two).

These three graduations can be grouped into clusters and represented as a scale, ranked by quantity and continuity of services hired in:

light hirers

unnamed energy company
Thorn-EMI
ICI
Pilkington
Sainsbury
Glaxo

intermittent hirers

IBM
British Steel

heavy hirers

Vauxhall
Kingfisher
Grand Metropolitan

Background to positions on the propensity to hire scale

The factors which account for a company's position on the scale are set out below. But a company's position could change. None of the light users, for example, ruled out more usage. Pilkington was careful not to use the word 'never' while the ICI informant noted that he might reconsider the position in extremis - if there was a predatory takeover bid - and 'one might say "I can do with more legs, I could do with more hands for a period of time" '. Thorn-EMI would reconsider 'if there was an issue which was so large that I needed extra resources to do the preparatory back-up work'.

The light hirers

The anonymous public affairs manager worked for what was then the UK's largest company and if they invited someone '. . . to come and hear your point of view . . . they would almost always come'. Access was not a problem.

> The company culture also did not favour outsiders being privy to important and sensitive decisions and operations . . . even if I had wanted to, I don't think the system would have permitted me to bring in an outsider [lobbyist] of that kind.

For the Thorn-EMI respondent, the light usage flowed from previous background.

> . . . when I was in the civil service myself and from my knowledge of Ministers, if there was an important issue, they preferred to speak direct to the people involved with those issues, direct to the the experts. So I myself wouldn't employ a third party to speak about anything which was important to this company.

For ICI, the explanation was the in-house arrangements. These were based on the local works of ICI in which 106 MPs have a constituency interest and where local managers have responsibility for relations with MPs, local councillors and officials, and MEPs. The respondent said:

> . . . we reckon that our ability to get information across or our ability to form relationships with Government must be based on the coal face . . .

At the Millbank headquarters, there was another set of relationships aimed at central Government and this followed from an emphasis associated with the first ICI chairman, Sir Alfred Mond, himself an MP: 'there was an acute awareness in ICI of the significance of our legislature.'

> So my Chairman regularly sees members of the Cabinet. He regularly sees MPs whether they be our own MPs or MPs with a particular interest in something which will affect ICI. He, on a sort of quite frequent basis, goes into the House of Commons to give, not opinions, but to talk to backbench committees, for instance, about whatever they want to talk about. He sees a lot of senior civil servants and his Board do too. . .

The respondent himself sometimes briefed Ministers but, to use a Biblical simile, he did this in a John The Baptist mode of preparation.

> Because, ultimately, particularly Ministers but most people in Government want to talk to boards and it's a very important message as far as I'm concerned because you then know not in terms of detailed issues but in terms of corporate strategy they're talking to the horse's mouth.

Another layer of ICI lobbying is the Chairman and Board meeting Permanent Secretaries: in the case of the Chairman,

> . . . he would see most of the important Permanent Secretaries several times a year.

and:

> . . . directors would see senior civil servants in the departments in which they have an interest. For example, our environmental board man: I suppose he goes into the Department of the Environment or they come here at senior level at least once a month . . .

Behind senior management - and sometimes overlapping - were 160 'monitors' - the internal jargon for issue experts.

> That expert . . . it's no good him sitting in an ivory tower. He's got to be able to go to talk to the civil service, talk to Government, talk to MPs. . . . As a source of knowledge, he is really vital in the briefing process of Government because they want to hear people from the coal face.

Pilkington followed the same self-reliance path because it also believed that the decision-makers want to talk directly to the 'coal face'.

> I can't think that I would particularly use them [lobbyists] to put Pilkington's views over because it's very much my view and it's been formed on the back of opinions expressed to me by Cabinet Ministers and ex-Cabinet Ministers and various other citizens. In the end, if a company wants to express a view, that comes better from the company than from somebody hired to do it, however much more elegant the mouthpiece might be.

At Sainsbury, 'direct access to Government' was done by directors and the company secretary. But the company is 'very pragmatic' and with a resources-for-tasks approach and a communications audit coming up, the hiring of lobbyists was not ruled out.

The pharmaceutical industry's close statutory and structural relationship with Government was the pre-determining factor making for limited hire by Glaxo. For example, legislation required Home Office licensing and inspection of animal experimentation. Chrissie Kimmons said:

> We are not allowed to sell a medicine unless and until the Government has granted us a product licence. . . Profitability and prices are determined by the Government. Contrary to public perception, this is an industry where Government sets our profits and there's day-to-day negotiations with the Department of Health . . . So the law puts us into contact with different Government departments.

She added:

> The main reason we work with Government is that we have no choice. Government is our customer because it buys all our products and it's our regulator. We must work in partnership with Government.

The intermittent hirers

IBM policy was project-by-project hiring and like the light hirers, it used its own people in meetings with Westminster and Whitehall and its own notepaper in written communications. The respondent said: 'I think we've always had a philosophy, certainly in IBM in the UK, . . . that anybody who lobbies the Government under the IBM name should be employed by IBM.' From this starting point, the contribution of lobbyists would be 'much more advice and guidance and listening; understanding the mood of the moment from what is going on in Whitehall, what is going on in Westminster'.

The following example of a lobbying project was given. In 1991, the Merlin programme to build anti-submarine helicopters for the Ministry of Defence was announced. IBM UK headed one bid while British Aerospace and GEC led a rival one. IBM UK were worried that the theme 'you cannot let this very sensitive defence contract go to this nasty big American company' would be brought into play against it.

In these circumstances the respondent felt he lacked the internal resources to counter any intense lobbying from the other bidders:

> So with limited resources . . . I would feel that I never have enough resources as to what the mood is and what is being said in the corridors of power. So we would use an outside company to give us advice on: 'maybe IBM you should think of going to see so and so. How is this decision going to be made. There are all sorts of outside influences; what about going to that department and calling on X,Y, Z.' So it was very much advice and guidance.

He saw this involvement with hired lobbyists as an exercise in mapping the 'political geography'. The simile also indicated in a more generalised sense an expected behaviour from the lobbyist:

> . . . the way we tended to run those sorts of project is that we would probably review with them (commercial lobbyists) on a two weekly basis progress. We'd map out during the course of the campaign . . . what we needed to do and what research they were going to do for us. They would certainly explain the political geography and we would then construct a plan to go and make . . . calls and representations.

British Steel also saw the benefit of hired lobbyists as extra resource when there was a pressing task. They represent:

> extra pairs of hands and extra brains and if you're running a fairly small department and you're concentrating on some other fairly serious issues at the same time, it's quite a useful additional member of a team that you're talking about.

The heavy hirers

Vauxhall were susceptible to the resource argument as well. Their public affairs man noted that many potential clients of lobbyists 'may be hit with the most dreadful crisis which means they suddenly need an additional input'. Another version of the resource argument also applied to Vauxhall: hiring lobbyists was less expensive than employing staff.

Kingfisher and Grand Metropolitan were the heaviest hirers of lobbyists. The Kingfisher respondent employed IGA directly and, wearing his Sunday trading hat, used the services of GJW 'for planning how the Sunday trading campaign is going to be moved forward'. (GJW was also hired by Sainsbury on the same campaign). One possible explanation for his heavy usage lay in the nature of the policy debate about Sunday trading. It was an issue which had 'now gone past the civil servant level . . . it is a purely political issue'. The Government allowed a free Commons vote in autumn 1993 with a choice of three policy options. This made the support of MPs crucial: and IGA 'have come up with a target hit list of Members of Parliament that we Kingfisher should be looking at in respect of Sunday trading'. Thus the Sunday trading issue was one amenable to the sustained lobbying of all MPs. This is a context which illustrates specialisation in lobbying: here a good lobbyist is somebody who understands the Parliamentary process.

Grand Metropolitan was a multiple hirer and hired:

> . . . a variety of different organisations for a variety of purposes in a number of different styles. Some companies I know go for one big agency and channel all their business through them. I have, over a period of three years, gradually, rather slowly, accumulated a small portfolio of rather small, specialist agencies.

Tessa Marston deployed her lobbyists in London, Brussels, Strasbourg and individual European capitals. A major need was monitoring in the sense of knowing the development of public policy. She described this:

> It's much more a question of being aware early on that an official in the Commission is thinking of a directive on such and such a subject. So I need people who have got access to that kind of information rather than public information that's already on the record which we can pick up by other methods. What I don't want and what a lot of big companies offer is a rather expensive press cuttings service.

The analysis above has focused on explanations offered by clients about their degree of hiring - up from the minimal level of document monitoring. Now the argument explores what needs lay behind these explanations. These needs can be grouped under the following headings: the need of clients for the supply of access to decision-makers; the supply of representations to decision-makers; the supply of advice to themslves on policy, and the supply of administrative support. Lobbyists can be characterised as supplying services to meet these client needs. Individual clients took a range of negative and positive positions about these needs/services.

Lobbyists as suppliers of access to decision-makers

It can be argued (2n) that commercial lobbyists are selling to their clients access to decision-makers. The payment to some 35 MPs by lobbyists (Hollingsworth, 1991) suggested that they are keen to be in a position to offer to clients access to Members and by implication indirect access to the Westminster and Whitehall contacts of these MPs.

What is offered to clients is access through a third party, the lobbyists themselves. Charles Lewis talked about his hiring of Geoffrey Tucker:

> He's a former Conservative publicity man and he's got his own small business. He's in St. James's St. Geoffrey actually does know personally all the

> important Conservatives of his day . . . if you are involved with Geoffrey and you get invited to his birthday party - which is usually a fairly lively affair at Brooks or somewhere like that - you will actually meet Lilley, Hurd, Heath, etc, etc, etc.

The IBM man recounted an approach from a commercial looking for business who offered: 'Let us help you get to William Waldegrave.'

Such offers of access must be put in context: access to decision-makers and lobbying are self-evidently inseparable; and most, if not all, who lobby want access. A group cannot make representations unless it knows whom to address and where that individual(s) is located. The targeted receiver of their representations can then be accessed in person or on paper. It is clear from the context of client remarks on access and from what was offered by lobbyists that access in person was preferred. For example, the Pilkington manager, an active in-house lobbyist, differentiated his own role of government relations from that of public relations in the following way:

> David [a public relations colleague] is involved in mega-phone diplomacy. . . I'm about speaking to people one-to-one, giving them a written brief. . .

Thus it is unexceptionable that commercial lobbyists are offering access in person for that is a goal sought by the general category of lobbyist. Anthony Weale, an in-house lobbyist par excellence, whose company ICI practise a very developed policy of self-reliance, was proud of his personal contacts with decision-makers:

> . . . I may not have as wide contacts as any group of consultants whose whole life is to build contacts. Nevertheless, . . . I reckon I know well about 120 MPs and on good friend terms. I know as acquaintances at least another 150; so I'm up to a very large number of MPs. I know dozens of civil servants in all the departments that matter to us, at both senior and drafting level.

There was a similar comment on the need for access from Brian Millner of Pilkington whose company also followed a policy of lobbying self-reliance. He talked of the attempted hostile take-over of Pilkington by the BTR group in 1987:

> . . . I spent most of that two months and a bit within or very adjacent to the Palace of Westminster and I orchestrated the efforts of our constituency MPs and many others and I'm quite proud to say that during that couple of months a 150 MPs went in to bat for me in one way or another.

The opportunity of access by hiring lobbyists was sought by Charles Lewis at British Steel when he worked previously for Tesco and HTV. Sunday trading was the policy issue facing Tesco but the supermarket's lobbying lacked 'any real co-ordination'. Lobbyists Charles Barker were employed and Charles Lewis described them as 'a sort of facilitating device' and a 'very useful supplementary part of my armoury':

> They would arrange meetings with people where we didn't already have any real relationship or . . . where we didn't have the ability to open the door.

At HTV, he employed the lobbyist Geoffrey Tucker who arranged access to Ministers as described above:

> You'll be able to talk to them [current Ministers] and have your few seconds to say something which you hope will be remembered. It's very much a chance thing.

Tucker also arranged contact with a key civil servant on the issue which was agitating HTV. Charles Lewis said:

> The Permanent Secretary at the Home Office was a key figure in advising us and guiding us over the franchise round because that was the most appalling sort of cock-up. We did find that Geoffrey Tucker was able to arrange some very useful contacts for us with Clive Whitmore, the Permanent Secretary and Lord Whitelaw who was heavily involved in setting up Channel 4.

The crucial issue facing Kingfisher and the SHRC (Shopping Hours Reform Council) was Sunday trading and on this issue, the Kingfisher man said:

> IGA [commercial lobbyists Ian Greer Associates] have come up with a target hit list of Members of Parliament that we Kingfisher should be looking at . . . That is their job to come up with that list . . . where there isn't personal knowledge to facilitate the meeting of the target Member of Parliament or the target Minister and people within the group.

On the issue of access generally, he said:

> The key for anybody working on the political scene is over a period of time to build up your contacts and the art is to spot the rising star. Because if you can get to that person when he's an Under-Secretary of State or even a PPS, then you'll likely be able to build friendships which are going to be extremely useful when the guy gets into the Cabinet because he will know you and he will be able to trust you. So if these people are known to us then, we simply talk to their offices and fix up a meeting.

He added:

> If it's a Minister of whom we have no particular knowledge, then we would use our lobbying organisation to organise a meeting.

He added that 'we would make life slightly more difficult for ourselves in trying to get to know people that we don't know'. Access was a quality being hired:

> Bearing in mind that we're using two of the larger [lobbying] companies . . . Now these are people who are known in Government and have been known for

some time and are trusted. And if you have a situation where GJW phone a Minister's office on behalf of a client, they are likely to be able to gain access.

As argued above, commercial lobbyists are not the sole suppliers of access. Access is a *sine qua non* of lobbying and lobbying happens without hired lobbyists. It is also a quality of the UK political system framed in the setting of the constitutional right to petition. The Vauxhall respondent referred to this: 'So the entitlement is there and thank God we have democracy. I have, over the years, worked for companies where they also feel they have a right to lobby, as anyone else does . . . '

As described above, Glaxo have built-in access to decision-makers: but they take advice on the background of individuals to be lobbied. The informant said if the company was asked to give evidence to a Select committee: 'We will ask someone (a commercial lobbyist) "who's the Chairman of that Committee, who are the members of that Committee."'

Direct access by clients

The data also shows that clients perceive access to be a mutual activity between decision-makers and themselves. Lindblom (1977), Jordan and Richardson (1987) argue that access is wanted by government to influential outside interests as much as it is sought by interests to government. Thus access is a two-way street with government at times wanting entry to the decision-making rooms of powerful, private policymakers in the economy. In contradistinction to the brokered access via a third party (the hired lobbyist) described in the section above, this can be described as direct access by self-propulsion through open doors.

The ICI lobbying operation described above implies this. Their man put its relations with governments into the context that there are:

> very few pieces of legislation going through here or in Europe . . . or in the United States that don't have some effect on ICI. Therefore the power of government to help or hinder us is quite considerable; it's incumbent on ICI to make sure that if there is any way we can influence the process to the benefit of the company and the shareholder, so much the better.

IBM noted that '. . . being part of the fabric of the UK economy is fundamental [to access] and of course Government departments have to listen to you if you are an important part of the economy'. The same stance was adopted by the anonymous interviewee of what was then the UK's largest company: '. . . if you invited someone to come and hear your point of view at . . . , they would almost always come.'

The Glaxo respondent expected to be consulted by Government and reported that 'nine times out of ten . . . Glaxo was approached rather than the other way round . . . '

She said:

> If Government is about to change the law relating to the supply of medicines in this country . . . it is an extremely arrogant Government that says 'we won't ask anybody who knows what they are talking about 'cos they're bound to be biased'. . . I would expect Government for this industry or any other to say 'we're considering a policy that will affect your industry. Is it realistic? Is it practical? We don't have expert knowledge on your industry ... ' Government must consult interested, affected and relevant expert parties before it can reach a conclusion.

In an example of Glaxo's involvement in public policy-making, she told of the inter-departmental working party on pharmaceutical prices - 'the scheme whereby Government controls the profitability of the pharmaceutical industry . . .'. Her comment: 'Glaxo's on that negotiating team.'

The Pilkington respondent said of the company chairman, Sir Anthony Pilkington:

> . . . he does move, and several of his peers do, in the world where they will, as a matter of routine, sit down for dinner two or three nights a week with people who may be their equivalent numbers in other national or international companies or who may well include Cabinet Minsters or junior Ministers and so on.

Pilkington is the largest flat and safety glass manufacturer in the world with two thirds of its operations overseas. In the UK, its plants are in 21 Westminster and seven European constituencies. The respondent said:

> So for a start, I cultivate our relationships with the Members of Parliament and the Members of the European Parliament who represent those constituencies. I believe they have a right to know what we do in their patch: equally I require and indeed demand right of access to them.

The Thorn-EMI respondent, a former civil servant, had direct access: '. . . I know how the system works.' The Sainsbury respondent described the company as 'clearly a high impact company' and noted that 'we've got our own Peer group here. We've got two Lord Sainsburys . . . '

Grand Metropolitan's Tessa Marston, also a former civil servant, equally took the view that direct access by self-propulsion through open doors was on offer:

> . . . actually access isn't difficult. If you're a big company like us and you ring a civil servant anywhere and say 'we need to talk to you because this is important' as long as you don't insult people down the phone, they'll see you. So I don't actually see democracy as a problem. I think in open democracy that's as it should be.

What is the relationship between levels of direct, self-propelled access and levels of hiring lobbyists? It could be argued that a high level of direct, self-propelled access implied low levels of hiring. Indeed, of the companies with high, direct, self-propelled access, ICI, Pilkington, Sainsbury and the unnamed firm were light hirers.

But IBM had high, direct, self-propelled access and yet it was an intermittent user of commercial lobbyists. British Steel was in the same category with high, direct access and intermittent usage. The British Steel respondent noted about them:

> They're not necessarily doing anything that we couldn't do for ourselves but they are in position because they can help open doors . . .

But British Steel also had direct, self-propelled access. Sir Giles Shaw MP was a board member and a former Minister of State in the DTI. The respondent said:

> . . . he's here on our board: he's not just here for that reason but that's an added bonus because he can open doors more easily than a lobby company can.

Grand Metropolitan was at the heavy end of the hiring scale with five lobbyists hired: yet access to decision-makers was not seen as problematic.

Vauxhall and Kingfisher were at the heavy end also and used commercial lobbyists to augment the direct access they have. The Vauxhall respondent talked of his lobbyists helping to make contact when he was engaged on other tasks. The Kingfisher man had direct access:

> I have upwards of a 100 MPs that I can write to or speak to at any time and simply say 'Hey it's David' and expect to a) get through to them and b) talk to them.

Thus the data from the field suggests a range of positive and negative correlations between hiring levels and direct, self-propelled access. ICI, Pilkington, Sainsbury and the unnamed energy company have light levels of hiring and have high direct access. IBM UK and British Steel are intermittent hirers and have direct access while Vauxhall and Grand Metropolitan are heavy hirers and have direct access. Kingfisher have direct access yet they hire lobbyists to widen it to decision-makers not known to them.

The ability to walk through the open door to Ministers, MPs and civil servants is only a *weak indicator* that lobbyists are not hired. Generally, hired lobbyists augment the supply of access available to clients rather than create it.

But finally a note of caution on access and a reminder that it is a means and not an end to policy development. Charles Lewis previously worked for the television station HTV at the time of the1989/90 bid for the commercial television franchises under a system mainly driven by the principle of award to highest tender. He hired lobbyist Geoffrey Tucker who arranged meetings with a Permanent Secretary and two Ministers.

Charles Lewis commented:

> . . . whether any of these meetings really helped is a matter of debate. We certainly had them. We appeared to get some quite useful steers from them but the whole of that exercise [bidding for a franchise] was to do with money.

Here access had been gained through the lobbyist to major policy influencers at the highest level but the crucial factor to influence HTV's fortune was a factor (the tender principle) not susceptible to manipulation through access.

Lobbyists as suppliers of representations to decision-makers

Once clients are before decision-makers, do they use hired lobbyists to make their case? The data suggests not. The light hirers were emphatic that they did not need a third party to represent them.

Self-representation was also the policy of IBM, an intermittent hirer. For British Steel, its recently nationalised past meant that contact 'tended to be at a very high level between individuals' (2n). They also had a former Minister on the Board who 'can open doors more easily than a lobby company can'.

For the heavy hirers, the Vauxhall respondent kept the 'more senior contact to myself and the Chairman'. On occasion he asked his lobbyists to arrange meetings but 'I rarely ask them to represent me'.

For the Kingfisher respondent it was 'inevitable' that the lobbyists did some third party representation when arranging access to Ministers not known to the company. He added: '. . . but there is within the Kingfisher group a bank of personal contact' and as an individual he knew 100 plus MPs, as well as Ministers.

For Tessa Marston of Grand Metropolitan, there was 'not a completely categoric no but on the whole I take the view that the company should represent itself'. Her preference was to appear with a manager 'so that they [the decision-makers] can actually feel the operational reality of whatever it is that we're talking about'.

The sample, therefore, strongly suggests that hired lobbyists as third party representatives are allocated the subsidiary role of secondary spokesperson, if they are allocated any such role at all.

Lobbyists as suppliers of policy advice to clients

Of the heavy hirers of lobbyists, two - the Kingfisher/Shopping Hours Reform Council and Grand Metropolitan respondents - explicitly attributed to the lobbyist a clear role of advising on policy, defined here as a contribution of opinions and/or proposed actions on matters of strategic concern to the client. A putative advisory role can be inferred from the statements of four other clients (Charles Lewis talking of his Tesco experience, IBM, Vauxhall and Glaxo) but its extent is very difficult, if not impossible, to explicate. With the anonymous informant, the lobbyists failed to adequately advise.

David Ramsden of Kingfisher, in his role as deputy chairman of the Shopping Hours Reform Council, explicitly gave a policy advice role to his lobbyists. He hired GJW:

> ... and they are used in a strategic role. They are not used to provide the normal, run-of-the-mill Parliamentary programme but simply to be part of the management and the strategic team . . . planning how the Sunday trading campaign is going to be moved forward.

Indeed, the client does the implementation:

> GJW are used to agree with us a strategy that is necessary to ensure currently that the issue of Sunday trading and the Government's declared intention of introducing a Bill actually happens and that the announcement of that Bill is contained in the Queen's speech in November this year (1993).

The strategy was set and 'then largely we the Shopping Hours Reform Council get on with the job'.

Tessa Marston of Grand Metropolitan also involved her lobbyists as policy advisers. This was a nearly inevitable consequence of using them as gatherers of policy intelligence. She wanted, via her hirings, to be 'aware early on, that an official in the (European) Commission is thinking of a directive on such and such a subject'.

Then, with this policy intelligence, she said: 'I will often have a strategy session with one of these people' and:

> . . . one of the most useful things that I get from them is brainstorming. Two heads are always better than one if you've got a knotty problem. You have your intelligence; you have your business scenario; you want to know how to use the one to help the other. I can sit here and think great thoughts but the jamming with somebody else who is familiar with the scene is very helpful.

But policy advice by lobbyists was more difficult to explicate in the following circumstances. Charles Lewis of British Steel had previously worked for Tesco which was then developing its policy on out-of-town superstores. A firm of lobbyists were hired and:

> I think the main contribution was to relieve me of part of my day-to-day burden. . . A type of activity which I don't have time to attend to fully is . . . planning who we should invite to what and how we should address a particular group of people - in fact writing the words for a position paper on an issue which we were feeling strongly about and getting the right sort of style and the right design organised. So the lobbying company did a lot of day-to-day spade work and even printing the certain bits and pieces and letters and so on.

This section of the Lewis interview was an example of the difficulty of identifying the source and extent of policy advice when a shared policy development process with the client is not explicity flagged up. It can be argued that Lewis's statement 'writing the words for a position paper on an issue which we were feeling strongly about' is either an act of amanuensis or the act of policy creation in the first instance. If the former is claimed, the question arises why were such expensive secretaries employed. If the latter is claimed, it is almost impossible to imagine that the lobbyists developed policy ideas in a context which was not influenced by the extant policy of clients. Most policy-making is reflexive and incremental.

There is also the question of lobbyist self-image and survival instinct: even a half-way competent lobbyist could hardly fail to respond with policy ideas if his client said he was 'feeling strongly' on an issue. Finally to add to these difficulties of identification, there is the question of own role perception by the client and by the lobbyists: dominant and subordinate social roles flowing from the principal/agent relationship can get involved. The client may not welcome advice in a key area such as policy by a hired agent while the lobbyist may introduce ideas in a covert way to save embarrassing the principal. There is also the question of memory: can the source of ideas and initiative be accurately recalled.

The text also illustrates the multiplicity of roles open to the lobbyist and how difficult it is to separate them out, here, in particular, the contribution of policy advice. The Lewis text above portrays the lobbyist as an aide to the client in organising events; drawing up invitation lists; writing in the right 'tone of voice'; getting documents designed, and even physically produced. Another example came from Glaxo. Their respondent hired a lobbying firm for advice 'on tone mostly' but 'never' for strategic advice. She sent them drafts of documents going to Government because '. . . we are not professional politicans and I . . . use an agency to look at what I have written and advise me on its drafting: how it's written; how it's structured'.

She added that, in reply, they will say: 'Don't be daft, you'll really turn them off. Don't talk about your profits: profits are a dirty word; couch it in terms of patients . . . why haven't you picked up this point . . . you've got one paragraph on this but as a politician that's what my eyes were drawn to because that's politically important and you haven't expanded that point'.

But these roles above are matters of process which influence policy content. For example, the length of time allowed at an event for policy statement affects the amount of policy which can be declared and the lobbyist can influence both the time and the words. Expanding time or text can influence meaning and change emphasis.

Keith Lockwood of Vauxhall also used his hired lobbyists to write the first draft of briefing papers. The difficulties mentioned above in the Tesco and Glaxo cases re-appear here as they do in the case of IBM who had a project-by-project relationship with lobbyists. The IBM man described the role of his lobbyists as not being representatives: 'it's much more advice and guidance and listening, understanding . . .'

How to interpret these inputs by lobbyists? They could extend from the retailing of political gossip which had strategic significance to the recounting of a policy development which was in fact over-dressed and inaccurate speculation.

Not all lobbyists succeed in policy advice, as the witness of the anonymous public affairs manager showed. Government policy impinged strongly on his employer, an international energy company. He was faced with the need in the 1970s for 'finding a *modus vivendi* with a very pro-active Government' and then in the 1980s with a Government 'which then wished to privatise, particularly in the energy sector which traditionally had been very largely a public sector industry in the UK'. These 'political factors' created the need to lobby, mostly, as analysed above, in the self-reliant mode.

But a firm was hired for monitoring in 'the hope that because they dealt with other clients in other sectors that . . . there would be external wisdom that could rub off . . . '. It was hoped that hiring lobbyists would bring contact with 'somebody who had walked over that ground a bit already'. But the lobbyists had 'walked on the whole rather superficially because . . . they had only done work in depth for quite a small number of clients . . . '

Lobbyists as suppliers of administrative support

The data suggests that there is another category of service to clients: the role of administrative support. Document monitoring comes under this head and nine of the clients used lobbyists for that task. It may sound a dull, routine activity but its importance was noted by Heinz et al. (1993; 379):

> We found that interest groups devote considerable resources simply to monitoring the Washington scene. Contrary to the conventional image of representation as consisting primarily of advocacy, our sample of clients reported that they most often used representatives to keep track of developments and maintain contacts with allied organisations.

They wrote about the difficulty of predicting events in Washington and lobbyists 'reviewing vast amounts of information' (389).

The anonymous client talked of document monitoring as '. . . a minimal basis for employing lobbyists, merely as an arm, a convenience. . . ' He agreed that they were low level doers 'in the way that we used them yes; but they were bright people'.

Pilkington hired a lobbying firm 'in a very limited way', i.e. on the minimal basis of document monitoring. The British Steel informant Charles Lewis needed relief from 'part of my day-to-day burden' and the lobbying company 'did a lot of day-to-day spadework'. But the analysis in the previous section suggests caution in accepting this self-attribution of 'spadework' to the category of administrative support: such 'spadework' could or could not fit into other categories of service supplied.

The data from the Thorn-EMI respondent appears easier to assign. She did not hire lobbyists but she would consider it 'if there was an issue which was so large' that she needed supportive staff work. She said:

> I'm not suggesting that they would write papers to go to Ministers but they can do the basic research. Some of it may not be solely related to this company and this company's performance but they can perhaps get in touch with competitors who on this issue feel there was a joint . . . mutual interest. They could go to trade associations. They could pull things together from a variety of sources.

The Vauxhall manager was a heavy hirer of a public affairs company and his description of the relationship pointed towards a reconnaissance support role: 'I use them as eyes and ears'. More data for this support role can be adduced from Keith Lockwood's comments in the section below on value for money.

Sainsbury was active on the Sunday trading issue and hired lobbyists 'because we've had to talk direct to MPs'. And in execution of this, 'What they did was to arrange some receptions for MPs . . . and advise directly on where particular MPs were coming from on the issues'. Again the words 'advise directly' are problematical for they could carry meanings ranging from a report of names to an interpretation of views.

Lobbyists as fee chargers

Commercial lobbyists hire their services out to interests and, as described from one of the theoretical perspectives in Chapter Two, are a hyphen in the policy formation process: on their left is the client and on their right is the decision-maker. But their left side relationship can also be seen under the heading of business: the hiring of a lobbyist means the payment of a fee by the client and the delivery of services by the lobbyist. This commercial relationship brings into the picture questions of the effectiveness of the lobbyist and the value gained by the client.

As discussed in Chapter One, assessing the effectiveness of lobbying involves difficult judgements. The best that can be achieved is an approximate judgement about effectiveness. One approach to approximate judgement is developed here. It is for clients to measure the outcomes of lobbying against fees paid and where the clients perceive those outcomes to be worth at least the value of the fees paid, there exists the state of 'value for money'. Where there is value for money, there is effectiveness - at least for the client.

Such an estimate involves reference to opportunity cost: what other value could the money have earned and what outcome would have happened without lobbying. The problem with this approach is imperfect knowledge about alternative uses of the fee money and about alternative outcomes. A variant of this approach is to set a prefixed lobbying outcome (usually but not necessarily a policy outcome) against a fee. The problem here for both client and lobbyist is again imperfect knowledge: how to track in a causal way the linkages between the outcome and the lobbyist's actions. Below is an analysis of the data on fees and value for money statements made by clients with reference to the equations above.

The Glaxo informant reported that document monitoring cost between 'five and six thousand a year' and the 'tone of voice' service 'over fifty thousand' pounds because 'we have probably put in the last six months a dozen submissions to different Government departments or Parliamentary committees'. She thought 'we have always had outstanding value for money' and she reported that her Board had never challenged the expenditure. On the monitoring service, value could be reflected in the quantity of material sent to her. About 'tone of voice':

> How do you quantify the value of the right tone? . . . I send them something I have drafted and they come back saying 'incomprehensible twaddle; full of corporate jargon; I didn't understand a word of it'.

The anonymous client paid in the 1980s an annual retainer of about £10,000 which was annually adjusted for inflation - and 'sometimes a bit less than inflation to keep them on their toes'. For extra and unusual loads of work, an additional hourly rate was paid. Value for money was assessed by 'taking the views of three or four of us who regularly used their services' at corporate headquarters and the views of users in operating companies.

> But I think on the whole they didn't find them [the lobbyists] as useful as we did because I think they probably . . . didn't know what it was they wanted from them.

This data illustrates the problem of opportunity costs. The clients had no clear idea of what their budgets would otherwise have been spent on and what in probability would have happened without the lobbyists. Nevertheless, a judgement had to be made: the lobbyists were on an annual contract ('we weren't talking about very large sums of money') and they were retained for ten years. Value for money?

The anonymous manager said:

> . . . I don't think there were many graduations on that scale. One would have said: 'are they still doing the job?' Broadly speaking if so, no problem. . . They didn't bother us or upset us touting for business that they would have liked to do for [name of company] . . . I totally trusted the chap in charge which is a very wonderful asset. . . . Certainly. . . I was not myself ever put back to the wall and required to justify it (the fee).

Perhaps the safest conclusion here is that a judgement about value was avoided: substituted was a judgement that not much value for money was in play and that 'trust' in people obviated the need to make a judgement.

Charles Lewis of British Steel explored his previous experience of hiring lobbyists to talk about value for money. When the television company HTV was bidding for a franchise in 1989/90, the commercial lobbyist's fee was an annual retainer of £20,000 plus expenses. Value for money was assessed as follows:

> Basically, I don't know . . . whether you can say that you have got value for money if the lobbying company didn't actually deliver the result you wanted. They may have done all the work and they have done everything very thoroughly and very diligently but if the decision on that issue went against you, your Board would probably say 'well, that wasn't much use: we haven't had much value for money there'. . . I think in the main, in the companies I've been with, we have always got what we felt we should get in broad terms from the lobbying company. You don't have any great sort of . . . high flying expectation when you take on a lobbying company. You just hope that there will be some sort of benefit for your organisation and its objectives as a result of doing that.

The initial Lewis reference above was to a fixed target that the lobbyist had to achieve and it was significant that the ultimate corporate policy arbiter and paymaster - the corporate board - would take such an approach: they were responsible for outcomes. The rest of the Lewis statement suggests an approach close to the unnamed public affairs manager quoted earlier - a suspension of judgement and an act of professional faith.

IBM told of hiring a commercial for a project at the rate of £3,000 a month. On a later contract, the same firm - 'maybe they did themselves down last time' - charged £4,000 to £5,000 a month.

> So we asked the question 'why have you changed from £3,000 a month to fifty per cent more than that?' . . . they have actually come back and said 'well if you're not happy with that, let us charge you £3,500 a month flat fee and we'll keep showing you our time sheets and anything more than that, we'll put in a bucket. And at the end of the project, if we have been successful or if you IBM have been successful in winning the project . . . we'll add up the hours and we'll say to you: look, we actually did these amounts of hours extra. What would you like to do about it?' I mean they're opening the door to saying that we can say 'bad value, we're not going to pay you any more' or we could be so delighted we've won this enormous contract and all the wonderful help they gave us, we'll pay them for the extra hours or we'll do some extra deal on it.

This amounted to a 'success fee' (payment dependent on pre-agreed outcomes) which was not an acceptable method of payment if the lobbyist is a member of the PRCA (The Public Relations Consultants' Association), a voluntary professional association.

The length of the aforementioned IBM contracts with lobbyists was 12 months in the case of the Merlin project above and six months in the case of another. Such contracts illustrate the difficulty of fixing fees:

> We're about to embark on another one for about six months. It's hard to judge. .. these Government tenders with the best will in the world. They say it's going to be on a six month process. Very often it does slip in timescale and so we would go on employing them (lobbyists) as long as we feel we need to.

Kingfisher said that it paid out 'more than £60,000 a year and less than £100,000 a year' for all lobbying activity in the UK and Europe. Grand Metropolitan had two lobbyists on retainer and the others were hired on 'a daily basis of piece work'. In the market overall, their respondent said ' . . . there are people who would charge £250 a day and people who would charge £250 an hour'.

At Vauxhall, the lobbying bill was 'perhaps just into six figures' when the respondent joined the company in 1990 but the figure was 'just over £20,000' in 1993. Keith Lockwood saw the cost in these terms:

> It's quite low in terms of consultancy fees . . . If you think of the overheads, frankly I'm getting the work of two people plus a secretary; for £25,000 a year, it's actually quite good value, because if you think I had to employ these people . . . the rule of thumb on employment is something like two and a half times your salary is your overhead. If you look at it in those terms, there are occasions when consultants can be quite good value, particularly within a company where the headcount is under constant perusal and it's getting tougher.

On value for money, he started with the premise 'one would accept that lobbyists are running businesses'. He said that they operated a policy of market pricing - selling at the fee level the client will bear. He recalled his own time as a commercial when making these judgements as a client:

> Sometimes, I think it's important to say: 'do I want that bolt-on goody: do I really need that? Okay, you said you did five hours for me last week. What were you actually doing for those five hours.' It's actually quite tough to do that with a consultant . . . and I know very well that I should and must question those hours.

The above data from Vauxhall raises two issues. Firstly, the opportunity cost of hiring lobbyists is couched in terms of administrative outcomes and not in terms of policy outcomes. This refers back to the notion above that hired lobbyists supply a range of services to clients, strategic and non-strategic, which are often difficult to disentangle. Secondly, commercial lobbyists are businesses seeking maximum fee advantage from clients as well as political/constitutional hyphens seeking policy advantage for clients.

Lobbyists as sellers of services to clients

Most businesses have to put effort into finding new selling outlets. In the case of commercial lobbyists, this effort takes different forms.

The Thorn-EMI woman reported that 'once or twice a month' she got literature through the post and ' . . . we reply turning down the approach'.

> If I wanted to employ somebody to help I know from my own contacts those people who are effective; who've helped contacts of mine in other businesses. . . I would go by recommendation rather than . . . a cold call.

IBM received 'a fair number' of soliciting letters and telephone calls. Some of the latter are from people who:

> . . . can be quite aggressive and quite honestly do not do themselves much good because they don't understand the way we operate and they don't understand in fact that we've really got quite a good network already. Others are much more sensible about the approach, maybe approaching by letter as well.

He recalled an 'aggressive sales pitch' in which a lobbyist offered help in meeting William Waldegrave but coincidently did so just two days after IBM had the Lord President of the Council (William Waldegrave) to 'a very successful lunch':

> And you can imagine how well that went down. I don't want help in getting in front of anybody. I might like advice on who to get in front of at any particular time but we can do that ourselves. And I think my view is that if we have aggressive third parties doing things or trying to do things on our behalf, perhaps not the way we like to do things, then they're actually going to do damage potentially.

For the Grand Metropolitan informant, there was 'ordeal by lunch for a couple of months' by the larger lobbying firms when she arrived in post. Eventually her choice, with one exception, was for smaller firms, hiring 'a combination of skills and expertise in a small sort of boutique organisation that backs those people up'. These were chosen after a process of networking among non-competitive peers doing Government relations work.

Lobbyists and client perception of confidentiality and of conflict of interest

No client reported a failure by lobbyists to maintain confidentiality on company information. Grand Metropolitan had a confidentiality clause in its hiring contract. Charles Lewis of British Steel, who has previous experience at Tesco and HTV, reported that it was 'never' a problem. Perhaps one of the reasons for its maintainence by lobbyists is enlightened self-interest. This was broached by the IBM respondent:

> . . . on confidentiality . . . these people have to behave the right way; if there was going to be a lack of confidentiality, then they know that they are going to lose their job. We've had no instance of that sort of thing going on. It has to be a partnership and you've got to trust each other and the important thing is to work very, very closely with these people. Their approach, certainly the people we use, is: 'Tell us all your concerns, your warts and all, because at least if we understand, then perhaps we will be able to give you much better advice.' So we do leave ourselves open to our weaknesses which these lobbyists will understand but I believe that it's the only way of working satisfactorily with them because then they can help us perhaps combat that.

Self-revelation, especially of weaknesses, about the client's business position could, if revealed, reduce corporate advantage in the marketplace. Therefore it may be that clients grade information in terms of its confidentiality - i.e. power to reduce competitive advantage - and only release task-specific information to their lobbyists. This is a policy of information by need-to-know. The views of the anonymous respondent offered support for this. His company was involved publicly with a major corporate acquisition. He had a good and permanent relationship with lobbyists but ' . . . both for confidentiality and all other reasons we didn't use external political consultants for that . . .'. He expanded:

> . . . even if I had wanted to, I don't think that the system would have permitted me to bring in an outsider of that kind but there's no reason why a good senior lobbyist should be less reliable than a merchant banker. Quite frankly, the strength of the corporate finance culture was rather stronger than the strength of the corporate Parliamentary culture and therefore one wouldn't have chanced one's arm. I think one tried to take very, very few risks indeed. I had total confidence in the head of the firm, you know, who was a good man and had formerly been a general and one had reasonable grounds for thinking he was ethically straight up and down and I never doubted him for a moment. Even then though, an honest man can trip you up if he doesn't know that he is doing it. So there's always a risk.

Another aspect of confidential information release by the client is a prior understanding that its receipt by a lobbyist does not create for him a conflict of interests. This avoids situations where a lobbyist could be arguing before a decision-maker the opposing sides of an issue or be arguing the same issue for competing clients.

Clients need this prior understanding before hiring. IBM asked for client lists. Charles Lewis of British Steel said that he checked for conflicts of interest between a lobbyist's clients 'but never found any major problem'.

Lobbyists and client perception of their reputation

Whatever their use of lobbyists, clients are concerned about the reputation of those they have hired with the decision-makers and with their own peer group of government relations managers. On this aspect, the data revealed a wide variety of opinions and attitudes.

Charles Lewis sought views among decision-makers and got 'very mixed' and 'varied' answers. Among MPs:

> Very mixed. Some people are . . . perfectly happy to be open and frank about these things; other people are a little different. The fact of the matter is . . . a lot of MPs are members of lobbying companies themselves and they have to tread a fairly careful line.

Among Ministers and civil servants:

> They varied. If I asked somebody I had met what he thought of a particular lobbying company, he would say something like 'very effective; do their homework; very thorough; will present your case in a very sensible and full way'. But it's usually bound to get back down to personalities and there are lobbyists who everybody knows and nobody particularly trusts.

He said that criticism was usually cast in the words 'can't trust them' :

> Something usually reasonably mild like that; nothing particularly serious unless the company had been involved in some notorious case or affair of some kind.

For IBM, there were two checks on reputation. Firstly their respondent noted that lobbying companies carried out their own surveys and the people he hired 'have been very quick to tell us that they come out the most favoured amongst other Parliamentary service organisations'. His second approach was 'to ask some of my peers in other companies . . . We talk to each other a lot, certainly those of us who aren't in competition with each other'.

Checks with non-competitive peers were also done by Grand Metropolitan. So Tessa Marston said she 'gradually developed a feel from my contemporaries as to whom it was worth talking to and to whom it wasn't'. As regards their reputation with decision-makers, she said that 'many politicians in particular have a prejudice against lobbyists . . . sometimes unreasonably . . . ' This limited the direct representation lobbyists could do for a client. A former civil servant, she said: 'I suspect I would have been rather sniffy about dealing with a lobbyist. At that stage, I would have thought this was kind of offside in some way.'

The view from Thorn-EMI was that lobbyists 'varied hugely in effectiveness and cost'. The ICI man noted that 'there are a large number of MPs who know commercial lobbyists or consultant lobbyists very well'. An MP would 'in my experience prefer a good brief to a good lunch any day'. He noted that many lobbyists were ex-MPs or had worked closely with Parliament for political party central organisations. Lobbyists with civil servant backgrounds were less numerous. These varying backgrounds made lobbyists more or less effective on behalf of clients, depending on the nature of the task to be achieved. So about reputation: 'there's a bit of horses for courses in it.' The anonymous respondent said the same.

The Vauxhall man noted that incompetence could also apply to clients: there were 'good and bad lobbyists and there are good and bad in-house people as well'. About the former, he thought: '. . . I'm afraid that there are a lot of clumsy lobbyists around.'

Kingfisher believed:

> The Parliamentary lobbyist in this country has on occasion got a bad name. I don't think that that name is totally deserved because I think that reputation has to a large degree been imported from America . . . I believe that the best do a very good job indeed . . .

For the Pilkington respondent, there was great variety of performance and reputation. In his experience, he thought the attitude of civil servants towards commercial lobbyists was 'a bit sniffy'. He added: 'They tend to regard them as . . . hacks . . . whose services are for hire to the highest bidder.'

He expanded:

> I think there are people who have got excellent expertise . . . it's a moving scenario. . . it's quite fashionable for people who've either taken early retirement, courtesy of their electorate perhaps, from the House of Commons or European Parliament or something, to set up a consultancy. And there are some sharks; there are some charlatans but there are also some very good professional people who are very close to the ground.

Conclusion

This Chapter has analysed the data from a representative sample of company clients of commercial lobbyists and has constructed a quantitative scale of propensity to hire lobbyists. Lobbying was defined to include document monitoring and therefore all respondents hired or had hired a commercial lobbyist, building up from this minimal act of lobbying. The propensity measures the amount of need the client has for supply of certain functions: the supply of access to decision-makers; the supply of third party representation in front of decision-makers; the supply of policy advice, and of administrative support. The need of individual clients for any or all of these functions ranged from a negative to a strong positive. The need to hire and which services to hire in was influenced by the client's previous personal experience of the the public policy-making process and their existing contacts; in-house lobbying capacity; company culture about outside consultants and whether they insisted on representing themselves; the regulatory regime they faced; current Government policy towards the industry sector involved; the need for an outside sounding board on policy matters; business contracts to be won; whether Parliament was heavily involved in their agenda; the degree of European involvment and Government's desire to consult industry. These needs could change for it was noted by respondents that they were dependent on internal and external circumstance. Although the propensity scale was constructed as a quantitative measure, it can be used with caution as a general guide to the intensity of need for lobbyists' services.

The fees for lobbyists varied greatly from piece work rates of £250 a day via monthly charges of between £4,000 and £5,000 to annual bills of £20,000. Clients found it difficult to make judgements about value for money and none declared that they worked to any discrete method for sizing up this factor.

Some clients were subjected to marketing approaches by lobbyists seeking work but no client said that any of these approaches alone led to a hiring. Instead, they relied on peer group networking for opinion about lobbyists to hire. The sample reported no operational problems about confidentiality of company information in the hands of lobbyists nor were clients concerned about any actual conflict of interests involving themselves.

Clients reported that there were effective and ineffective lobbyists offering themselves for hire and that they had different skills to offer. They also reported the views of decision-makers as being in the range neutral to mildly critical.

Notes

1. The information about tinplate was given in a letter of 2 July, 1993 from Charles Lewis to the author. The former noted British Steel's previous status as a nationalised industry: 'Remember, until the end of 1988 British Steel was nationalised and contact up to that time and since has tended to be at a very high level between individuals.' The information about strip products and the plc was given in a telephone conversation of 3 October, 1994.
2. The Political Editor of The Times, Peter Riddell, argued (19 June, 1993; 4) about the Asil Nadir affair and lobbyists that: 'public affairs firms can use long-standing political and personal contacts with Ministers and the asistance of "tame" or retained backbenchers to gain a hearing, but little more.'

4 Lobbyists for hire: a profile (part one)

Introduction

The subject here and in the next Chapter is the hired lobbyist. The subject of the previous Chapter was the client: the focus now turns from the hirer to the hired in an attempt to build up a more detailed and operational analysis of how hired lobbyists go about their work than has hitherto been published in the UK. This Chapter looks at lobbyists by activity sector and by client preference; business getting; fees, and titles.

The lobbyists

In the period March 1993 to January 1994, interviews were had with Fred Morgan of Westminster Advisers; Peter Moore of Market Access International; Michael Burrell of Westminster Strategy; Dr. Martin Smith of Government Policy Consultants (GPC); David Perchard of David Perchard Associates; Simon Nayyar of Westminster Communications; Tim Rycroft of Good Relations; Charles Miller of The Public Policy Unit (PPU); Evie Soames of Charles Barker; an anonymous 'senior consultant' for a London public relations consultancy; Tessa Devlin of College Hill Associates; Tom McNally of Shandwick, and Patrick Robertson of Taskforce Communications. There were also meetings in 1991 and 1992 with David Wedgewood of Wedgewood Markham Associates; Jenny Jeger of GJW; Tom Watson of Hallmark Marketing Services and Douglas Smith of Westminster Advisers.

Fred Morgan was interviewed because of his relatively long experience and because he was a Labour Party member. Political affiliation has been thought significant because there is an assumption that most lobbyists are Conservative in their personal politics because of their largely private sector clientele and because commercial lobbying came to the public's attention mostly during the Thatcher administrations. This suggested in the words of Moore (1991; 26) that the political right 'may be attracted by the entrepreneurial character of an industry which apparently rose with the "enterprise" culture of the 1980s'. But Moore went on to note in his profile of GJW staff that, of the politically active staff, 53% were either Labour or Liberal Democrat and that of this figure, the Labour component was 29%. There was also some evidence of a lack of enthusiasm for commercial lobbyists from Labour MPs: a 1992 poll by *Access Opinions Ltd* showed that 33% of Labour MPs found such lobbyists very helpful or helpful compared with 54% Conservative MPs. Another 1992 poll, this time by Mori (1n), also reflected an anti-lobbyist bias by Labour MPs: all MPs in the sample ranked 'PR consultants' as the 11th most helpful source of information out of 18 but 30% Conservatives described them as most helpful against 18% Labour members. It was considered worthwhile, in the light of the assumption of a right-leaning personnel and of these figures, to interview a declared Labour supporting lobbyist.

However, the data from the interview with Fred Morgan did not show any differential lobbying behaviour which could be attributed to political affiliation. Another lobbying firm had two London Labour councillors as directors and it was suggested (2n) that matching Labour supporting lobbyists with Labour controlled local authorities helped when waste management contracts were put to competitive tender. The unnamed lobbyist said that he was an active Labour Party member and that in his judgement some 15% of lobbyists were Labour activists (3n). Sometimes political affiliation does lead to party political action: Shandwick reported in its 1992 accounts that two staff were seconded to the Conservative Party for the general election campaign (4n).

Only one lobbyist, Ian Greer of Ian Greer Associates, turned down the invitation to be interviewed and he maintained his refusal after a second request (5n). Only two refused to answer a question and the question in both cases was about fee levels. The anonymous lobbyist chose silence because he was the substitute for his managing director and did not want his views to be regarded as the official position of his employer. Five of them had offices in the 'division bell area' of Westminster; three were in the City of London; one was in Mayfair. There were two women lobbyists.

In all cases except three, the interviews were with the individuals initially approached. The exceptions were the unnamed above, Westminster Communications and Good Relations.

The lobbyists interviewed had varying lengths of personal experience of the activity. The range included eight; two; seven; six; four; three; eight; twenty-one; four; one; seven and six years.

As a fincancial backdrop to these meetintgs, *PR Week* (1993, April) published a league table of 1992 fee income of the largest 150 public relations consultancies in the UK. Lobbying firms were either indirectly included where they were part of PR groups or they were mentioned in their own right as independents. The Shandwick group was first with £23,400,000 and Lowe Bell Communications, owners of Good Relations, were second with £15,008,000. Countrywide Communications, part owners of Government Policy Consultants, was sixth with £8,187,978 and seventh was The Grayling Group, owners of Westminster Strategy with £6,008,212. College Hill Associates had turnover of £1,728,989 and were placed 28th. Westminster Advisers were 147 with a turnover of £166,889.

Lobbyists and their clients by sector

What is the balance of clients by public, private and voluntary sector? Westminster Advisers had 12 clients spread over all three sectors while Market Access estimated private companies were 60% of clients; public bodies 12% and charities eight per cent in 1991. Their respondent judged that since then numbers of 'charity pressure groups have died out somewhat'. In the transport specialism of Market Access, 30% of clients were in the public sector and the rest in the private but 'they're not necessarily big businesses . . . thirty, forty, fifty people'. All of College Hill Associates' 60 clients were in the private sector: the majority were 'blue chip' publicly quoted companies and there was one trade association. Tom McNally said his current employer Shandwick and former employer Hill and Knowlton 'tended to have mainly commercial clients'. He thought growth areas were contracted-out parts of the civil service, local government and 'foreign public bodies including foreign governments'.

The client list of Westminster Strategy stood at 52 in August 1993. The following is a breakdown by inspection of title. Sixteen could be identified as public or private companies (e.g. AEA Technology and National Westminster Bank), another five were trade associations and professional associations were three. Local authorities numbered 16; nationalised and public sector organisations one each. There were three charities/pressure groups (e.g. Amnesty International); one common interest group (e.g. Business in Sport and Leisure) and one trade union (e.g. Police Federation). Six were put in the miscellaneous category (e.g. Chartex) following difficulties of title identification.

The Westminster Strategy lobbyist estimated an equality of private and public sector clients. He said:

> We work for the Association of County Councils and a large number of individual county councils. We work for several London boroughs. We've done quite a lot of work in the health service and we do quite a lot of work for quangos of one sort or another. . . quite a lot of work for trade associations . . . probably our largest trade association client is the Japanese electronics industry . . . a lot of work for companies relating to privatisation. So we do quite a lot of work for companies that were once in the public sector but are no longer.

and:

> There has been a trend in our business: local government has become a much more important part of our business than it was two years ago.

Michael Burrell added that 'on occasion' they turned down clients. Conflict of interest was one reason and he gave the example of regional electricity companies with differing policies: here the potential client could be given recommendations which could be in conflict with advice to other regionals. Unease about the client's operation meant that 'once or twice we have turned down clients because we simply felt extremely uncomfortable with the subject area'. Internally staff were given the 'right' not to work on some accounts for reasons of conscience.

He also noted that sometimes commercial lobbyists were likened to barristers in that both accepted a changing series of cases. But he rejected the comparison in that the legal system imposed a prior obligation to ensure that all were offered representation, an obligation which did not apply to lobbyists. Secondly:

> in practice you cannot give really good advice to clients to whom you feel hostile: so it makes sense not to try to work for clients you're totally out of sympathy with.

Government Policy Consultants (GPC) employed seven people in the UK and seven in Brussels. A partial list of their 1992 clients broke down into the following categories: five companies; two trade associations and three public sector organisations (e.g. London Zoo) and three which could not be securely identified by title. Individual clients included (summer 1993) South Yorkshire Passenger Transport Executive, the Bingo Association of Great Britain, and the Association of Plastics Manufacturers in Europe. At the time of interview, GPC's Martin Smith said their balance of clients was significantly in the private sector and:

> We currently don't do any work for the voluntary or non-commercial sector. The budgets available to most clients in the voluntary sector are fairly small and at this stage in our company's development I want to concentrate on developing the commercial momentum of the business here.

At Westminster Communications, there were 47 clients listed in summer 1993 serviced by 12 staff. An inspection of titles yielded the following. Twelve were public or private companies (e.g. London Underground Ltd. [Development Directorate] and Standard Life Assurance) and 11 trade associations. There was a healthcare organisation (Denplan) and three professional assocations (e.g. Chartered Institute of Public Finance and Accountancy). There were two nationalised industries (e.g. British Railways Board); five local authorities and five other public sector organisations (e.g. Civil Aviation Authority). Common interest groups such as Royal Automobile Club numbered two; and six clients fell under the miscellaneous heading because of difficulty of title identification.

David Perchard Associates had all their clients in the private sector bar one - the Department of Trade and Industry. The Charles Barker respondent had 'very little' clientele in the public sector. She said that there had been more in the 1980s, such as the British Airports Authority, when the bulk of the privatisation programme was passing into legislation. In the future, the Next Step programme of hybrid public/ private state agencies for the civil service might produce more. Private sector clients were split equally between individual companies and trade associations. One charity had been on the books for 20 years.

For the Good Relations lobbyist there was a:

> broad balance between large private sector companies and the public sector and quasi-public sector organisations, such as local authorities and recently privatised former Government bodies. There is not a great deal of representation from the voluntary sector but as between the other two, I would say it's a fairly even balance, probably sixty : forty in favour of the private sector.

Private sector clients were 'predominately individual companies'. He worked on between five and 12 clients with one other colleague, the latter concentrating on product-related issues, such as food safety for the client NutraSweet.

For the unnamed lobbyist, probably sixty or seventy per cent (maybe even higher) of clients were in the private sector and 'by and large they're big business . . .'. Another view expected that the client list would always very largely be big business.

Charles Miller said about his client list that '. . . predominantly, it will be big business'.

> That will be two hundred companies or consortia who come together to work on a particular issue. . . trade associations . . . they may be 20% of our turnover each month. Non-UK companies . . . about 15%. Local authorities and local authority related bodies, perhaps ten per cent . . . But certainly the bulk, a good 60%, will be individual big organisations . . . we don't currently work for any voluntary organisations.

Of public sector clients, there were 'a lot of them on our books' in summer 1993.

> These are people like British Rail; local authorities, quangos like the Sports Council, English Heritage and the National Heritage Memorial Fund and so on. Recently privatised public sector bodies also form a large part of our client list.

He added that public sector bodies had become 'somewhat more confident' about using lobbyists. But:

> They have to run the gauntlet of the National Audit Office. We certainly have one public body who still for all sorts of reasons . . . have us down on their books as something like interior decorators. Most of the others are quite frank about it but they will not call us lobbyists. They will say we are political consultants; we're local government advisers; we're policy advisers, advisers on consultation. Anything but using the L word because that implies that public money is being spent to lobby the provider of public money.

The data has revealed a greater diversity of clients in terms of sector than has been published before. Public regulatory and funding bodies such as The Takeover Panel, the Civil Aviation Authority, English Heritage, the Sports Council have hired lobbyists, along with bodies about to be privatised or recently so - British Rail and British Gas plc. Two lobbying firms represented some 20 local authority bodies.

These bodies made up ten per cent of the clients of a third and 30 per cent of a fourth lobbying firm.

But despite this diversity, it is clear that the private sector provides the bulk of clients and that the clients from other sectors are a dilution of a great predominance. Moore (1991; 27) had reported 'the overwhelming importance of individual firms' in the composition of one lobbying firm's client list. Grantham and Seymour-Ure (1990) had also previously found evidence for this strong bias towards the private sector. Out of 83 examples they gave of current or former clients of 16 lobbying firms, only 18 were in the public sector (as identified by title). But it should be noted that some of the latter have been clients for a long time. Grantham and Seymour-Ure listed The Takeover Panel as a client of Westminster Strategy in 1987/8 and it was still so in summer 1993: the same applied for British Rail Board and its InterCity division as clients of Westminster Communications.

The predominance of the private sector is likely always to exist and is, in part, a consequence of the ability to pay for a professional service. But the degree of predominance fluctuates over time as the analysis above suggests. Ironically, public sector bodies appeared to be a larger proportion of client lists even at a time (mid-1993) when that sector was shrinking.

The impact of Government policy on the public sector is the proximate cause for the proportion of public sector clients. It is a reasonable assumption that the local authorities who have hired lobbyists at a time when the Local Government Commission is reviewing their functions are reflecting a defensive reaction to what could be a negative outcome for them. Support for this assumption is implied in *The Independent* newspaper report (6n) of 24 August, 1993 that the Audit Commission was unhappy about such hirings. The same variable of Government policy accounts for the presence of ex-nationalised industries on client lists. Here the agitating factor is often active regulatory regimes. For example, in August 1993, the Monopolies and Mergers Commission recommended a partial break-up of British Gas plc, a move welcomed by the company's regulator Ofgas. British Gas was a client of Westminster Communications (as was the Audit Commission summer 1993).

Theoretically this 'governmental agenda for change' factor has links to the disequilibrium concept set out by Holtzman (1966) in Chapter Two but challenges it in that the cause of the disturbance in the pattern of relationships of an interest is not another interest but government.

The good client

The section above looked at the lobbyist/client relationship from the technical aspect of client ownership: another, more personal perspective on that relationship is the lobbyist's preference for certain client behaviour. What is a good client for a lobbyist? Data generated by this question offered insights into optimum relationships as defined by one side in the supply of a professional service: it suggested that lobbyists prefer working to clients who bring forward a matter of substance, who have some understanding of the political system and who allow their advisers autonomy.

For Westminster Advisers' respondent 'a good client is a) one that has a good case; b) one that listens to you and c) one that can afford to pay you. For Westminster Strategy, there was also an economic specification:

> A good client is a client who pays the bills . . . we are a business and that's the fundamental . . . is a client who has something interesting to offer the Governmental process in term of knowledge, expertise in a subject area and one who understands the value of advice and is willing to listen with an open mind and be prepared to change their minds. There's not really much point in hiring consultants if you think you know how to do it. So it's that quality of humility really that says 'I'm not a specialist in lobbying: you are. This is my problem: give me some advice on how to handle it'. Inevitably, it's all about personal relationships and trust and so you seek to develop a rapport with each client.

Evie Soames for Charles Barker also listed an economic dimension: a good client is 'one that sticks with us year after year and doesn't complain, pays their bills on time'.

The Westminster Communications respondent echoed the attraction of ' . . . a client who has a substantive policy issue to address' for 'it is very difficult to do anything for a client who doesn't actually have anything useful to say'.

Tom McNally of Shandwick also talked about substance: 'A good client is someone with a big problem but with a real willingness to use what we have to offer and build us into the management and planning structure'. He noted how 'a resentful in-house department' of public affairs could hamper the lobbyist's performance and then block access to directors.

He characterised the 'worst' client as saying: ' "here's a bundle of money, go and get this for me" which isn't how it happens and isn't how it should happen'.

David Perchard preferred working for companies rather than trade associations 'because they have a clear idea of what they want, make quicker decisions and all in all you generally see more results of your labours'. The good client had clear objectives; was decisive; had an agreed division of responsibility with the lobbyist and did what she said she would.

> A good client is actually interested in what we do; not simply retaining us as a sort of security blanket. They make their own contribution. And they tell us what they're up to.

Clarity of mission by a client appealed to the Good Relations informant: ' . . . a clear idea of what they wanted to achieve. Other qualities were: ability to take advice; act on it within the agreed order of priorities; enthusiasm to want to drive the project forward'.

Tim Rycroft said empathy for the lobbyist was also appreciated:

> A good client understands that the area in which we work can be maddeningly vague. Sometimes private sector companies can find it irritating, I think, trying to get results in this arena because it doesn't seem to work to any sort of logical process: which I suppose is why they come to us in the first place. But I don't think that necessarily makes it any easier for them to cope with what seems like a completely arbitrary way of doing things, which it often is of course.

Understanding the political process was also a feature of the good client for the College Hill Associates' lobbyist: 'People who expect something to happen because you buy them lunch are nightmare clients because it just doesn't happen'.

She added:

> A good client is someone who doesn't give up and who isn't of the disposition that you have to be with the Tory Party to succeed . . . you need a client that's interested and recognises that change can come about but it's not as a result of one meeting or of three meetings but of a continual programme . . .

For the Public Policy Unit informant, Charles Miller, the good client gave the lobbyist some measure of autonomy - 'let the dog bark' - and has understanding of how decision-making works, and is responsive: 'there's nothing worse when you have a case which requires very, very urgent decisions being made than a client who's never there'.

'We're a distress purchase': the business of getting clients

Commercial lobbyists are professional advisers running businesses. Some of these businesses are substantial: Westminster Strategy employed 35 people and had a £2m turnover in the summer of 1993. Westminster Communication had 47 clients and 19 staff below board level. Shandwick plc says about itself in its brochure Global Reach-Local Focus that it 'is both the leading and the largest organisation in the world, solely dedicated to public relations consultancy'. How do they recruit clients? How do they engage in business development?

For the Westminster Strategy respondent:

> Mostly by word of mouth, reputation. The main source of new business is existing clients either in the sense that they ask you to do more and more or in the sense that they recommend you to other people . . . you get some clients from advertising in specialist publications like Vacher's, that's not really significant. You get some clients from what one might call marketing activities . . . I do quite a lot of speaking at conferences about lobbying and that quite often leads to new clients but it's mostly word of mouth.

The formula was similar for College Hill Associates. Tessa Devlin said 'good work means referral... If you work on a competition issue ... and it's successful, word will get round town that these are the chaps to employ for a competition issue, for a MMC inquiry'. Cold calling (an uninvited approach on potential clients seeking work) was 'not often successful but often we will see something in the paper and write a letter on that basis'.

Business development was similar for Westminster Communications: 'Principally I suppose they come to us on strength of our reputation and I stress that they come to us rather than us going out cold calling ...' Other routes included winning competitive tenders; references from existing clients and from sister company Citigate Communications.

The process is similar for Good Relations, now part of the Lowe Bell group which according to its 1993 brochure had an income of £16m. Tim Rycroft listed three ways:

> The ideal is to be referred from one happy client to another. Frequently, we're involved in beauty parades in which we competitively pitch against the other organisations in our field. And sometimes existing clients who may be using us for other areas of work discover that they have a need for public affairs work and the brief expands to include that.

For the Shandwick informant there was no one single way of getting clients ('There's self-publicity, advertising, networking, cold call letters') and it was an activity that took up a third of his time. The comparison was with 'running up the down staircase because in many ways we're a distress purchase'. He thought 'companies tend to hire us because they've got a particular problem and as that problem recedes, they either downgrade our activity or drop us altogether'.

'Clients have come to us mainly by word ...' said Charles Miller of the PPU which listed 16 lobbying staff.

> Very rarely have we found clients generated by publicity . . . they're not generated by impersonal contact. It is very much personal contact, catching people at the right time. We now have a chairman who's had a recently high public profile and who's done a lot of marketing for us and that has made a big difference.

Martin Smith of GPC which employs seven people thought that the 'best way to get clients is by word of mouth and personal reference'. GPC has been trading since January 1993 and previously operated as Countrywide Political Communications from 1989. He said that '... a lot of business does change hands'. He gave examples of referrals - introduction to new clients from a third party - in the following circumstances: referral from a competitor because of conflict of interest; referral by a large law firm, and by a Government department. In addition, a promotional brochure was mailed out, occasional booklets and speeches published and 'direct telephone selling' done on a trial basis. He summarised his approach as 'conventional marketing techniques and private networks' which took up between 10 and 30 per cent of the firm's time, depending on the state of the client list.

Westminster Advisers had been in existence for two/three years and for Fred Morgan, clients 'come to us almost entirely'. He said: 'We don't do any advertising at all. People ring us up or write to us or meet us and ask us to do some work for them'.

> I think this is the result a) of being fairly well known in the industry; b) Doulgas [Smith] in particular writes articles for magazines and newspapers and appears occasionally on television, and c) he and I . . . speak at meetings . . . which attract potential clients.

Westminster Advisers had between 10 and 12 clients (summer 1993) and operated an element of client selection:

> . . . people talk to us about their problems and ninety nine times out of a hundred we will want to continue that discussion and want to accept them as clients. But after discussion . . . we might feel 'well this really isn't for us or quite frankly between you and me we don't like this bloke' and in that case we won't proceed.

Peter Moore, who had worked for GJW, said many clients went to them through referrals. There was also the identification of political problems in newspapers or on the professional 'grapevine' and 'then you make your approach, explain who you are, what you can do, how you think you can help'.

He worked (summer 1993) for the newly established transport section of Market Access. Getting clients was a large part of his work: 'you've obviously got to be quite aggressive about it to get this unit off the ground . . . it's a new commitment on the part of the group to develop the specialism in transport policy'.

Cold calling, such as direct telephone selling, was a 'less successful route but sometimes it works' for Charles Barker. Referrals and competitive presentations against other lobbyists were the majority sources of new clients, along with shared business with the other two divisions in the larger Charles Barker group.

The above suggests that lobbyists seek clients and that they do so along a passive/active continuum from reliance on referrals of potential clients by satisfied clients to competitive tendering and cold calling on the telephone. Firstly, it is noteworthy that this search for clients mirrors the search for effective lobbyists found in the data from clients. For example, the IBM lobbyist referred to a 'network of government relations people . . . we will compare notes' and the Grand Metropolitan respondent 'asked about amongst my peers . . .'. The Thorn-EMI respondent said that 'if I wanted to employ someone to help, I know from my own contacts those people who are effective . . .'.

Secondly, the balance of the data suggests that most business development is at the passive end of the continuum and that this distribution forbids the use of a pro-active term such as 'client search'. But this balance reflects a particular stage in business development by most of the sample. They are mostly older or larger businesses with a track record.

It is therefore significant to note who was specially active in getting clients. Martin Smith of GPC and Peter Moore of Market Access were building businesses, as was Tom McNally who had been at Shandwick for six months and was establishing himself (summer 1993) in a job which had two previous occupants in 18 months.

Above all, wherever these lobbying businesses stand in the passive/active continuum, they all want more clients. The interview question was 'How do you get clients?': none said that the question was inappropriate.

Lobbyists and fees

Lobbyist charge fees. They work in a marketplace which matches the suppliers of advice to those looking for it. The business development described above is an expression of that market as are the advertisments by lobbying firms in periodic supplements in *PR Week* magazine. Lobbyists seek a profit either as independent firms or as part of a larger private or public business. But one asserted that lobbyists do not sell their services to the highest bidder because they do not have perfect knowledge of what the fee levels are of their competitors: largely they are tendering blind.

Tom McNally of Shandwick plc described the market circumstances of summer 1993:

> . . . I think fees have levelled off in the last two or three years as recession has bitten. It hasn't stopped the flow of public affairs work but certainly in the heady days of the eighties fees were tending to creep up whereas they have levelled off as . . . company budgets have come under stress and competition has intensified. But there is a point beyond which you can't go without going out of business . . .

The ways in which fees are calculated and their levels show variety. For Westminster Advisers, the first step is a reconnaissance of the work to be done and the result may be that 'we could quite easily do some work for somebody for two or three thousand pounds'. A basic feature of fee charging that runs through the data is the length of contracted work measured in time: this can be sub-divided into two categories. Fred Morgan described them:

> One does things either on a project basis: they say 'we want this done . . . we think it ought to take three months' and so we spend three months. Or we are asked to do a much wider job for which we might charge an annual fee. Annual fees are getting now much less usual.

Another organising principle for fee charging is range of service bought. Peter Moore said:

> . . . you can have the stand alone monitoring account which would usually be on a retainer. Speaking for the whole industry, I suspect . . . somewhere between £500 and £1,000 a month for that. More common is to combine that with a consultancy service . . . Fees can either be a monthly retainer . . . figures between £2,000 and £5,000 a month are probably common though . . . some companies do specialise more in larger accounts which may have some degree of exclusivity in terms of other companies in the same sector . . . You'd be bound to the one company which could be up to or around £10,000 a month quite easily.

He said exclusive working 'was probably less common now than in the . . . eighties when there were things like take-overs and . . . and there was a lot more money flying around'.

For Westminster Strategy the fee structure had developed pragmatically. Michael Burrell said: 'the way one has built the business is instinctive' and later 'you try to reach a fee agreement that suits both parties'.

> . . . maybe 60% of clients are on annual retainers and they will vary from in our case £500 a month to currently a maximum of about £11,000 a month. But the average monthly retainer would be £3,000 or £4,000. Then project fees which you try and base on how much work is involved. Occasionally we charge people on the hourly rate basis and that will vary depending on the seniority of the person involved but we are very flexible.

Flexible fee structures were also a feature for GPC. Martin Smith said: '. . . there are virtually no two clients who work on exactly the same basis'.

> We prefer to work on a retainer basis, not just for the obvious financial reasons but also because we generally believe that's the best way to work with clients because one isn't then always engaged in firefighting . . . We also have project clients . . . Any variation on these two themes is ultimately obtainable through negotiation.

In the previous 18 months, GPC had done projects from £500 to £26,000, the former accepted on a loss leader basis. The latter client was a Canadian utility and the work involved 45 interviews with individuals in German industry, government and the media 'on a very precise set of environmental policy issues in relation to power generation'.

Client uncertainty about hiring a public affairs consultancy was a key feature in the fee charging policy of David Perchard Associates. From 1987 until the beginning of 1992, most of his clients had not hired a consultancy before. David Perchard explained:

> They were not convinced they needed public affairs consultants: maybe their trade association could do the job for them perfectly well. So it was necessary to demonstrate that there was a finite kind of fee there: so we went for flat annual

> fees. And the trouble with that is that the more enthusiastic you are, the more likely you are to be reducing your hourly return by over-servicing the client. Certainly we did that and we have gradually moved over to an hourly rate and we set a very small retainer . . .

The retainer varied between £2,000 and £5,000 'but in general we prefer to work with an hourly rate and we top off our time in quarter of an hour segments and bill accordingly'.

Westminster Communications also used hourly and part thereof rates: charge time is broken down into six minute segments within an agreed monthly total and timesheets kept by all 'up to joint managing directors and the Parliamentary and non-executive directors,' said Simon Nayyar. Hourly rates are combined with a fixed monthly retainer 'previously agreed . . . '

Tom McNally reported variety of practice on fees. His previous employer Hill and Knowlton was 'almost entirely time sheet based' while Shandwick 'are much more annual retainer'. He thought that the trend was towards time sheets. There was also a cycle in the political year and fees reflected that. 'So it's not . . . five K a month. It may be one K one month and eight K another'. Another factor making for uneven payments was the appearance of a threat to the client which called for work of '12 or13 K' a month. In these circumstances '. . . obviously if the issue merits it, companies will say "never mind, get the result." ' In normal circumstances, companies would say 'look, we want to be kept up to speed on what's happening but we don't want that to cost us more than two, three K a month'. In circumstances perceived as dire for the client, such as a reference to the Monopolies Commission, fees could amount to £250,000. 'That's probably the top end of anything I've earned'. With an 'average distress' facing a client, he thought the fee would be around £10, 000 a month. 'Bread and butter' clients paid about £30,000 a year.

Good Relations charged monthly retainers as well as for project work 'whereby a brief is agreed for a certain amount of activity which may be defined in terms of time or by set objective for a fixed fee'. They also charged by hourly rate. The majority of fee was earned by retainer; a 'large minority' by project work and 'a very small minority' by the hour, with a preference not to work by that latter method. Retainers ranged from £1,000 to 'several tens of thousands a month'.

At the PPU, the fee range was similarly wide. Charles Miller said about a recent month that the lowest fee charged was £325 and the highest £28,000. Work was either on a retained basis or an ad hoc one. He said: '. . . high fees are always charged on ad hoc work. That's when you have a Monopolies Commission inquiry or a take-over . . . and you have to throw people at work all hours of the day and night. A lot of writing, a lot of telephoning. That's where it clocks up'.

The fee charging model operated by PPU was the law firm. The fee rates were equivalent to lawyers.

> We have a bulk of people in this company who because of the policy of our recruitment would be ranked as junior partner level and above in a law firm and

they are charged accordingly. And we have another tier who would be called researchers or junior consultants charged at another level.

Hourly rates were used. Charles Miller explained: 'All our thinking is done by the hour or by quarter of an hour units. Everybody keeps a timesheet. . . We bill our clients monthly as I think all lobbyists do or very occasionally on completion of a project'.

College Hill Associates had a preference for retainer fees 'for commercial reasons' and the majority of clients paid on that basis. Tessa Devlin said:

> Our recommendation in almost all cases would be 'if we are retained, then we will constantly be looking out on your behalf . . .'. Project-based clients are often those that have a specific problem: perhaps they're being investigated by the OFT; they're trying to avoid being referred . . .

Fees were time based. She explained: 'We certainly keep time sheets and client reports . . . someone will say "what on earth did you do that week" and you will go "this is exactly what we've done".' Annual fees for 'a straight monitoring account' were £15,000 to £20,000 but 'if it's something with an issue that is current and big and is part of somebody's platform, then that could reasonably double. But fees are always calculated: it's not something that is pulled out of the sky . . . We know what our time is worth. We can judge by looking at a problem or an issue how much time that will need a week'.

Another view was critical of the charges made for monitoring, judging them to be excessive for the supply of information already in the public domain. The same view indicated fees of between £5,000 and £8,000 for policy advice and high level political access.

Charles Barker was flexible in its fee structure. Evie Soames said: 'We work on all those bases - retainer basis; project basis; man hours basis; monthly basis; retainer plus man hours during a campaign. All kinds of different arrangements because it's an uncertain political life so we can't plan exactly our programme and our fees like my colleagues in other disciplines. . . '. But the majority of clients were on retainers to which might be added an ad hoc project during the Parliamentary session. Fee levels were at the same level as those for public relations.

Another charging principle is success fees. These were a matter of some sensitivity inside and outside lobbying circles for it makes an explicit link between public policy-making and making money for one of the participants. One of the interviewees said that they worked 'occasionally with a success fee attached' but did not want that statement to be attributed. A representative body for some lobbyists, the Public Relations Consultants' Association (PRCA), bans such fees in its Code of Conduct but Peter Moore believed that they are charged 'throughout the industry'. Evie Soames said: 'I know lots of people do. I'm not very keen to do so but I may be persuaded to change my mind'. She reported about opposition to these fees that 'a great many of the great and the good are saying that this is perhaps rather a blinkered, old fashioned attitude'. She would not accept a 'no foal, no fee' basis of payment: 'I might accept an add-on sweetener but I don't think I would try and change minds for nothing'. The PPU lobbyist had 'no compunction at all' about charging success fees but added '. . . clients rarely want them'. Tom McNally said that Shandwick do charge them but that Hill and Knowlton do not.

Tessa Devlin added that she was against success fees: 'because it doesn't make commercial sense. Does that mean you work for a year towards a goal, you take them . . . a long way forward and the end result is the Government still puts an amendment into a Bill and you don't get paid?'

For Westminster Strategy, Michael Burrell said '. . . we don't have success fees'.

> We would not agree to an arrangement whereby we were paid in the event of success and not in the event of failure or paid more in the event of success because I think there is just a small risk that perhaps, particularly younger, junior people might be tempted to go beyond what would be appropriate because of the financial incentive and I think it's very important to guard against that.

Fees for lobbyists have been touched on in previous UK academic literature on commercial lobbyists but not as extensively as here. The previous references have been indirectly reported as industry averages and not attributed to individuals or described as the operating practice of individual companies. The data on fee structure above is an extension to the literature.

The use of success fees also raises a question of appropriateness: is it a matter of concern that a player in the public policy process should have a personal monetary interest in the outcome of that process? The Westminster Strategy lobbyist raised the question and ruled out success fees as a consequence. None of the others raised the question.

Lobbyists: nomenclature and self-perceptions

Chapter One showed a sensitivity by some lobbyists if their work was described publicly as public relations or lobbying. This sensitivity is reflected in these meetings with lobbyists.

The most negative reaction to the public relations description was given in a non-attributable conversation after an on-the-record interview: 'If you describe me as being in public relations, I'll issue a writ'. It was not clear from the context whether irony was being employed.

But for Fred Morgan of Westminster Advisers 'lobbying is very much like public relations in the sense that the area is very, very wide'. For Michael Burrell of Westminster Strategy, the question 'are you in public relations' was 'an extremely arid, pointless debate' with a partial case to be made for inclusion and exclusion. For Evie Soames of Charles Barker the 'arid' debate was over.

> I used to mind. I used to spend hours in the seventies and the early eighties saying: 'we're completely different. We must have nothing to do with the PRCA. We must have nothing to do with the IPR (Institute of Public Relations). We are a completely different profession'. But I think that was all a waste of time. We're in the communications business... I do quite a bit of press relations when it's necessary as part of our campaigns.

The Westminster Communications respondent talked exclusively of the 'role of public affairs consultants'.

For David Perchard, lobbying was related to and overlapped 'a little bit' with public relations.

> We're always very keen not to be described as public relations consultants because it implies presentation rather than substance and what we're doing involves analysis and a fair amount of intellectual contribution.

> David Perchard used the self-descriptor lobbyist 'sometimes but not often'.

> I don't say that I'm a lobbyist; I say that I am a public affairs consultant. However lobbying is one of a number of activities we perform as public affairs consultants . . . I am a lobbyist in the same way that I'm a car driver. It is one of the things that I do.

Tom McNally of Shandwick was 'most certainly' in public relations and in a 'specialist part' of it but recognised that some colleagues saw themselves as 'political counsel'. He did not object to being called a lobbyist: 'I do not spend all my time lobbying. It is one of a number of options open when one advises a client'. He gave the following example of non-lobbying work: telling a client that legislation was inevitable and that it could not be resisted or amended.

The Good Relations respondent gave a qualified answer to the question of relationships with public relations: 'yes but again public relations is a slightly unsatifactory label for what we do'.

He hesitated to call himself a lobbyist and did so 'only when I can't think of anything better'. He thought of himself 'as being a political advocate' but recognised one perception of that title as 'a bit pompous'. The public affairs and government relations titles were not 'really entirely satisfactory' either. For Martin Smith of GPC, the title 'public policy consultant and government relations consultant' is not satisfactory but lobbyist is a term people will understand 'but it will also have extremely negative connotations'.

Charles Miller of the PPU did not call himself a public affairs consultant 'because I don't know what it means' and was relaxed about calling himself a lobbyist ('I don't mind . . . I have no pride'). He was not in public relations but it overlapped:

'. . . all lobbying firms that I know use PR. The question is whether it's the servant or the master . . . PR can be part of lobbying but lobbying isn't part of PR'.

The brochures issued by the lobbyists for promotional and business development purposes were much more coy about using the word 'lobby', if they used it at all. There was a wide resort to semi-technical, semi-jargon descriptors such as 'public affairs' and 'government relations'.

* Westminster Advisers was 'a partnership of senior consultants specialising in public affairs and government relations work' and bound by the Code of Professional Conduct of the IPR.
* 'Market Access helped companies do business with Government' in a folder entitled The Market Access Public Affairs Group.
* '. . . Westminster Strategy is one of Britain's leading specialist government, political and media relations firms'. It also benefited 'from its membership of the Grayling Group, one of the United Kingdom's top ten public relations organisations'.
* 'Government Policy Consultants (GPC) is a specialist public affairs consultancy' and 'GPC takes public policy and government relations consulting seriously as a business'. Among its services are 'government relations advice and assistance including lobbying the UK Government and (sic) European Community institutions'.
* Westminster Communications Group had 'Public Affairs and (sic) European Community divisions; '. . . all the consultancy specialises in integrated public affairs and public relations campaigns'.
* Good Relations was 'The Leader in British Public Relations for over 25 years'. It is part of the Lowe Bell Group: 'We specialise in consultancy, public relations, government relations, design and advertising'.
* The Public Policy Unit were 'Political and Regulatory Advisers'.
* 'Charles Barker's Public Affairs Groups provides ... consultancy and information services on legislation and policies . . . '
* 'Shandwick Public Affairs is a specialist company within Shandwick, the world's largest public relations consultancy'.
* Taskforce Communications are 'Consultants in public affairs' and they note the 'strong interdependency' between public affairs, public relations and media services.

The print publicity references above clearly indicate a reluctance to ascribe the titles 'lobbyist' or 'lobbying' to the work of individuals or of corporate bodies in a public way. This hesitation reflects the negative or at least ambiguous connotations discussed in the literature. These connotations are in common usage (7n) and lead to hesitation by individuals and corporate organisations to use titles which would put at risk their social prestige. But individuals are content to use 'lobbying' and 'lobbyist' in discussion as generic descriptors of their work and of the general field. All the clients and lobbyists met received a briefing note which only used the descriptor 'lobbying' and none queried it. The questions were framed in the same way and only one lobbyist refused to discuss her work in its terms: one declared a preference for the word 'communicate'; and another talked of lobbyists 'to use a term which I really don't like very much'.

Conclusion

This Chapter is part one of an analysis of data from a representative sample of individual lobbyists working in London and environs. Their clients were mostly in the private sector; usually large plc companies but trade associations were also represented. The number of public sector clients was largely determined by Government policy towards the sector, especially in regard to privatisation, regulation and competition policies. The proportion of public sector clients on lobbyists' lists was therefore a fluctuating quantity and appeared to be a higher rather than lower quantity at the time of the interviews (mid-1993), largely because of the local government review. Voluntary sector clients were very few.

Lobbyists preferred clients who bring a substantial matter forward; who understand that the political process is unlike business, and who allow their agents autonomy. Keeping and getting clients concerned all lobbyists, with some lobbyists more active in this business development work than others. Those establishing new businesses or re-establishing old ones spent much time on this work - up to a third. A variety of business getting techniques were used, with referral by satisfied clients to new clients being a favoured one.

There was also variety of fee levels and of fee types in play in the competitive market-place for lobbying advice. There was no industry-wide scale and lobbyists charged what the market bore. £250,000 had been charged to clients facing very threatening circumstances, such as referral to a regulatory body: the lowest reported was £325 as a loss leader to get new business. Fees were structured by time in year, month, hourly and sub-hourly units; by stand-alone project; and by outcome. The latter were known as success fees; were fairly widespread and raised a question of propriety: should players in the public policy process have a personal monetary interest in the outcome of that process. Annual retainers were the favoured fee structure of lobbyists but the hourly time sheet was becoming more common.

Lobbyists had mixed feelings about being called public relations people but were nearly always sensitive about being publicly called 'lobbyists'. In print they always preferred some other title. They were privately hesitant to self-describe themselves with the 'L' word. But they were ready to use it when generically and impersonally describing the field.

Notes

1. The source is Mori, 32 Old Queen St., London, SW1 9HP. Tel: 0171 222 0232.
2. Non-attributable information given after a recorded interview.
3. Non-attributable information given after a recorded interview.
4. The Report states p 14 that the direct cost of their services was £101,000.
5. In a letter of 1 October, 1993 to the author, Mr. Greer said that topics covered by this work have 'been well covered in many similar projects and articles in the past few years'. In a comment about fees, he added that the 'way in which they are agreed is obviously a commercial decision on the part of both parties'. On 5 October, an article appeared in the Guardian newspaper on p 6 under the headline 'The power and prestige of Ian Greer'. Its authors were described as profiling 'the leading player linking politicans with companies seeking a path to the powerful'.
6. The Independent newspaper of 24 August, 1993, p 4 under the heading 'Auditors call halt to council campaigns'.
7. The editorial on p 5 of *PR Week*, 26 August, 1993 was entitled 'Shed light on a shadowy world'. It described lobbying as a 'shadowy world' and was a call for 'greater transparency' in the relationship between politicians and lobbyists. It said: 'The word lobbying is rarely seen in the press without being preceded by the phrase "shadowy world of." In fact it is taken as read in many quarters that lobbying is, and by its very nature will remain, a secretive mechanism by which back door deals are constructed. A mythology has been created, with the lobbyist as the spider at the centre of a web of whispered intrigue. Yet examination of the "abuses" of the system reveal a tiny number of cases to cause real concern'.

5 Lobbyists for hire: a profile (part two)

Introduction

The focus in this Chapter remains on the lobbyists but now from the following vantage points: what they say they do for clients; a proposed new typology of lobbying behaviours; a review of services supplied to clients; self-perceptions of relationships with decision-makers, and of giving value for money to clients.

'The cerebral and the arms and legs' - a range of services

This section examines what lobbyists say they do for clients. The interviews offer a detailed, information-rich, 'thick' description of their daily operations. This fullness of data has confirmed that there are many discrete activities bunched together under the single label lobbying. The literature has stated that lobbying can be broken down into separate but linked activities and data confirms that disaggregation.

Chapter Three broke down lobbyists' work into services supplied in response to client needs. Another breakdown is suggested by the data in this section: the categories lobbying process and lobbying content. As regards process, all the lobbyists said they did a range of separate but linked activities (monitoring; gaining access; making representations; policy analysis; support work, and media relations) which are grouped here under the single descriptor lobbying. None claimed to do an activity which was not done by another lobbyist and all demonstrated that they did a range of activities common to lobbying. Also there were, in the language of marketing, 'unique selling propositions' on offer from individual lobbyists: claims were made of presentation expertise, skilled policy analysis, inside knowledge of the decision-making system.

As regards lobbying content (issues and policy), two lobbyists (David Perchard and Charles Miller) claimed pre-client specialist knowledge of these and one (Martin Smith) said it was fostered by client demand. The majority tendency among respondents was that lobbyists seek clients first and not issues and then principally service their process needs. Few commercial lobbyists claim to be issue and policy experts.

Before looking at what the lobbyists say they do, it is worth reviewing the issues lobbied about. The overwhelming impression is of a great spread of public policies.

Included are UK building regulations; deregulation of civil aviation in Europe from the point of view of English regional airports; EU policy on packaging and on environmental issues; the deregulation of bingo advertising; food safety; profile raising for a public sector body likely to be privatised; getting nuclear submarine refitting work for Devonport Dockyard; working for Plymouth City Council on changes to Parliamentary boundaries; local government reform; maintenance of the direct flight between Plymouth and Heathrow; running the National Lottery; reform of the Sports Council and of the Civil Aviation Authority; British airports policy; building a new airport; European aviation policy; planning issues involving science parks; rail link to the Channel Tunnel and to Heathrow; clearance for food additives (1n); the reference of fragrances and of CDs to the Monopolies Commission; access to the gas distribution market; de-regulation of London buses; the use of 44 ton lorries for access to railheads or on all UK roads; Sunday trading options; the future of milk marketing; the case for computer game manufacturers in a reference to the Office of Fair Trading; photosensitive epilepsy and any links with computer games; Group Four, their handling of remand prisoners and prison privatisation; Crown Estates and consumer matters; a television company explaining the impact of new technology; Labour Party corporate tax policy and the two types of water company.

This was the issues background to the generalised question: 'what do you do for clients?'

For Market Access, Peter Moore said:

> . . . you start off at the basic level with providing a monitoring service. . . Some clients come to you: they want to write to a Minister with a problem. You may just have to help them draft a letter and put it in the appropriate language and the appropriate terms and make it the appropriate length. Sometimes the detail that is interesting to them might not be interesting to the Minister and would not even make it past the officials into his box for the weekend . . . Prepare briefs for Members of Parliament, Peers, officials on a client's particular case; help to arrange meetings with officials, Members of Parliament . . . You can advise on Parliamentary procedure.

Later he added: '. . . you often find yourself just advising clients on the phone for anything from five minutes to an hour on a whole range of issues, depending on how much they've got to talk to you about . . .'.

For Michael Burrell of Westminister Strategy, his organisation offers the long menu. Westminster Strategy '. . . is a lobbying company which helps people put a case to Government'. He expanded:

> . . . from one end, basic monitoring through analysis of the significance of that information; to advice on what to do with it; to helping to fix meetings; to advising clients on how to handle meetings; to going to meetings with clients and interpret what's being said to them . . .

He believed that '... there should be no privileged access for one sector or one company as against another'. Rather than contacts, what Westminster Strategy offered to clients was:

> an understanding of how the system worked; who are the decision-makers; and when is the right time to make representations; what is the best tone of voice to make those representations in. So it is about understanding the system and how to present to it, not about contacts.

For Martin Smith of GPC there was a menu on offer and it had a centrepiece:

> ... policy analysis is central to it because unless we understand in some detail the client's business and how it relates to trends in public policy, we don't feel comfortable in doing the job. It is a question of wanting to be confident that we can anticipate, deal with anything that might come along. We do also engage in lobbying in the sense in which that term is generally understood. For example, the Private Members' Bill on the de-regulation of bingo advertising was entirely done by this office. That is to say we did the analysis; we supervised the drafting of the Bill; we lobbied on the Bill; we dealt with the Home Office; we dealt with the Gaming Board ...

He developed a three boxes image of the services offered: box A is monitoring and intelligence; B is policy analysis, and C is 'representation, lobbying' and the latter is 'an activity which we do probably only 15 percent of the time and for some clients not at all'.

Clients choose their own menu of boxes:

> Some clients will only want box A; they want to know what's happening. Some want A and B; they want to know what is happening and why it's happening; and some want A, B and C to understand it all, know it all and get their oar in somewhere. The best clients want all three but some unquestionably only want one. A client that only wanted boxes A and B (was) Electricité de France during the privatization of electricity. They wanted to know what was going on; who the players were; where the policy fault lines were; but they did not want anybody to say anything to anyone about their interest at all. They certainly didn't want to represent their views.

He favoured 'the development of genuine policy specialisms and the policy specialisms that we develop follow the clients. It has to be that way round because somebody needs to be paying for us to become the world's leading expert on the draft directive on the incineration of hazardous waste ... '.

Later, he added:

> I have one or two people in Brussels who know more about the politics of waste and waste management than I would guess anybody does, because they spend all their time working on those subjects. Every draft directive, every policy

statement they are absolutely familiar with and also on a country-by-country basis could tell you precisely how the the position of Lei Amici della Terra varies from Les Amis de la Terre or Friends of the Earth, that degree of special knowledge.

David Perchard Associates also described a menu:

> ... the first thing that we do is keep abreast of developments in whatever field it is we're working on and the most important thing is to plough through the endless paper; to talk to decision-makers before they're making their decisions so we can give people advance notice of what's likely to happen: to summarise all of this in as much or as little detail as the clients want ... we have somebody who spends a lot of time travelling with the European Parliament; attends most meetings of the Environment Committee ... most meetings of the Economic Committee and almost every plenary session which keeps us up-to-date with developments ...

Tom McNally of Shandwick offered clients 'a variety of activity' and 'the basic bread and butter is to monitor activity' in London and 'increasingly' in Brussels and Strasbourg. Clients could do this themselves 'but the sheer volume of material that comes out of Government needs to be filtered if busy executives are not to be swamped'. Next on offer 'is analysis and counsel'.

Simon Nayyar of Westminster Communications, also offered clients variety of service:

> a number of discrete activities. . . First and foremost intelligence gathering. You can't hope to influence the decision-making process if you don't know what's happening. Secondly profile building: unless an issue or a client and its interests are known or understood, one cannot make an effective contribution to the policy debate. Opinion forming, putting across the key substantive policy issues in a way that is easily assimilated by decision-makers who, not least because of their own time constraints, will have a very short time frame in which to take in the information and indeed often fairly low boredom thresholds. And then there is the issue of strategic advice; having gone out in the corporate decision-making arena establishing a view on the way ahead, identifying the objectives and then offering advice about how most effectively to meet them.

For Westminister Advisers, Fred Morgan said:

> Usually there is a specific problem that they (clients) have (i.e. the building regulations). And these come up about every four or five years. There's a revision of a section and the potential client might be concerned about what's going to happen at the next review; might be concerned with what's happened in the last review, and will want us to influence the development . . . in one respect or another.

He elaborated on how they exercised their influence:

> We do it in a number of ways. First of all attempting to influence the civil servant and the Minister. If that proves impossible, influencing Members of Parliament and getting pressure put on the Ministers by Members of Parliament.

For Good Relations' Tim Rycroft, the centrepiece of their menu of services was familiarity with the decision-making system:

> We sell our knowledge and expertise at finding our way round the political process. . . it breaks down into the cerebral and the arms and the legs. . . Some clients need us to be their arms and legs. So today for a client I am attempting to book accommodation and security passes for party conference; to book dining rooms; to send out invitations. . . And then that ranges all the way up . . . to purely advice and guidance.

He offered to clients that '. . . I do know the political and Parliamentary process very well'. A colleague had policy specialism in the area of food safety and European regulations on food additives but:

> I think we would all feel that it's best not to get too drawn into a speciality because Good Relations sells its public affairs as being broad-based. We don't try to sell ourselves as being specialists in any particular area and . . . one of the tasks of a consultant is to be able to assimilate a client's business and to understand it very quickly and to deal with it.

For the PPU's Charles Miller:

> They [clients] want to find out what's going on inside system . . . Second thing is putting cases together. . . Third is advice on advocacy: in other words how do we go about winning this case or actually acting as advocates, negotiating with Whitehall, with Members of Parliament. The putting together of cases and the negotiation side as distinct from advice on strategy are . . . areas where we are nearly unique. The common law (of lobbying) is that advisers should advise. That's largely grown out of the fact that lobbyists . . . haven't become experts on particular subject areas whereas there are some now in our profession who're real experts in aviation, in local government, in energy, whatever; who are speaking sense when they advocate a case on a client's behalf.

Charles Miller argued that all lobbying firms 'would say they have an emphasis rather than a speciality'. He added:

> Our emphasis is away from pure Parliamentary work. It's on balance . . . getting at the system where the system makes the decisions rather than letting the tail wag the dog all the time. . . You go where the problems and the decisions are.

Evie Soames of Charles Barker said her work was '... a mixture of campaigning; lobbying; information; intelligence; advice, contacts; analysis of political developments, forthcoming legislation' and split equally between London and Brussels.

For the unnamed lobbyist, lobbying was 'getting the right message into the right ear at the right time and we can advise on that'. He did not see his role as a direct, face-to-face advocate for a company: rather a facilitator. He gave the example of a client who was interested in running the National Lottery:

> They feel they're best suited to do it so we are involved in advising them on the political implications of actions they may take, have taken, want to take. Should they be involved meeting people other than those they have already seen? What should they say to them? And arranging meetings, arranging dinners, breakfasts, whatever it happens to be. Writing letters, drafting letters to go to Ministers.

He recounted the work of a colleague who kept a 'watching brief' for a client who faced queries about health issues related to children. So that colleague 'will be writing letters to MPs and countering things said in the press'.

For Tessa Devlin of College Hill Associates, her work was also a range:

> If we use as an example the work that I do for this [water related] trade association... in the first instance we keep abreast of whatever's happening and that would include keeping in contact with the Government . . . sponsoring department; with MPs; with any political manoeuvring within the political parties; and certainly with the regulators. It's maintaining relationships with people so when the DOE has a question or a politician has a question, they think 'ah, who was that person who helped?' and they come to the water companies for answers. And that positions our client as an adviser to Government.

The above data emphaises the multiplicity and diversity of the activities done under the single descriptor lobbying. Nobody ruled out doing any of the activities of lobbying: their work is client-led and they will service client needs. They let clients 'pick 'n mix' from the range of activities offered. They are professional advisers in the sense that they have a principal and agent relationship with clients and work to the latter in a structured relationship of query/advise/agree action. But most of the data suggested work which is focused on lobbying processes rather than on content. By and large, commercial lobbyists are not experts on issues and policy.

This emphasis flows from the logic of the market-place in which lobbyists are hired. Being businesses, it is sensible - as *homo economicus* - to offer services that appeal to a maximum of potential clients. All clients do not face the same issues but they all face the same decision-making process in the UK and EU. Lobbyists for hire can therefore maximise their span of potential clients through process expertise rather than issue and policy expertise.

The balance of the data also suggested that most lobbyists worked behind their clients as background advisers and not mainly as their public representatives. This follows, arguably, from the process emphasis because the substance of public representation of a client is issue and policy matters.

Backgrounder and foregrounder types

The data also suggested another related conclusion: that although lobbyists do not rule any type of activity out, they tend to work around a particular cluster of activities rather than another. They do not exhibit work 'no-go' areas but they do have work preferences. These clusters can be further thought of as Weberian ideal types, defined as conceptually pure types of rational action (Hughes; 93). No actual lobbyist copies all the behaviours of the type but many lobbyists copy a number of them, albeit in somewhat degraded form. Lobbyists can also be expected to have behaviours recognisable of more than one type.

Conceptualisation of the data suggests two ideal types of lobbyist.

the backgrounder type: working as the unseen adviser; monitoring corporate and official documents in the passive sense of spotting references and issues; giving policy-making sovereignty to the client and offering marginal comments on policy; drafting documents which the client will then send on to decision-makers: suggesting to the client who the relevant cast of decision-makers is; perhaps effecting the introduction of the client but then not being present at representations with decision-makers; giving advice that is about processes; comfortable with minimal autonomy vis-à-vis the client:

the foregrounder type: working as the visible adviser; a policy expert; already critically monitoring the external environment as part of their own views on public policy; offering their policy expertise as a resource to refine or even create client policy; ready to represent the client publicly and alone to decision-makers; ready to run public campaigns via the mass media; comfortable with maximum autonomy vis-à-vis the client.

The **backgrounder** is less visible to participants and observers of the policy-making process than the **foregrounder**: the former is more reactive to clients, the latter more proactive.

It is not implied that one of these types is precedent, more influential or superior in any way over the other. Which behaviour a lobbyist employs and whether he 'borrows' from both types is contingent on a number of factors to do with performance in a particular set of circumstances. This Chapter has shown, for example, in the data from Westminster Strategy and the PPU that a lobbying exercise can include little advice on policy but strong, pro-active advice on presentation; or strong advice on policy but none on mass media campaigns. Secondly, commercial lobbyists can propose behaviour but clients decide. Also, the social context in which the two types are used as an interpretative device is critical. For example, the lobbyist can be very active with the client in policy development and thus of the foregrounder type but be nearly invisible to the decision-maker. The latter is a combination of lobbying behaviour explored in the next Chapter.

The data presented in this work offers examples of behaviour which fit the two ideal types above and in its totality is the empirical foundation for the conceptualisation. Such a conceptualisation hopefully offers a tool for more fully understanding the subjective data collected from social actors called lobbyists and any added understanding is the reason for the conceptual development. But it must be stressed that these ideal types cannot be used as benchmarks for counting lobbyists under the umbrella of one or other type. Ideal types are not constructs in the same epistemological category as data. Instead, they are conceptual tools which offer patterns for discriminating amongst lobbying behaviours described in the next two sections in terms of services lobbyists offer.

Gaining access to and making representations to decision-makers

Access to decision-makers is defined here as the capacity of clients to reach the relevant decision-makers with oral and written messages on public issues affecting them. They can do this independently as the self-reliant clients in Chapter Four, 84-88 demonstrated but the focus here is access for clients mediated by their lobbyists. Two aspects of access should be singled out: a) oral and written messages and b) identifying the right decision-makers in the public policy process. It should not be assumed that posting or faxing messages is an easier operation than speaking them. In either case, the necessary condition for success is transmitting to the right receiver. But the general preference by UK decision-makers for an opaque cover over the locus of decision-making makes finding both oral and written routes somewhat problematical. Nor should it be assumed that a face-to-face meeting is more persuasive than a well-drafted sheet of A4. The data below illuminates these points.

Making representations is defined here as the persuasive presentation of a client's case in person, by proxy or by document to the relevant decision-maker. Again it should not be assumed that representations in person are more effective than representations by document. Effectiveness lies in the cogency of the represented case in policy and in political terms: the delivery vehicle is secondary.

Although conceptually, access and making representations can be separated in part (the focus for access is discovering the right recipient for message delivery: the focus for representation is delivery of a persuasive case), they actually overlap in lobbying practice and are treated jointly here. The commonalities can be identified as a shared focus on right message content ; right form, whether written or spoken and right timing. This section treats both commonalities and differences together on the grounds that the data shows that the two concepts are often operationally fused into a sequence of acts. For example, clients write persuasive letters, drafted by their lobbyist, to civil servants identified by their lobbyist; clients walk into the rooms of a Minister or of a civil servant identified by their lobbyist and speak a persuasive case shaped by their lobbyist; doing both at a time chosen for impact. Another example of fusion is when the lobbyist meets the decision-maker by chance or socially and speaks for the client.

The analysis below shows up the access and representations work of hired lobbyists and illustrates backgrounder and foregrounder behaviour analysed above.

Fred Morgan of Westminster Advisers illustrated access/representations fusion:

> Seeking to influence the Conservative backbench committee, we would find out who's who in that committee. We would assess how sympathetic or unsympathetic they are. We would have a look at the biographies of the members of that committee. We would talk to the client about that committee. We would then write to the secretary of that committee and seek to persuade them to give the client the opportunity to address that committee.

Would he describe his role as a backroom one?

> I would not say always backroom boys but that's where we would prefer to be . . . there are different styles. You might go to another lobbying company and they tend to be front men. Certainly my predeliction is to remain in the background.

Tim Rycroft of Good Relations shared this backgrounder preference:

> Our approach is always that it is better that the client should do it themselves [fix up meetings] even if they do it on the basis of a draft that we prepared and told them where to send it; how to send it and when to send it. It is a general rule of public affairs that people who run the political process prefer to be dealt with direct rather than through intermediaries. However, there are times when clients want us to do it for them or aren't able to do it themselves and in those circumstances we will do it . . .

He was ambivalent about ease of access: 'It isn't easy; whether that means it is hard, I'm not sure'. He noted that it was easier in the EU to the point that the Commission '. . . looks much more favourably on the input which lobbyists can give'.

> The Commission . . . will often hold hearings on new policy initiatives and invite interested parties along to come and tell them what they think and it's much easier to do it that way than have to fight one's way through layers of bureaucracy to find the decision-makers to make the case to them. So I suppose in that sense (of a UK/EU comparison) . . . access is difficult . . . but it isn't a major obstacle because the vast majority of decision-makers in the end would like to make their decisions on the basis of being well informed as opposed to being ill-informed. And there is usually . . . a way to get information to them.

Another view of access as relatively easy was because Ministers were friends in many cases and a former Cabinet Minister was available as a channel for the highest level contacts. For Market Access's Peter Moore, access was also not a problem: 'access is surprisingly easy really: if you've got a good case; if you've a genuine reason to go with it'.

> Now if we've got a client that doesn't have a legitimate reason to approach a Minister or an official, we would tell them 'look, go back and do your homework and then come back and then we can tell you what to do'.

He described some access work as 'preventative medicine stopping them (clients) going in at the wrong level or making sure they go in at the right level'. He described a backgrounder scenario:

> . . . I would say that a huge proportion of our work, does not involve going in and seeing a Minister. It might make a Minister aware of what you're on about if you're into the Minister with an inappropriate message. Then you just find that your work's counter-productive; so you either advise against it or you avoid it and you only use their time if you judge that it's an appropriate and relevant issue for them.

He said that 'we might arrange [a meeting] if the client wasn't confident to do it themselves and didn't have the phone number or something . . . just because it was easier to do that'.

For example, his managing director was an ex-civil servant: '. . . so it's just logical, sensible and easier for him to do it . . . knowing his way round the department and its various ways'.

He added that some lobbyists will see Ministers independently of clients: '. . . a lot of lobbying companies will have occasional dinners or lunches or breakfasts . . . to which they will invite a Minister along and just go through a round robin of issues that they know are going to come up at some point'.

For Westminster Strategy, Michael Burrell estimated that 'of our current client list, about ten per cent perhaps would not use us for access: so the other 90 per cent would'. He amplified:

> . . . clients are very proud and therefore routinely, particularly at the beginning of a relationship, they will say 'oh we meet Cabinet Ministers every day of the week: don't need any help on that thank you'. And pretty routinely one discovers that that's a load of old codswallop and even it it isn't . . . they are meeting the wrong people. Fine, by all means have a drink with a Cabinet Minister but actually, without going overboard on this subject, it is generally the civil servants who are more important or it's maybe the junior Ministers who are more important; or maybe it's a different department or set of departments from the ones that naturally occur to the client.

Fixing up meetings was a 'routine part of the job', he said. About the personnel at these meetings:

> I guess there are three basic possibilities. There's the client going in by themselves; there's us going with the clients, or there's us going in by ourselves. And the vast majority of cases would be the middle one of those . . . The client and us going in together: the client on the whole making the case; us listening hopefully with a degree of sophistication and ready to intervene if - as does happen very occasionally - the client completely dries up. There are some clients who prefer to go in by themselves. As for us going it by ourselves, it really depends what you mean. I think we would very rarely have a formal meeting where we were formally putting the case on behalf of someone else but we would every day of the week bump into contacts and have a chat about things and one of the things one would talk about is one's clients.

He estimated that 60% of his firm's lobbying time was spent with civil servants and 40% with politicians:

> It does slightly vary over time. In other words, you might spent more time with MPs where the Government has a small majority than you would where the Government has a large majority. But most of the work we're involved in is detail . . . MPs simply don't have the time to get to grips with detail even if they have the inclination or the interest, so mostly you are dealing with civil servants in particular areas. . . In very many cases the media will also be an important part of the equation.

This reference to the size of the Government's majority is supportive of the 'fragile majorities' concept: small majorities imply a concentration of lobbying effort on Parliament and increased workloads for lobbyists as clients sense that they are more likely to win concessions.

Getting access was 'relatively easy' for Tessa Devlin of College Hill Associates but:

> It's dependent on giving them (decision-makers) enough information at the start so that they think that you're not going to waste time and it's using a number of different mechanisms and possibly phrases when you open the door, so that you're comfortable with them and you don't offend them and then you work within the protocol or hierarchy that the Civil Service have.

Who made representations was a matter of judgement but there was clear preference for the client to do so:

> I maintain firmly that no one sells the client's issue with client's objective as well as the client. I can know the brief backwards and I still won't do the same justice because I haven't spent my life working on that particular issue. So I always recommend that the client is there. There are some occasions like a presentation in front of a backbench committee where there are so few

> committee members that I would send in the client alone but . . . I would have prepared their brief and vetted it and scrutinised what they were about to say and wait in the corridor for them.

She estimated that 60% of representations were client and her together; 30% client alone, and ten per cent her alone. She arranged the meetings with decision-makers. Contact with Ministers was the least frequent: it was then equally split between officials and Parliamentarians, including Peers. But how are the relevant decision-makers identified?

> . . . the majority, of course, I would know by books and by reputation. Civil servants that cover areas for which my clients are interested I would know personally through the work I've done for them. But in all cases, I would say it's not a personal connection that carries a client's issue forward. It's a solid information: it's getting the person who wants to hear you. Of course, if you happen to know Michael Portillo, then great.

Tom McNally pointed out the converse: that Government wanted to know the thinking of large companies. He said: '. . . I always point out that most companies have the right of access simply by their size or their capabilities'.

He saw the amount of access he could arrange as part of his professional capital and his firm had a 'rolling programme' of hospitality for Ministers, civil servants and senior journalists. When representations were made 'most often I would advise clients to go on their own, having being well prepared by us'. Preparation included 'everything from media training . . . to preparing a chief executive for the kind of fast ball he might receive in front of a televised Select Committee'. He thought that the lobbyist alone making the representations caused 'resentment on the part of the recipient'.

David Perchard had a more foregrounder approach. It has been described above how his staff attend the EU Environment Committee and track developments on packaging issues. 'More time is spent speaking to legislators on (clients') behalf than arranging meetings'. These direct representations flowed from the firm's specialist knowledge which allowed them to say to clients: 'this is what is going on; this is why you should care about it and this is what we suggest you do about it'. This was specialist knowledge conferring lobbying power and was in contradistinction to the generalist who could only say to the client: 'this is what is going on: isn't it interesting'.

Access in Brussels and Strasbourg is 'not difficult'. He explained: ' . . . all you've got to do is find out the right telephone numbers and there's endless directories to encourage you to do that . . . '.

But in some circumstances, he introduced clients directly to decision-makers. He said:

> We tend to wheel in the clients in two ways. Sometimes we organise a guided tour of Brussels, occasionally Strasbourg, so that the client can meet a number of people whose work affects them and get a first hand feel for what it's about.

> At other times we will want to deliver a particular message at a particular time and it's always much more persuasive if it comes out of the client's mouth because he's got all the detail and information to hand. He's got the passion for his particular case.

Charles Miller implied that access for the PPU was not a problem as its employees came from Government and that such a background was 'a basic pre-requisite for joining the company'. Something over 50% of representations were done by the PPU alone or with the client present. Explaining this balance, he said:

> Many [clients] are highly professional and [it's] just for you to give them the information they need in order to help them to do their job better: but an awful lot of them are trained to do other things and simply don't have the experience or ability or the confidence to put over a case well.

Both Perchard Associates and PPU claimed policy expertise (a foregrounder characteristic) and it is noteworthy that they do significant amounts of direct representation themselves with decision-makers. Depth of subject knowledge allowed a lobbyist to hold his own vis-à-vis a decision-maker. As David Perchard said about lobbyists emphasising a service in access rather than in policy knowledge: '. . . once you've delivered the party line, you haven't got any supplementary conversation because you don't know enough about the business'. The GPC respondent also claimed policy knowledge but did not emphasise representing clients alone.

For Simon Nayyer of Westminster Communications, access was a 'very detailed, very sophisticated analysis of not only decision-making processes but MPs . . . officials and a whole raft of other decision-makers . . .'. Representation was 'a very flexible combination' of all three variants - client alone; lobbyist alone, or both together. But the necessary condition for any successful representation was the case: 'unless you have a well founded case there is no point going out to talk to decision-makers. It is a waste of their time and a waste of your own'.

A flexible approach to representations (with both foregrounder and backgrounder characteristics) was also the way of Evie Soames of Charles Barker:

> No norm, depending upon the relationship of the client or depending upon our knowledge of that particular industry and depending upon standing. On some subjects, on some industries, on some trade associations, we are known as the representative so we go and see the officials and the officials will ask to see us. On other times, like the big corporate clients . . . it might not be appropriate for us to be at the meeting.

Access was not a problem: more problematic was whom to access and the general political balance of power when access was gained. She said:

> If we're trying to reshape a White Paper or heavily involved in the consultative process . . . it's obviously the officials who are the target . . . much more time is spent with officials, with the departments than with Parliament because

> Parliamentary lobbying is . . . not usually productive. But of course (Parliamentary lobbying) is a bit more productive now for the threat of a rebellion is much more of a powerful weapon than it has been for a long time; so we will be doing more in Parliament in this next session. . . (because) if one's hoping to stop a department in their tracks over something that one finds is . . . going to be detrimental to the client interest, . . . one more productive route now is to go via some MPs so that they might flag up some opposition.

Whom to access was also more problematical for the anonymous informant. He said:

> . . . rather than approach every MP on an issue, we use knowledge that we pick up in our daily reading of Hansard or by using the reference books that are available in every library to say 'who really has an influence and can bring pressure to bear on this issue?' And therefore we may target 25 people rather than 250, only those with a direct interest. Now because you've already filtered out those that are more likely to be interested in the subject, you're more likely to have a sympathetic hearing. What's also important is the level at which the approach is made. It is probably more important for the chairman of a company to see a Cabinet Minister than for a senior manager. A board member you can argue either way. . . The big constraint is time and who the Ministers are prepared to see and the specific interest they've taken on individual issues.

His backgrounder preference was not to represent the client directly: '. . . we feel that the strength of representation is diluted by it coming through a third party' and 'we're more likely to mention things in passing rather than act as the advocate ourselves'. He added: 'We will advise and probably go in with but we're not the expert'.

Lobbyists, clients and policy

The data indicated that 12 or more of the lobbyists gave policy-advice to clients, i.e. advice on either their corporate policy and/or the relevant public policies. But how does this square with only three of them *claiming* issue and policy expertise? In reply, several points need to be considered. Policy advice is a sensitive activity in that policy is the key variable in lobbying, the subject of attention by all players. In an advisory relationship, the rewards and risks of giving good or bad advice are high with the explicit consequence of work continuing or work diminishing. But commercial lobbyists describe themselves as being in the general category of corporate advisers; and in terms of their own marketability to clients and their own prestige vis-à-vis competitors such as lawyers, they have to offer a policy advice service. Yet the data indicated that lobbyists are generally wary of giving policy advice, except for a minority who explicitly present themselves as policy experts. Generally, the advice they give to clients is more often about lobbying processes. Secondly, this bias is added to by the difficulty of separating out policy advice and presentational advice - a difficulty also met in Chapter Three. The foregrounder/backgrounder typology helps, however, in understanding the separation.

The Westminster Strategy informant made the case for separation but showed the difficulties:

> There is a very fuzzy line between presentation and policy and it's hard to say really when one is advising on one and advising on the other. A lot of the time we are asked to draft papers or comment on the client's drafts and very often we are asked to help on policy in the sense that a client will say 'my objective is' or 'my preferred point of arrival is' and we will say 'well it maybe that that is just politically out of the question; you're not going to get that but you might be able to achieve this; now that's not exactly what you want but it's quite close to it'. It tends to be a dialogue on policy but they are the experts on their policy and we are the experts on presentation and that really is the broad dividing line. It would be entirely inappropriate for us to be setting policy for major plcs or indeed a range of other institutions but entirely appropriate to offer advice on how those policies should be presented.

Simon Nayyar also noted the inextricable mixture in practice of policy analysis and presentation and said their role stretched over both: 'presentation comes atop the analysis'. He defined the firm's offering to clients as a series of functions including strategic advice where this was 'having gone out into the political market place . . . having identified key issues and objectives and having made a significant contribution, hopefully in one's own right, to that evolving policy debate'. The implication is the lobbyist influences the client's policy and that influences the public policy debate.

The Market Access respondent implied that his advice to clients could amount to a veto on presentation of their policy to decision-makers: 'if we've got a client that doesn't have a legitimate reason to approach a Minister or an official, we would tell them'.

The difficulties of separating out advice on policy and on tactics/presentation were also underlined by the College Hill Associates' informant who advised on both. Tessa Devlin said:

> any time that the client would be thinking about putting a statement, I would review that statement and say 'if you say this, this will be the implication. If we turn it around and phrase it in another way or bring in another point, then this will be what you accomplish . . . Will this rile the Labour Party? Will this actually bring them on side and give you a further network to use in furthering associations?'

For her, policy and tactics are:

> so closely entwined it's difficult to differentiate because tactics are applied to absolutely every policy decision. So policies can change and be tweaked to ensure they carry through the right message. And I don't think that is a bastardisation of a company's policy. I think it actually helps because often people in an industry don't see what they're saying.

For the GPC lobbyist, policy analysis was an explicit part of their service in the sense of analysis of public policy in areas of client interest. Martin Smith (in line with David Perchard) wanted input into client policy and looked for clients 'that are keen for us to work with them on policy analysis as part of their internal corporate affairs activity'. He added:

> in other words not a bolt-on, not a sort of who-do-we-need-to-meet, who-do-we-need-to-send-an-annual report-to but very much part of their internal long-term planning for the future, being part of a team which helps them to form a view . . .

The Good Relations respondent linked monitoring (a lobbying process) to policy advice. He went through document cuttings every morning. 'I will then fax them to the client or ring up the client and say "there's something here that I think is important and this is what I think you ought to do about it." ' The same link between monitoring and advice was made by the PPU. Its informant Charles Miller distinguished between monitoring as 'ex-post facto summaries' and 'detailed pro-active intelligence gathering' with his firm specialising in the latter. Another policy input was via '. . . putting cases together - that's anything from vetting the arguments that clients have put together to starting de novo, handling economic research, market research'. Charles Barker also linked monitoring, analysis and advice in that reporting public policy events to clients involved 'a certain amount of analysis'. The same link was made by the anonymous lobbyist: '. . . seeing a paper coming out of a think tank helps you know what is going on but it is actually monitoring as well'.

For Tom McNally of Shandwick, 'analysis and counsel' lay the other side of monitoring events for a client and meant 'that you are at a senior level influencing the company's response to political and Governmental policy and indeed in a quite legitimate way helping to influence that policy' where policy could be either the clients' or the Government's.

'Part of the machinery of government almost' - lobbyists' perceptions of relationships with decision-makers

It is clear from the data below, which is new in the UK literature, that the subject matter under investigation here is plural: there are *relationships* of varying quality and these relationships vary because of a number of identified factors in the data. Those factors, given by respondents about their own behaviour and about their perceptions of decision-makers' behaviour, are: inter-personal chemistry; departmental attitudes; length of the relationship; frequency of contact; mutual benefit through information exchange; perceived competence of the lobbyist; disclosure or not of their clients by lobbyists; perceptions of lobbyists' knowledge; the party politics of politicans; the perception of lobbyists by decision-makers as closely involved with Government; the perception of lobbyists as profiting from information given by officials. These factors appeared in the data with differing frequencies but the most recurring (Westminster Strategy; Market Access; Perchard; Westminster Communication; Good Relations; Charles Barker; the unnamed lobbyist; College Hill Associates and Shandwick) was the claim that lobbying provided mutual benefits to the public policy process.

There has been some previous work on the perceptions of decision-makers about their relationship with hired lobbyists but there was no picture, only the lightest of sketches. Now the data here has painted a picture of variable and mixed attitudes and behaviours.

Fred Morgan found positive responses: 'Certainly as far as Westminster is concerned, I personally find that everybody accepts the lobbyist as part of the machinery of Government almost and there doesn't appear to be any antagonism or concern whatsoever'. The same smooth passage was experienced by Simon Nayyar for the following reasons:

> . . . we are absolutely transparent about who our clients are and what their interests are and I think we serve, certainly MPs, a thoroughly useful and helpful role. We can significantly cut down on their mailbags and help to shape and model issues into their quintessence . . . And the point . . . helps significantly to reduce the amount of time that MPs have to devote to an issue because we have already helped a client to focus . . . arguments.

For Peter Moore, the quality of relationship depended on personalities but also 'an element of . . . departmental psychology comes into it'.

> There are certain . . . departments and areas that have a thing about lobbying or lobbyists but generally it depends on the individual. There are people that you will hear any lobbyist worth their salt say 'Oh God, not so and so' . . . because they have got an attitude problem about lobbying . . .

These attitude problems extended to civil servants and Ministers: about numbers, 'you're tempted to say one in fifteen/twenty people . . .'. The difficulty was exacerbated when the lobbyist was specialising: 'you'll find yourself coming back to the same group of people. So even though there might only be one awful person in twenty, he's the awful person who have to deal with all the time'.

But the majority attitude is 'not a problem'. He added:

> . . . it's not an issue even . . . so long as Ministers have their code of conduct in mind; MPs have their responsibilities to constituents and their constitutional

> responsibilities are minded; as long as lobbyists don't overstep the mark in terms of what they do to achieve clients' end, then no, it generally isn't an issue.

He noted that there was 'slightly more doubt on the Labour side because . . . it's seen as a big business thing, private sector dominated'. Overall he argued mutual benefit to lobbyists and lobbied:

> when you get plugged in seriously to a particular policy community . . . there are people to avoid but you also know there are an awful lot of people who are lobbyable, open to an approach as long as it's a legitimate approach and a relevant approach and are perfectly glad, not least MPs. They're more than happy to receive briefing or advice and again the messages go both ways. Its not just about us trying to get information out of them . . . we can often pass on useful messages from departments as often happens; you know 'tell so and so to cool it on such and such'. And you can do that quite usefully and everybody avoids a nasty public mess . . . money isn't spent on administrative and other arrangements to get to a stage where there's only going to be a problem anyway.

He elaborated the mutual benefits:

> There are clauses mis-drafted in legislation all the time by accident or oversight . . . that would cripple or seriously damage commercial or other interests. And it's often a matter of just pointing those out . . . even if they're going to stick to the principle.

Mutual benefit was also invoked by Michael Burrell. The alliance of client policy knowledge and lobbyist presentational skills 'strengthens the quality of representations'. If that alliance was effective:

> that should lead to decision-makers receiving presentation either oral or written that are clearer, crisper, more to the point, less ambiguous, less time-wasting . . .

Evie Soames of Charles Barker detected a party political difference of reaction: 'There's not much criticism now in the Conservative Party. There's still some lingering remnants of the Labour Party who feel that we are sort of parasites and that what we are providing for large companies, individuals and the voluntary sector can't afford. . . there is that sort of argument that occasionally gets raised but not by all that many people'.

She developed the theme of involvement with Government:

> I think most people realise that we're a kind of fact of life and the more there is open government and the more there is consultation, which are the Government's objectives after all, the more they know they're going to need companies, trade associations, commercial interests . . . like ourselves to help them.

She thought that civil servants 'on the whole' were as accepting as politicans. An anecdote: ' An awfully nice Under-Secretary I spoke to yesterday, I couldn't believe how outspoken he was 'cos he wasn't somebody I knew at all well beforehand'. But a problem area for the hired lobbyist could be replying to detailed questions: 'It's just occasionally . . . you feel you aren't the person; that if it's going to become a technical discussion, then they might just as well discuss it with a technician'.

The anonymous lobbyist also made a political analysis. About MPs, 'there are some who wouldn't touch them [hired lobbyists] with a barge pole'. With civil servants 'there is a range of reactions':

> some civil servants regard lobbyists as stepping on their territory; developing policy; trying to make decisions that they should properly take. Other civil servants recognise that the lobbyists very often can fulfil a vital function. You already filter out those interested in an issue, knowing through experience and background perhaps what the civil servant wants to see. Not in the sense of what is the answer they want: but how can they process a piece of information. You can provide that a lot quicker and a lot easier. They recognise that companies or individuals have a legitimate interest and two pages of well reasoned brief are far better than being sent out to seek information . . .

This lobbyist also noted a departmental dimension to attitudes. As between the reaction of politicians and officials, he judged the latter 'more favourable but it can depend on the department'. He said 'the Treasury gets many submissions before budgets and probably regards everybody as a pest'. Stressed elsewhere was an ideological compatibility with decision-makers, reinforced by personal friendships and previously established working relationships.

Martin Smith of GPC thought that the perceived competence of lobbyists and the disclosure of interests by them influenced the attitudes of decision-makers. On the first: '. . . a civil servant will not be as impressed by the clients we've got . . . but by whether we sound as if we know what we're talking about'. On disclosure, he gave the example of representing a regional transport authority to a civil servant while having British Rail as a client and not disclosing that fact when the conversation was about funding the Channel Tunnel rail link: 'there would be an element of failure to disclose there which that civil servant might well be expected to see as material in assisting him or her to decide how much to tell us'. He operated rules of disclosure in dealing with decision-makers.

David Perchard estimated that the three people in his firm were in contact with a 'couple of hundred' decision-makers in the UK and in the EU, including 10-15 contacts in both the German and French Environment Ministries. Attitudes varied.

> The moment you talk to decision-makers for the first time, if they don't know you, they don't know the company, they are usually suspicious and I would say rightly so. The important thing is to demonstrate straightaway that we have knowledge in the subject and that we are in the business of information exchange rather than a suction pump. As the relationships progress it becomes that much easier. We are always very keen to be regarded as insiders rather than

> outsiders. Pat (Perchard staff member) has a great and general interest in public policy and she's the one person who has a background which is entirely in politics in the public sector. And she can take part in the gossip on equal terms with them and they know that she is a good source of information on packaging policy issues.

Several MEPs had consulted him over the European Parliament's report on the packaging directive and 'we had one MEP who asked us actually to draft some proposals for him'.

He drew a picture of involvement with policy development. His firm took part in the UK Government's re-cycling advisory group 1989/1991; and the DTI had been a client of the firm. With the latter, '. . . we have the kind of relationship with them where they know that if they phone up for a bit of insight into the way the industry is thinking or the way things happen, then they will get something which is fairly reliable'. The European Parliament had also asked him to make a presentation at a hearing on the environment.

He added about the DTI:

> They also know that if they don't want to make fifty phone calls but want to get an idea into circulation, if they tell us then we will tell a lot of other people unless we're especially asked not to. So that's the kind of relationship that we like. We want to be the oil in the wheels of the machine to help Government and industry understand each other better.

Tim Rycroft of Good Relations believed that with decision-makers 'there is a general suspicion about intermediaries, which is understandable, which is why we advise our clients to do things directly'. He expanded:

> We always approach these people (decision-makers) from the point of view of saying 'well, they have a job to do and how do we approach them in a way that will help them get their job done'. For example if a civil servant is putting together a paper for a Minister, the civil servant is aware that he or she will have to include some information on the other side of the case. . . Now by providing that information in a way that we know is useful to the civil servant, we're helping him or her to get the job done. And so while you're not always going to be welcomed warmly for what you're doing . . . if you approach it in the right way, you usually get a very businesslike response.

He asserted that one disadvantage of a lobbyist being a subject specialist was dealing with the same group of decision-makers and ' . . . it may mean that they just get more and more irritated with you constantly phoning up and telling them different things'.

Tessa Devlin also reported some civil servant hostility but in the context of an estimated 90% being 'helpful':

> sometimes you find civil servants who don't want to speak to you because they think that you're a consultant and they are giving you their intelligence for which you are charging and making a profit. I did have one chap on the phone who said 'alright . . . so you're going to sell what I tell you and you don't know anything about it'. And my response was 'if you think your job would be made better by 35 different people calling and asking this question, fine. . . you know that I'm here to try and make things quicker and easier and I won't waste your time because I know what I want to ask: I know how you work'. And he was fine after that.

It was 'harder to say' about politicians: the helpful majority was 'probably less than ninety per cent but . . . that's just because of the disposition of politicians'. She amplified: 'they're interested in their constituents. They're interested in making sure they're re-elected and so that changes their perspective. A civil servant is interested in the issue'.

Offer an expert helping hand to civil servants was the advice of Shandwick's Tom McNally to his clients: '. . . one of the early things that we would advise . . . is to offer to the civil servant in the department concerned as much information, ideas that you can, within the realms of commercial confidence, make available. Because you'll have a friend then in terms of the job that they've got to do'. Even so, he thought that the increased amount of lobbying meant that officials were becoming 'increasingly jealous of their time'.

'One of a great many voices in play' - lobbyists and their perceptions of value for money to clients

In their business role, commercial lobbyists have to be concerned that their services generate sufficent levels of satisfaction in their clients: if not, they will lose fee income. Chapter Three looked at value from the clients' stance: here the focus is on lobbyists.

How does the lobbyist measure the value he generates in exchange for his fee income? What is his/her perception of how the client measures the value received for fee expenditure? Is measurement possible? Is value for money the marketing equivalent of effectiveness, an indicator of goal accomplishment? Is there a more subjective 'feel good' factor for the client in the calculation of value?

The first point is that hired lobbyists face a situation common to any hired adviser: the most important assessment of value is by the client and the question therefore becomes 'does the client measure my value by advice given, work done or by happenings in the external environment?' The choice of answers available to the client reflects the complexity of the operating environment. For example, the advertising campaign may be executed as planned but there are unsatisfactory sales: counsel's opinion is persuasive but the court case goes against the client. For the lobbyist, the case is well constructed and access gained but the policy development is against the client because of intervening variables. In the language of the doctor/patient relationship, treatment is agreed with the patient and carried out but there is no cure.

The data below shows that lobbyists declared that they were working mostly to client definitions of value for money rather than their own. This is no more than sound survival sense in a principal/agent relationship. But handing over entirely the assessment of value of professional services to clients is a high risk strategy for a lobbyist. He can reduce this risk to professional survival by influencing the client's choice of assessment criteria and, in particular, by urging the client to follow a twin-track approach to value assessment: measure observable and attributable goals, e.g. winning a tax concession, meeting a Minister; and assess more imponderable goals, e.g. awareness creation, shaping opinion.

Following this twin-track approach to value assessment, the lobbyist therefore knows that when his role in external events is being reviewed, in one set of cases he can claim any successful outcome as his own: in the other set of cases, he can say that he '. . . is one of a great many voices in play (Martin Smith)'. This allows a flexible, ambiguous and complex answer to the value question. At the level of a business, this duality is a rather satisfactory situation for the lobbyist: when the cure works, claim success: when the cure does not work, the other voices can be called in to account for failure. But in the aftermath of no cure, it is still important that the client should have a 'feel good' factor. This is one reason, the data suggests, why lobbyists will sometimes introduce clients to a lot of decision-makers, i.e. to impress them with the lobbyist's contacts and to try and build up reserves of goodwill with the client. There was one strong dissent from this approach, one which stressed that the policy outcome of lobbying was the only one worthwhile for clients.

Tom McNally looked at outcomes but saw complications in claiming credit. He said about legislation that 'one can look to a whole range of changes which we were in part influential in obtaining'. He gave the examples of the Broadcasting Bill and the ITV Association; the Water Act and the Water Services Association, and a reference to regulators which 'doesn't take place or is severely muted'. But even in these relatively clear-cut circumstances, lobbyists can never prove 'our input was the decisive factor'.

For Fred Morgan, the value question had to be client framed and it may include both measurable and imponderable benchmarks, such as awareness creation. He said:

> the best value for money is if we achieve all the things that the clients desire and certainly if one doesn't achieve anything he desired, I don't think that would be value for money. Sometimes their requirements are . . . perhaps less objective, less hard. For instance, they may feel that Government doesn't and Parliament doesn't take any notice of their industry and they want to make an impact on Parliament or on Ministers not to require any particular advantage but to be there when there is a problem.

David Perchard shared this client-centred definition of value: '. . . what really counts is . . . not what we think they ought to have but what they think they ought to have'. But events can sometimes show that the client's calculation of value was misjudged. He noted ' the quality of advice that we give . . . we can best measure by looking back over the files a year or two later' to compare advice given with policy outcomes. He found himself saying:

> . . . we said that would happen and it did and I'm afraid too often there's an element of 'I told you so' here which we don't always communicate to the client . . . but one of the hard facts of life in business is that public affairs is the sort of thing that operates for a Wagnerian timescale.

He noted that clients in general tended to ignore potential threats until they loomed large 'by which time it is much more difficult and expensive to stop'. But there was business advantage in this procrastination ' . . . because if we were successful in stamping on every dinosaur while it's still in the egg, then the number of hours that we had to work would be rather less'. Clients act later rather than earlier 'nine times out of ten'.

A client-oriented definition of the value was offered by Tim Rycroft: 'the most important measure from our point of view of value for money is if the client is happy'. He described:

> if the client feels that we're doing the right things for them; things they expected us to do or the right level of activity, or delivering things that we have undertaken . . . then that represents value for money. They feel they are getting the service they asked for.

But he said 'the service' is difficult to define for three reasons. Firstly 'because very often our work is aimed at preventing things happening rather than making things happen and one can never know whether we were instrumental in preventing them happening or whether they would have been prevented from happening anyway'. Secondly there was serendipity:

> I could have a chance meeting with somebody who turned out to be very important to one client and discover something of enormous value to them that they couldn't have found out any other way and that thirty second conversation could be worth the entire month's fee or the entire year's fee if it comes down to being that important to large commercial organisation which some of these decisions are.

The third definitional difficulty was the converse of the above: completing an agreed plan of action and not winning the policy argument. Tim Rycroft explained:

> on the other hand, one can work as hard as possible; fix up meetings with all the right people, make sure that their case is put in the most effective way and they might still not get what they're looking for. Certainly in the practical sense of us having done the work that we'd undertaken to do and done it to the best of

> our abilities, they're getting value for money: but they are not getting what they set out to get.

Charles Miller also thought about client reaction to agreed work not producing the desired outcome: 'the important thing is their perception of whether they've been given the right professional advice'. But in the last resort, value was getting the required result for the client: the 'most obvious' value was '... you're after money from Government and you get it'. He added:

> second most obvious is where you're after a very concrete result. Get us assisted area status. Get us this tax concession. Get us an extension of relief from blah, blah, blah. Well, if you've done most of the work, then you can say 'well, I've done it'. Often of course you're a member of a team which may include bankers and lawyers, the in-house people . . . in which case it's very difficult to tell.

He said that value for money was more measurable for lobbyists who claimed to resolve problems and who say 'we did it for you' rather than for lobbyists who say 'you are now better perceived inside the system'.

Tessa Devlin confronted the above dichotomy as follows:

> . . . I suppose it would be very rare for me to devise a programme that would end with a yes or no answer because part of the relationship with Government is develop a dialogue. It might mean that you don't have success on a measure ... but ... you've positioned the client as an adviser to Government so that next time it comes round you're in a much better position.

She related the value question to trust between client and lobbyist: 'I believe that I give value for money because I'm honest in what we can achieve for the clients. I never lead them down the garden path. I give them a really direct steer about what is achievable and that means they can trust me and trust . . . in business is value for money'.

For Peter Moore, the client definition of value was also in the forefront: 'providing the service that the clients want and that places them in a political environment where they can best promote their commercial case'. Market Access attempts to gauge its service provision through a 'process of consultation with a client':

> it's just good politics. You send out a questionnaire every now and then and say 'are you happy with the service; where's it weak; where is it strong; where could it be improved; what do you think we've done for you; what do you think we have achieved?' I suspect this is very rare in the industry. I think it's a good thing because it is so difficult to say 'well, we did that'. But there are some things when you can say 'I did that'.

Martin Smith could have agreed with the latter sentence: for him there were satisfactory 'measures of effectiveness' for some lobbying activities. He gave the example of the passage of a Private Members Bill on advertising bingo steered through by his firm: '... we got it onto the statute book. Now there you have an outcome which is 100 per cent measurable'. But he did not claim that this example was representative '... because clearly if you are working on Government legislation or still more on European legislation, then you are one of a great many voices in play'.

He gave the example of the European plastics industry, another client, as 'a sort of midway point' of effectiveness. He said that the industry:

> ... has a highly specific set of interests in relation to proposed legislation on packaging and packaging waste and there will be very specific outcomes in terms how much the industry will be expected to recycle of its product by the year... ninety eight, two thousand, two thousand and five. In other words, what is ultimately enshrined in the directive will be able to be placed alongside the industry's objectives at the start of this process and we will be able to say ' well, it was forty per cent succcessful or fifty per cent successful or sixty per cent successful ...'.

This quantification could not be applied to other work 'where it's very difficult to measure effectiveness and I think we have to talk through the process with the client beforehand so that this is understood'.

Simon Nayyer identified another form of quantification as the 'train spotter approach': it is one which could produce the goodwill reserves referred to above. He said that in this case some clients:

> ... will assess the successfulness of their work and ours by the number of Ministers and the number of Select Committee Chairmen they have seen in a month.

But for other clients, 'the process is rather more sophisticated ... what impact one has had on opinion forming and in moving a particular policy issue forward'.

Evie Soames for Charles Barker put the value question into the context of economic recession: '... everybody expects us to do more for less'. In this context clients 'are pretty good at ensuring that they get value for money... and so many people are constantly propositioning and canvassing our clients ... one doesn't sign up for a year and sit back and think "that's going to be safe as houses"'. Client do ask the value for money question. She described 'a constant evaluation process' where work is planned and progress gauged at monthly meetings; where client and lobbyist review annual programmes after nine months and the former then 'decide whether they want to do more or less or anything the following year'; and where 'the question is addressed when we re-negotiate the fee or re-negotiate the contract'.

Conclusion

What commercial lobbyists say they do can be typified mainly as lobbying process work (monitoring; enhancing policy presentation; arranging access; arranging representations and executing media campaigns). They offer clients a range of services, presenting lobbying as a set of discrete activities which clients can 'pick 'n mix' to suit their needs. Lobbyists are client-led but they want clients to choose more rather than fewer services. A small number of lobbyists claim to be issue and policy experts as well.

Commercial lobbyists do not refuse to supply any lobbying service if asked by clients to provide it but they have their work preferences. These preferences are revealed by the field data as clusters of activity around some rather than other lobbying services. For example, most lobbyists will fix access for clients but some will get clients to do it after advice on whom and which departments to access. All commercial lobbyists will advise on how to persuasively present a case but most do not want to present it alone. On policy, all lobbyists want to improve its presentation and some want to amend its content. But generally they prefer to involve themselves with the processes of lobbying (access and presentational activities) rather than with issue and policy substance.

These clusters of preferred activity, attracting majority or minority practice and participated in by individuals differentially, can be conceptually re-grouped into two ideal types of lobbying: **backgrounding** and **foregrounding**. In themselves, these types cannot be used for counting lobbyists completely under one heading but they do allow a better understanding of the actual access, representation making and policy influencing practices of lobbyists. Conceptually focused definitions of lobbying activity lead to a deeper and fuller analysis of lobbying in practice.

Commercial lobbyists have various relationships with public policy decision-makers, with an identified range of personal and structural factors making for the variations. The factor most mentioned as making for positive relationships was that lobbying brought the mutual benefit of two-way flows of expert information to public policy-making.

Because they are hired for their services, commercial lobbyists are concerned about how the paying client values their services. Ultimately, they are ruled by the value judgements of their clients but they respond to the complexity of the operating environment by sometimes claiming credit for both measurable and imponderable outcomes.

Note

1. *The Independent* newspaper, Wednesday, 8 September, 1993, p. 9 reported under a headline 'Food dye lobbyists keep best of British' that lobbying had prevented the banning of colour additives by the EC in the case of certain foods sold in the UK, including canned and mushy peas, kippers and cheddar cheese.

6 Lobbyists for hire: the decision-makers

Introduction

This Chapter is the fourth to analyse the major role players in commercial lobbying. The previous three Chapters examined the hirers and the hired: the focus now turns to the objects of their attention, those who influence and make public policy, collectively known here under the title 'decision-makers'. This is the first time that in-depth interview data on the views of UK civil servants and special advisers about commercial lobbyists has been published. Haug and Koppang (1993) reported that they were working in Norway in the same area.

Decision-makers are the third set of actors in the lobbying process after the clients and lobbyists. With their inclusion, data about hiring lobbyists can be triangulated from three viewpoints. They can be segmented into four groups - backbench MPs, Ministers (current and former), special advisers to Ministers and civil servants. MPs and former Ministers are relatively easy to interview via the Parliamentary culture of access to the public. Ministers were unlikely to be interviewed on the grounds of workload and of their discretion limiting the quality of the data. The First Division Association (FDA), the trade union which represents civil servant grades one to seven (the grades involved with lobbyists), is in a position of overview about lobbyists and Liz Symons, the Secretary General, gave their view.

Ten meetings were had in all. Two of the interviewees were Under-secretaries and four were special advisers. The interviewees were Kenneth Carlisle MP; Robert Dunn MP; Sir Anthony Durant MP; John Mills, Under-secretary at the Office of Fair Trading (OFT); Cliff Grantham, special adviser to the then Secretary of State for Education, John Patten; Eleanor Laing, special adviser to the then Secretary of State for Transport, John MacGregor (her views are reported but not attributed); an anonymous former special adviser, now a commercial lobbyist; Bill Robinson, former special adviser to Chancellor Lamont; an anonymous Under-secretary administering a major national reform programme, and Liz Symons, general secretary of the First Division Association.

The issues decision-makers above were lobbied on included routes for new roads; defence contracts on a new tank and torpedo; abortion; Sunday trading; local government; fair trading and consumer protection; deregulation and reform of the Consumer Credit Act; prison privatisation; homosexual age of consent; dangerous dog legislation; rail privatisation; tax on Scotch whisky; tax on potato and wheat crisps; Post Office Counters' privatisation and the national lottery.

The FDA reported that grades seven (principal) and five (assistant secretary) were the officials most frequently to be at the receiving end of representations. The principals were likely to head up a sub-section (e.g. toxic chemicals) while the assistant secretaries headed up the section (e. g. pollution): the principals would field telephone enquiries; the assistant secretaries would be at a meeting with clients and/or lobbyists; while the Under-secretaries (grade three) would be present if the matter had major policy ramifications. In the first instance of contact, if there was a need by the lobbyist for information, the civil service grade executive officer would be the official likely to give it out.

On access to special advisers, discussions were had with Jeremy Mayhew (1n), a former DTI special adviser, and with Cliff Grantham (2n), a special adviser at the Department for Education (DfE). Mr Mayhew said that he had little contact with commercial lobbyists because he had only accepted representations on the party political aspects of policy and all other representations he had directed to civil servants. But he had not been impressed generally by what he had seen. He had noted that some lobbying was done in a way to impress clients - for example meeting Ministers - when the more effective functional route would have been meeting civil servants.

Mr Grantham had been a special adviser for three years at the Home Office and the DfE: before that he had been a research assistant to MPs; a lobbyist who founded his own company Westminster Briefing, and an academic author on lobbying (1989; in Rush (ed.) 1990, and with Norton, 1986). His general impression was that the number of lobbying firms had probably peaked; that lobbying effectiveness was difficult to evaluate; that concentrating on, in Miller's phrase (1988;17), the 'dull offices' of Whitehall was productive, and that lobbyists should not forget that public campaigns influenced Ministers as well as private representations. Another pre-fieldwork briefing was had from Kay Dixon (3n), personal assistant to Cliff Grantham above and formerly secretary to the late Robert Adley MP, a declared critic of hired lobbyists. Her view was that the latter complicated contact between an MP and the interest by requiring extra time and effort to fix up meetings through a third party when contact could have been bilateral and administratively easier.

Contacting MPs started at a time when one of them, Teresa Gorman, criticised Members in their role as objects of attention for commercial lobbyists. She wrote in *PR Week* (28 October, 1993) that:

> I conclude that our monster plcs and super-quangos have public affairs budgets that have to be spent. The lobbying firms merely provide a conduit for the allocated sums to be spent regardless of results. The number of MPs supplementing their incomes by collaborating in the 'influence business' enhances the mirage of substance.

Two days earlier (26 October), the Channel Four programme *Checkout 93* (4n) estimated that 'consultancy fees' to MPs totalled some £11m a year; reported that they were known as 'the school fees factor' and that they averaged about £11,000, with one MP rumoured to earn £60,000.

John Townend MP, Chairman of the Conservative Backbench Finance Committee, declined to meet. Sir Bryan Carsberg, Director General of Fair Trading, was the only other prospective interviewee to decline. His office wrote (5n) that he 'very rarely' met hired lobbyists and that if intermediaries are involved 'in the arranging of meetings, they tend to be lawyers representing companies . . . '. The letter added: 'Circular letters from lobbying organisations are invariably placed in the waste paper basket'.

A range of reactions: MPs

One theme which ran throughout the interviews with lobbyists in the preceding chapter was their assertion that commercial lobbying was an accepted and valued part of public policy-making. But several clients interviewed in Chapter Three reported a range of positive and negative views among decision-makers about commercial lobbyists. A range of official reactions was also reported in Chapter Five by the lobbyists themselves. A range was also found in these interviews with decision-makers. Exploring these varying reactions is the major focus for the following analysis of the data from MPs.

More positive than negative: '. . . they do oil the system'

Robert Dunn MP was (November 1993) Chairman of the Conservative Backbench Transport Committee. He worked for J. Sainsbury plc before his election in 1979 and was an adviser to them until 1983. His constituency of Dartford, Kent, is along the route of the proposed Channel Tunnel rail link to London and 'after 1988, because of the rail link issue in my constituency, I gave an undertaking that I would take on no commercial interests while I was fighting British Rail and that remains the position today'.

He noted the growth of hired lobbyists since his election and thought of them as 'signposts' for MPs pointing the way towards 'private interests from the commercial sector'. He assigned to them the general role of introduction agents:

> I've always seen the positive view that . . . they do oil the system. . . . they bring people together in a way that it might not be so easy to do. There's been tremendous growth. I think it's very important . . . that we do have this . . . given the various sophisticated rates of change. Sometimes you do need a briefing from people who are within the industry concerned . . .

He was lobbied 'in a variety of senses'.

> Sometimes by organisations such as Life and Keep Sunday Special . . . Transport organisations obviously wish to come to see me to make their views known and some lobbyists in the private sector who have a transport client may ask to see me or give me lunch in order to meet them. And I have been lobbied on a regional basis too when I've gone to lunches and found most of my colleagues from the County of Kent at the same lunch . . .

At these lunches:

> we have a meal which normally leads to a presentation from the chairman of the (host) organisation as to where there are problems with his industry, where his industry's going and what the Government is doing right or wrong in that industry.

He said that he had never been approached by a lobbyist personally in the House (6n): instead he would get 'two or three' lunch invitations a week and would accept 'about one in three'. An MP had to be 'selective' and he accepted that 'there's no such thing as a free lunch'. He said that 'there's something in it for someone somewhere'. He believed that the process 'can be a two way traffic'. He said:

> There are occasions when I will accept an invitation because I'm interested in meeting the people that they're prepared to introduce to me. Perhaps in other circumstances that introduction may not be so easy to arrange or bring about. Sometimes, it's been lobbying for precise things. And sometimes it's come out in the conversation that 'it may be helpful if the Government did X, Y, or Z' and 'have you realised that this is the effect of Government policy.' . . . but it's always up to the MP as to what he or she does about that. You say 'well, that was a waste of time': you might say 'that was a good idea and that was useful'.

But he noted that he was not aware of any 'follow-up' after such lunch/ presentations:

> that's what I find fascinating about it. . . . the two come together and then it might be a question of following up, saying 'well, you had the lunch, can you help in any way.' I'm not aware of that happening to me.

He elaborated on the value of this lobbying:

> my view is that I've gone along to learn and I suppose the principal of the (client) company . . . feels that they're satisfied that they've done their best to persuade legislators that there's a rift somewhere in policy. And I suppose the proprietor of the agency (the commercial) feels that they've done their job by bringing the two interests together.

He said the role of commercial lobbyists at such lunches was that 'they've held the ring'.

More negative than positive: 'They're just paid hacks'

Kenneth Carlisle MP was Minister of Defence Procurement for two years and of Roads for one year and he accepted being lobbied: 'that's part of one's job as a Minister.' But he was lobbied directly by the interests concerned and not by hired people. He said:

> as a Minister you're not really lobbied by these groups [commercial lobbyists] at all. I never was once. I was lobbied by people who built ships or manufactured weapons . . . or people who had an interest in how we used our land, like English Nature. I was never once approached by a professional lobbyist and indeed as a Minister, you wouldn't listen to them. They have no right to come and see you. They're just paid hacks. The people who come to see you are the people . . . to whom the arguments mean something.

If a hired lobbyist had come to see him as Minister, he would have said: 'no: I want to see the principal. I don't see someone secondhand. I always see the people who are interested in getting some particular result.' He said that he would see an MP or Member of the Lords 'who had some connection with a company or movement . . . but if there was a material interest they would always have to declare it'.

He said that 'very few' MPs did this 'but if they did so, they'd have to declare their interest and it wouldn't make much difference unless they had very good arguments . . . '.

He added:

> and one always discounted that but . . . that was part of one's duty to listen to all sides of the argument, to see as many people as possible.

He said that he was not known for his views on hired lobbyists: rather 'that was the accepted view in Government. And I would have thought that every Minister would be exactly the same. It's inconceivable to me that a Minister would actually see a lobbyist.' He thought the same about civil servants: '. . . it just doesn't happen'; instead they met the clients directly.

As an MP, commercial lobbyists did not lobby him individually: they wrote instead 'but I seldom read what they have to say'.

Kenneth Carlisle did not think that they were 'particularly effective' but they 'probably play a useful role in that they do get the issues out'. For him effectiveness lay in knowing whether to approach civil servants or Ministers and in constituents using their MPs. He added:

> as a MP, you can get hold of the Minister and therefore there's no point in going for a lobbyist if you go direct to the Minister. So the lobbyist might get hold of me in order to try and bend my thinking so that I can . . . take the point of view to the Minister or put pressure on Government to change their views.

He noted that 'a lot of companies seem to feel that they need someone to represent their interests in Parliament . . . but I think it's best for them to use their MP'.

He ranked a campaign by GEC to buy one of the company's torpedoes and secondly the campaign for the Challenger 2 tank as two of the most effective lobbies he had known. GEC concentrated their lobbying on constituencies where they had factories and 'therefore they made . . . a very, very powerful lobby but they didn't use consultants as far as I know'.

More neutral than for or against: 'They're a little help: they're no hindrance'

Sir Anthony Durant was Chairman (December, 1993) of the Conservative Backbench Environment Committee and was the object of lobbying directly by organisations or via hired lobbyists as intermediaries. Generally there has been a 'marked increase' in the amount of lobbying and he had no objection to the hiring of lobbyists and was not put off by their representing multiple clients. He added that 'now the intermediary process is also very much on the increase, I suppose I could have lunch every day if I really set out to do it'.

Overall, he assessed their contribution to his work as: 'they're a little help: they're no hindrance. . . they're part of life.'

He accepted about two lunches a month and did not find them 'effective' in altering his opinion. Instead:

> I would say that they have stimulated my interest . . . a subject has been on my backburner but they brought it to the front . . . It doesn't influence what I'm going to do about it. It does at least bring it to my attention. So to that extent, they are providing quite a useful service.

He added that 'thirty letters from my constituents on an issue have a bigger effect on me than lunch, dinner and tea'.

He was ready to be lobbied if the subject interested him personally or as Committee Chairman: 'sometimes the persuasiveness of the approach by the intermediary has an effect.' But:

> I don't think Members of Parliament are as influenced as everybody thinks they are. I think they make their own judgement. We have only one skill and that is judgement. We have no other skill.

He thought the lunch invitation was the most frequent form of approach and most of the clients were businesses. The lobbyists were well briefed and at lunch 'they conduct the session'. Some of them specialised in environmental questions. He reported that they did not go to the constituency to stimulate interest and that if they did, 'I wouldn't like it' and that MPs could spot a standard letter.

He said lobbyists found it 'always a much more difficult thing for them to get to see Ministers but they do'. He described the process:

> They usually have to couple it with two or three tame MPs who take them along. But I would say that (influencing Ministers) is more difficult because the Minister is well aware of what they're up to and he's surrounded by batteries of civil servants who are going to advise him. It's very difficult changing Ministers' minds and you can only do it (with) the other aspect of Parliament which is important . . . the numbers' game.

He thought that the amount of lobbying by commercial lobbyists was 'probably near peaking':

> I think there's a boredom factor creeping in with Members of Parliament . . they are pretty cynical human beings who are dealing with humanity every day of the week and so I think the impact these people are having is beginning to diminish by the amount of it that takes place. The more it goes on, the more Members say 'oh no, not another one'.

He reported that the Select Committee of Members' Interests was concerned about:

> the intrusive nature of them hanging around this place. I don't think they are going to be criticised for taking people out to lunch. I think hanging about here; bombarding with paper; weedling their way into Committee Rooms and so on: that's the side that is causing Members of Parliament concern.

A range of reactions: civil servants and special advisers

The views of MPs have been well aired in the Reports of the Commons' Select Committee on Members' Interests; in journalism by MPs themselves; by Shaw (1990), and in the introduction by Austen Mitchell MP to Jordan (1991).

But the views of special advisers have not been researched nor those of senior civil servants (the only known published exception to the latter group was a survey in the *Government Report* [1987]); or the views of a body representative of senior civil servants, such as the FDA. Hence this chapter is structured to separate out the views of these sub-groups from those of MPs. The general conclusion of the new data is that a) hired lobbying is a recognised part of public policy-making but within limits; and b) some lobbying behaviours are preferred over others.

Special adviser Cliff Grantham believed that commercial lobbyists 'are an accepted part of the Parliamentary landscape' and 'now they are drawn upon by decision-makers'. For John Mills at the OFT 'they're perceived as fulfilling a function' and 'if they weren't there, they'd probably be invented'. And 'there is this feeling in Whitehall that these things can be useful for the civil servants themselves: therefore let's go along with it'.

Liz Symons of the FDA reported that her members made 'very little' comment about commercial lobbyists and what there was 'has not been terribly praiseworthy'. She said:

> What members do talk about is being lobbied by the Child Poverty Action Group, lobbied by Shelter, lobbied by Oxfam. They talk to me about being lobbied by people who are genuinely committed to the causes for which they're lobbying, rather than being lobbied by the professional consultancy which will take all-comers for money. And I don't think they cut much ice with members . . . (who) are far more likely to want to talk to the people really concerned with the matters in hand.

The anonymous Under-secretary noted that the hirers of lobbyists in his policy area appeared to believe they were getting value from hired lobbyists: but he doubted the value they gave to their clients. As somebody courted by them, he saw some usefulness in them because periodically they came up with new information.

Liz Symons underlined the need for civil servants having good contacts with interests: 'there are very close relationships between civil servants and pressure groups . . . if they are genuinely doing their job, both of them know each other.' Her concern was for 'consultation with those who were genuinely committed to the causes for which they were lobbying rather than going through an extra stratum'.

The anonymous ex-special adviser, now a commercial, gave a more positive evaluation:

> those lobbyists who wine and dine the whole time, I don't think that is the approach. The approach that I used to find the most useful (as special adviser) . . . is a sort of professional, well researched approach to case making . . . It's not twisting people's arms and trying to get them to do something they wouldn't otherwise . . . the best you can do . . . is ensure that your case is properly heard in the right places.

He had seen the hired lobbyists as 'an extension of the company they were hired by' and 'it is a good thing that Whitehall, Westminster is open to the outside . . . just doesn't sit in an ivory tower'.

A similar image was used by Bill Robinson, former special adviser on tax to Chancellor Norman Lamont: an open Whitehall with information flowing in. He said:

> people sitting in the centre arguably are only as good as the information they are given and lobbyists are throwing information at them so that's not bad.

He saw lobbying as 'inevitable' and 'at its best it's a useful source of information.' This theme of commercial lobbyists as an information source linked all the respondents in this section of the fieldwork and supports the Norton and Grantham thesis (1986) that they are a 'hyphen' between public policy-makers and private interests.

While analysing the data below, it is important to be aware that the perspective of the respondents vis-à-vis hired lobbyists is similar to that of mariners towards icebergs. For both groups, there can be much that is not visible.

Commercial lobbyists can advise clients on access, presentation and policy content behind the scenes and hardly offer any public sighting to the decision-maker. It is a behaviour which fits more with the backgrounder type developed in Chapter Five. Equally much is not seen by commercial lobbyists. The value put on the information they pass on is, in the nature of things, not usually known. Decision-makers can have an incomplete view of lobbyists; lobbyists can have an incomplete view of special advisers and civil servants.

Berry (1993; 346) has elaborated on this phenomenon of partial sighting. He reported that the 'hired gun' type of lobbying with lobbyist and decision-maker face-to-face is 'small' in the UK. He estimated that one in ten lobbying firms do this head-to-head lobbying while the norm was 'their primary role as advisers and policy experts'.

'Good lobbying is best conducted if it's not so naked' - seeking contact

It is well reported that MPs are lobbied. They are legislators; they are the traditional focus for lobbying and they are accessible. For the lobbyist, they live in an open field. But the reporting of lobbying of civil servants and special advisers is scarce, if not non-existent. For the lobbyist, both these groups, in comparison with MPs, have dwelt behind walls of anonymity and discretion. The data below suggests that the walls have crumbled in places.

John Mills spent three and a half years in the Downing St. Policy Unit which was a 'prime target not just for lobbyists but for everyone with anything to sell or to offer . . . and part of our function at the Policy Unit was to act as a conduit for . . . ideas from outside the normal channels'.

He made a general distinction in approaches:

> there is a constant intercourse between officials in a whole range of jobs and their clients in the particular market place with which they are dealing. . . I would hesitate to call that lobbying . . . there are elements of lobbying: everyone is trying to pedal their own ideas but it's not all lobbying. Some of it is simply . . . the conduct of business, the development of good relations and so forth.

But besides this normality, there was something more self-interested:

> there was plenty of what you might call naked lobbying: people with a vested interest or a self-interest who simply wanted to see all possible channels to convey their views to people they perceive to be in positions of influence . . . So I think one does have to draw up a kind of scale of lobbying activity from

the normal, almost routine, day-to-day contact between organisations, institutions and Government ; and the more set piece lobbying occasions.

He gave an example of 'naked lobbying' in changes to the scope of the Consumer Credit Act as a result of de-regulation:

> we've had many submissions from all sorts of trade associations, all making various proposals in their own interest but wrapped up in general public policy wrapping paper. Except for one submission from the (name of trade association) who simply said: 'We make no secret of the fact: these regulations are an absolute bind and they make it very difficult for our (members) to advertise their attractive mortgage offers . . . Please would you remove them just for us.' That was a naked lobby and they made no secret of it and it was very unsuccessful because it was so naked. And it's probably the case that good lobbying is best conducted if it's not so naked; if you're not simply perceived as presenting a selfish or a vested interest.

At the OFT, John Mills had been lobbied directly by interests and by hired lobbbyists. 'Very senior people in organisations can always lobby on their own behalf' and he had seen that at Number Ten. He said 'a lot of lobbying goes on concerning competition policy' and:

> some of that comes through these lobbying firms but I would hazard a guess that most of it is done at senior company level. And I think it is probably easier for a company to do. If it's fighting its own corner in a competition investigation, that company has got to plough its own furrow and know what it's talking about.

'Naked lobbying' also appeared in the lobbying done to the anonymous former special adviser: for him it was 'shameless lobbying'. He talked of the dichotomy between lobbying with a 'public policy dimension' and the 'shameless' variety'. He used this distinction in filtering out people and issues he would not deal with:

> If I felt there was a side issue that was relevant to Government policy or had an implication for Government policy, then I would see them. If it was somebody saying 'well, I'm a company and I want for my own interest to achieve xyz', I really couldn't be interested because I wasn't paid to represent the interests of a particular company. I was paid to ensure that my Minister was properly briefed and was able to take informed and wise decisions.

He noted that the public interest and the private could correspond and that the 'good lobbyist will identify his own interest with those of public policy'.

Bill Robinson, special adviser for two and a half years, talked about '. . . quite a lot of people were obviously quite anxious to make my acquaintance, who were jolly nice to me . . . '. He did not regard the number of lobbies as excessive: 'I certainly did regard it as being one of my jobs to be the conduit of outside ideas into the Treasury and so I would see people. I was not inaccessible.' He noted that the Treasury was organised to receive representations on budgets: five Ministers, three special advisers and the civil servants in FP division who 'would just start to canvass views'.

He elaborated:

> part of the whole budget-making process is about seeing outside pressure groups, feeding their ideas into the Treasury and there's quite a wide team of people who will field them. I mean The Scotch Whisky Association gets to see the Chancellor: not many do. But there are five Ministers, anyone of whom is prepared to see lobbyists and if they don't make it as far as a Minister, they get fobbed off with a special adviser.

Cliff Grantham had been lobbied at both the Home Office and the DfE by a 'combination' of direct approaches from interests and via hired lobbyists. In the case of the latter, the 'most effective form of contact' is for the initial contact to come from the lobbyist and then contact to be 'directly with the organisation concerned'.

He saw his role 'to act as a conduit between Ministers and the world outside, particularly from the party perspective but more generally as well'. He would take a dim view of a lobbying firm representing opposing interests but had not come across that duplication (nor had the former special adviser). He did not find the contacts 'intrusive because after the initial approach I had a high degree of control as to whether I wanted to have a meeting'.

One respondent reported six approaches a week from hired lobbyists and the same number again directly from interests: what was being actively sought from the contacts by the respondent was twofold: information which had a party political resonance and data which had a significant policy impact but which was hitherto unknown.

'They came in themselves but I think with a hire lobbyist in tow' - how the decision-makers are lobbied

John Mills had contact with between six and eight commercial lobbyists and 'on the whole they have been people of quite high calibre and they're all people who seem to be ambitious'. How do they make contact? 'They ring you up and invite you to lunch . . . '. Another respondent favoured the contact sequence of telephone call, letter and office meeting, with lunch being seen as an inefficient use of time.

John Mills described the contact strategy:

> they have built up a huge range of contacts among Ministers; among MPs; among special advisers; among the politicos whether Labour or Tory, among a number of senior civil servants. They soon smoke out which civil servants are open; which ones are not. They soon smoke out who is really influential in a particular area. It's not always the most senior. They're also quite good at

> smoking out who likes a free lunch. And being absolutely blunt about it, I think most middling, senior civil servants do like a free lunch because there aren't many perks in the civil service and . . . a free lunch can be quite agreeable.

But he thought there was a right and a wrong way for the lobbyist to handle these lunches. A 'right turn off' was lunch with the 'firm or lobbyist who sits you down in a smart restaurant and no sooner have you ordered a bit of grub than he starts peddling his wares'. Instead:

> if you can establish a good contact, your general impression is to come back to the office and say 'here is someone who is quite forthcoming, who's got a point of view, their firm is important in the sector or their association . . . let's put him on our list of contacts . . .'.

He described behaviour at meetings:

> The person from the lobbying firm will take a very low profile. They might try and guide their clients towards certain questions but the lead in the meeting is from the client. The lobbying firm had almost done its work by fixing the meeting; has probably briefed the people on the civil service background. So I've found in set-piece meetings they've taken a slightly back seat role, rather like the officials when Ministers are present: speak when you're spoken to.

John Mills made a distinction between the lobbying approach of 'very senior people in organisations who can always lobby on their own account' and '. . . middle-ranking people who are a bit diffident about it . . .'.

> . . . because they're not quite sure where to aim their fire; they're not quite sure who is who; they're not very sure whose telephone number is whose; they haven't got a directory, and they feel they need the comfort of someone to do it for them . . . They are well able to present their own case . . . but sometimes felt a little ill at ease until the ice had been broken.

He related these needs to his time at Number Ten and to opportunities for the lobbyist:

> . . . the skill, or rather the value, of these lobbying firms was in a sense breaking that ice for people in [the] private sector or public sector authorities who just felt unsure of themselves in Whitehall.

He developed this point about coming into contact with Whitehall. At that stage 'I think there is a feeling of helplessness and someone who can hold your hand and help you chart a course is probably not without some value'. In this context, the contacts of lobbyists are particularly attractive to clients newly in contact with Government, a point that Liz Symons believed to be part of their attraction to interests 'out on a limb from central Government'. One respondent confirmed this by saying that some lobbyists were particularly well known and how this expedited direct representations.

Bill Robinson said contact was 'nearly always a telephone call, sometimes a letter'.

> On the whole I would talk to anyone on the phone and if after talking to them for a bit, I thought there might be some sort of case for what they were putting forward, I would have them in to see me.

He had regarded himself as a special adviser on tax as a fiscal issue rather than tax as an issue with political consequences. He knew:

> the Chancellor's mindset on these issues quite well, so that if someone could show that there was a genuine non-neutrality . . . if they could make a prima facie case over the phone . . . I would say 'yes, I'm very sympathetic, why don't you come and see and then you can provide me with some ammunition'. I'd be prepared to take up those battles inside the system.

By example, he 'actually fought quite hard' for the trade association of manufacturers of potato and wheat crisps, two similar products taxed differentially. He recalled the meeting: 'they came in themselves but I think with a hired lobbyist in tow who may have been the man who set up the meeting.'

He sensed that interests contacting Whitehall for the first time were more likely to have an internal government affairs officer or to have hired a lobbyist. His major perspective was fiscal but he was aware of lobbying in the background.

> I became aware of the hired lobbyist, of which Ian Greer Associates were the most prominent but just because they were so very active in holding little parties actually. That seemed to be their main activity.

He remembered lunches at the Conservative Party conference and drinks parties on the lawn of Dean's Court, Westminster.

The ex-special adviser talked of a contact strategy which was usually 'the company chaperoned or shepherded by a professional lobbyist'. But he noted how it worked:

> in most cases, it was the company themselves who were doing the advocacy and no doubt the lobbyist behind the scenes briefed them as to what they should say or not say. . .

Companies wanted contact with Government for one of three purposes. The first centred on a particular message the company wanted to transmit. The second was more 'educational' and was a visit to a factory to see equipment being made and to meet the company board. This was a welcome variation: '. . . when you're dealing with papers the whole time. . . it's very useful to actually try and get a concrete handle on something.' The third purpose in his experience was about exporting and the lobbyists wanted '. . . high level political help if there was a trade mission somewhere and they wanted to ensure that the Minister visiting that country was properly briefed'.

Contact by lobbyists was orginally by phone but '. . . in the main they wanted face-to-face meetings or either to come along and they would talk and then leave you with a paper'. He hardly socialised with them, the exception being an annual party by a big lobbying firm which he called 'a political get-together and general networking':

> there was very little attempt to transact business. . . I don't think they saw it that way and certainly the people who went to those occasions didn't.

Sometimes lobbyists wanted information from him and 'I'm afraid I got a reputation for being singularly unhelpful because . . . there was no mileage . . . imparting knowledge to them'. He did not see contact as a 'two-way process' and this made me 'very unpopular I think'. He was 'ultra cautious' in the release of information to lobbyists in case it could be used against the interests he, as special adviser, represented.

The anonymous Under-secretary told of two contacts a day from hired lobbyists in his area (7n). It was mostly by phone with a follow up-by letter where there was some substance to set out. The point of this initial contact was to arrange a meeting, mostly over lunch. He accepted mostly on the basis of 'personal chemistry' - if he liked or respected the lobbyist, he would accept. He did respect some for their policy knowledge but they were few.

He was aware that lobbyists contacted the special advisers in his Department but he judged the latter's influence on Ministers to be weak. He noted that Ministers in general said that they did not like hired lobbyists but he also noted that Ministers accepted their social invitations and talked about them. He told how Ministers might come in on Monday with 'fun ideas' but whether that was the influence of partners, lobbyists or hard thinking was unknown.

Liz Symons reported civil servants saying about contact with hired lobbyists that 'they were there' at meetings but her members 'didn't know what they were there for and they didn't want to speak to them; they wanted to speak to the people paying the bills'. She reflected that '. . . you could have the same thing about lawyers and all sorts of other people but people don't make the same [anti] case'.

In the experience of Cliff Grantham, the initial approach was usually a letter or a telephone call. He then made a judgement 'as to whether I think it is going to be in my interest to see and to hear direct from those concerned'. He thought that most lobbyists were 'wise' to the attraction of concise briefing material and 'so on the whole, the material that does arrive tends to be short and succinct and precise'. But he was critical of lack of follow-up: 'so there's a great-to-do at the time of the approach; material's prepared; perhaps an introduction to a particular client, but very little sort of continuous follow-up.'

Why decision-makers let themselves be lobbied: 'the art really lies in filtering out naked self interest'

John Mills said there was no special civil service code of conduct towards hired lobbyists and that the general rules about propriety applied. He saw contact with them as, in part, a relationship of mutual benefit:

> the civil servant's job is to understand what is going on out there and the art really lies in filtering out the naked self-interest in the points that are being made because . . . that is how policy is formulated and how understanding grows. So, it's not entirely a one-way process.

He developed this concept of mutuality:

> it's wrong to assume that Government or bits of Government instantly know their way round the economy, around the public life in the UK: they don't. Even less so when it comes to Brussels . . . and it is a value to a thoughtful civil servant, especially a senior or grade five and above . . . to build up contacts so that when a problem arises or there's a little issue or sensitivity, you can ring up someone . . .

But there was a limit to mutuality expressed as exchange of information: it was appropriate when the subject matter was

> the general development of public policy for a sector or for overall issues or in relations to Brussels where it's a great help to know that you've got the private sector or whoever on your side.

Information exchange, however, was inappropriate when the matter was specific to a firm:

> if a company rings me up here and refers to the fact that they've got their case on the Director General's desk, I would be very guarded. And I certainly wouldn't reveal his hand. I would just give them what is in our public statement.

But mutuality also took another form. He gave the example of being phoned up by lobbying contacts saying: ' "Look I've got this frightful national association on my back and they're paying us good money but they're desperately keen to get their point across" and I said "OK, look, half an hour next week." ' He added:

> bit of give and take and the lobbying firm appreciates that; doesn't try it on all the time but it helps you build a good relationship with them so that if there's a sensitive issue, you can say 'look . . . you're getting nothing from me on that' and so you can keep a relationship going.

But this 'bit of give and take' cannot operate where there is no perception of reciprocal value by the official:

> there's nothing worse than being rung up and told 'look we have a delegation of widget makers who want to have two days' lobbying in London and we're fixing the programme. Can you give them half an hour?' It's just a complete and utter waste of time. But if it's sector specific or if it's a group who you have a particular interest in . . . then your own antennae suggest that these people can be useful to make contact with . . . sometimes it works and sometimes it doesn't.

Another respondent also objected to attending meetings which lobbyists had organised largely to impress their clients. And the objection extended to them 'pressing their luck' to get access on the basis of acquaintance.

This theme of being 'used' was also taken up by the anonymous Under-secretary. He let himself be lobbied to get access to previously unknown data. But he disliked the process he had to go through to get it. He felt used instrumentally by the lunches in the sense that he knew his presence was boasted about by lobbyists to their clients. And while he was not puritanical about lunch (the interview with him scheduled for 3pm started a little late because he had attended a lobbyist's lunch), he felt that he had to 'pay' for the hospitality with information.

He noted that the information he gave out was mostly in the public domain or was only one enquiry away from it and he was surprised that clients were not aware of this. He was often pressed on policy advice but apart from his own occasional indiscretion, he never revealed what he told Ministers. He regarded that discretion as a constitutional duty.

Bill Robinson thought the job of hired lobbyists was 'to act as a bridge between the political and commercial world'. Cliff Grantham talked the same language of liaison when he said that part of his job was 'to keep eyes and ears open and . . . to act as a flow, a channel of communication between organisations and Ministers'. He noticed that interests without professional lobbying advice had a 'rather scatter gun approach and sent voluminous material'. In consequence 'consultants can actually facilitate a process and keep the level of paperwork down and that leads to a more efficient system'. Another respondent talked about lobbyists being 'an open line of communication' with the outside world and how, like accountants, they can help business make technical issues more understandable to external audiences.

The anonymous former special adviser also saw the value of contact outside Government and valued it in part as a counterpoise to advice from the civil service:

> it was helpful to me being an individual without massive resources to carry out research. One way of finding out whether the advice coming up from the civil servants was legitimate or not was to get the arguments that were being flung around outside and testing those internally to arrive at a view as to whether a proposal that was being made was in fact the correct one.

Perceived influence and effectiveness

The perceived influence and effectiveness asked about in the interviews was that of hired lobbyists and not the influence of the interest represented. The difficulties in making this distinction were looked at in Chapter One and they obtrude here again. In some of the replies, it was clear that the distinction between hired and in-house lobbying was elided where respondents wanted to make a point common to all lobbying types. This theme of effective behaviour for the individual lobbyist is explored particularly in the American literature as exercises in attribute listing. Appendix Two brings together the attributes nominated by the decision-makers talked to.

John Mills did not think commercial lobbyists were influential in public policy-making:

> there are some very good exceptions where well organised lobbying really can turn things on their heads but by and large, it is in one ear, out the other. You might note one or two points; you might reflect on one or two things. You might want to follow up one or two points, draw them into a sort of brief for a later date. But the times when I think you come away from these meetings saying 'My God, our policy was completely wrong: these guys are right' I would say was very rare. I think that the lobby firms know that too.

But there was a form of effective lobbying. For him, good lobbying generally was the antithesis of the 'naked lobbying' he described above and therefore 'if you are not perceived as presenting a selfish or a vested interest', there is a perception of effectiveness:

> what good lobbying is about - and this is where some of these private companies come in - is in insuring that officials or Ministers or MPs . . . are aware of the concerns, perhaps in a fairly general sense, of these organisations. So that when a particular crunch point comes, they (officials) say 'better check what they think'.

Lobbying was effective, he thought, when the civil servant could say: 'whom do we want to talk on this: I know, I'll ring so and so whom I met last month.'

In line with his general proposition that outside contact was essential for policy-making, he reiterated that 'in most areas of public policy, you can't create policy in a vacuum':

> you have to be in constant communication with interested parties and interest groups . . . one is often sitting in one's 'ivory tower' saying to oneself 'well, who do we talk to about this'. And if you've actually got a ready-made list, you're half way there and I think good lobbyists know that.

Making contact between Whitehall and interests not used to such contact was an advantage of hiring lobbyists said Liz Symons: 'if I were lobbying on something; a one-off issue from outside all the machinery of Government; didn't know the ropes; didn't know where to start, may be it would be worth considering [hiring lobbyists].'

Cliff Grantham said that their role in public policy-making was 'overall not significant' and he added: 'they probably can in particular instances play a significant role but taken in totality, I would think their influence is more on the modest rather than significant scale.' He developed the theme:

> ... there has been undoubtedly some successes on the part of consultancy firms influencing particular decisions. I suspect when they have influenced decisions, there's probably other factors at work as well. It is very difficult to quantify precisely ... very often they're pushing at an open gate and then there's a certain change of direction taking place anyway and they may come in and help move that forward. But I think taken across the board I would say their influence on the whole is there but it's quite modest.

He cited the Financial Services Bill of 1985/86 as an example of modest influence when there was a 'small army of consultants' lobbying and 'I'm sure that some of the detail of the Bill was amended as a result':

> but these are very often technical drafting points. I think just in terms of the broad direction of major policy issues, the ability of the firm (of lobbyists) to change the direction of the Government is very limited and doesn't happen that often.

Another respondent made the same point about amending detail: lobbyists could effect 'changes at the margin' but changes to the core of a policy were not known to him. But it was also pointed out that lobbyists' influence could be great in certain Parliamentary circumstances. The unwhipped vote on the Sunday Trading Bill was quoted. Other circumstances were where the Government was caught between two competing political imperatives, e. g. strong constituency pressure and a legislative obligation from the EU. Within this 'change at the margin' paradigm, some 30% of lobbyists were thought effective by one respondent.

The anonymous former special adviser did not think they were influential as individuals because '... in so far as you're a decision-maker sitting there and the people who are doing the talking are the companies ... I suppose you don't really think about the lobbyist behind it all'. Rather '... the effectiveness of the lobbyist ... is always apparent in how well briefed their interests were likely to be. Were they sensitive to what my agenda was likely to be? Did they understand the realities of decision-making?' He recounted an example of the crude approach by one lobbyist who 'tried to strong-arm me down the phone ... by sort of saying "this is an issue you should be looking at and if you're not looking at it, you're not doing your job properly" '. He called this approach 'really very counter-productive'.

He reiterated the belief that the effective lobbyist is singled out by 'not simply pursuing their own agenda but addressing the Government's agenda and is seen to contribute to that agenda'.

He continued:

> there is a view that lobbyists are leeches on the body politic and to some extent that may be true of some people. But they can also fulfil a useful function in that no Government employee or civil servant likes to develop policy in a complete vacuum and in so far as lobbyists can facilitate an input from outside, then they are making a positive contribution.

Companies did not lobby on their own behalf without hiring, he said, because managers are employed 'to look at the bottom line and are very busy people'. It followed:

> it's not time effective for them to spend time thinking about what is the right time to go and see somebody; what is the right message to take them: and therefore in that sense people who either had worked in Government, who knew the way the system worked, could actually make the relationship (with Government) a lot more productive.

The anonymous Under-secretary was currently administering a major reform programme and had previously worked in two Ministerial private offices. He did not know of lobbyists overturning or amending the central features of a major policy(8n): and it was constitutionally appropriate that it was so. He gave the example of the poll tax. But lobbyists had overturned particular instances of policy and he gave planning decisions and road schemes as examples. He introduced 'proportionality' into the evaluation of lobbyist effectiveness in the sense that the lesser features and particular consequences of policy were open to review but not the pre-suppositions and principles of policy. It was proportionate and appropriate that lobbyists could influence the former. He noted that this power to amend was susceptible to pressure from groups of MPs and to the degree of resolve Ministers showed towards their own policies.

But if lobbyists were unable to change the core of policies, were they effective in changing particulars? He believed that some were because of their policy knowledge and process understanding but most were not because they gave 'superficial and presentational advice'. Lobbyists could advise on whom to write to and when and on the draft of a letter, but most had little policy advice to give in their own right as subject specialists. He thought there were two sources of that advice available to lobbyists who could then pass it on to their clients. The first was MPs and the second was the shrewdness of the effective lobbyists in 'interpreting my discretion'. The good lobbyist also listened for what was not said and interpreted the silences in the context of their own reading of the policy map.

Bill Robinson judged that lobbyists were influential in so far as they introduced issues and cases to policy-makers - i. e. the hyphen function. He expanded:

> everybody knows where they are coming from: so in that sense their views carry no weight but they do influence affairs to the extent that they introduce people who have a genuine case to make to the right official quarters where they will get a sympathetic hearing.

He found their performance 'quite variable' in their ability to master their clients' case but 'it was quite hard to separate out the contribution of the client and the contribution of the professional lobbyist'.

The 'ability to master the brief of the client' was important because the Treasury 'really hate bullshitters'. He explained: 'if people come up and don't know what they are talking about, they get very impatient and write them off very quickly'.

He argued that the main task for the lobbyist was getting the client introduced to the right decision-makers, followed by selecting the right person in the client body to make the representations. In that sequence of effectiveness criteria for an individual lobbyist, the ability to completely master the brief was highly desirable but not essential.

Concerns in the relationships

The amount of hospitality to accept; a possible 'americanisation' of UK lobbying; the quality of relationships between Whitehall and other, especially non-metropolitan, parts of the public sector; and ambitious claims by lobbyists of what they could achieve were mentioned as concerns.

For John Mills, there was a question to be raised about the public sector hiring lobbyists and it was:

> because those parts of the public sector, like education, like local government, feel they can't otherwise get into Whitehall. I think Whitehall's at fault because they ought not to have to go through those mechanisms (lobbyists).

Access to Whitehall by other parts of the public sector was also a concern for the anonymous Under-secretary. His judgement was that many non-metropolitan organisations were either or both unconfident/ incompetent in their dealings with Whitehall and turned to the London-based lobbyists for process guidance and for emotional support. He accepted that in part it was caused by central departments showing 'user unfriendliness.' His response in his own case was to sponsor or organise events which brought Whitehall and the interests together in direct contact.

Another concern was the danger of an 'americanisation' of lobbying in the UK: the continuous and intrusive hospitality of Washington was, he thought, better avoided in London. He noted that while there was no formal Civil Service statement of propriety vis-à-vis lobbyists, there was awareness about the difficulties of judging the appropriate amount of hospitality to accept. Liz Symons of the FDA agreed that there was no official position on propriety.

Bill Robinson also touched on the example of the USA, where he judged lobbying had become excessive. He did not like American practice 'where huge amounts of money are spent and there is an awful lot of junketing . . . to influence the decision-makers by giving them nice trips'.

About the UK, he said 'obviously one is worried about undue influence and one's worried about corruption'. But:

> I must say I didn't see anything in my two and half years inside that led me to think there was a slightest whiff of corruption about British Government.

He went on to talk about the 'very well established pattern of taking senior civil servants out to Wimbledon and Lords and out to lunch . . . of which the quid pro quo is that the civil servant in question will spend some of the time listening to the reasons why we should or shouldn't cut mortgage interest relief or whatever. . . '.

He continued:

> . . . civil servants aren't terribly well paid and don't have an incredibly enjoyable existence: I think the odd decent lunch and visit to Wimbledon is a reasonable perk for the job. And they're all immensely upright people who wouldn't allow themselves to be persuaded by anything other than a good argument and the most they will do for these people is - if there is an argument worth hearing - put it down on paper and see it gets to the Minister's attention. So I think on the whole . . . the system works quite well.

Most lobbying is for business interests, he agreed, but it did not follow that the latter had 'undue' influence:

> you could argue that the big battalions are representing more people. So the amount of influence, as it were, per person . . . I don't think is undue. If one pensioner gets the Minister's ear for ten minutes, you might say that was undue influence.

For the anonymous former special adviser, the focus of concern was not the lobbyist - 'provided that everybody knows where you are coming from . . . '. But:

> there are much more constitutional issues for MPs . . . it's important for them that they represent their constituents and if they also take on consultancies, it's very important that should be known and people can take a view as to why they're pursuing a particular course of action.

Conclusion

The interview data (new in the public domain for civil servants and special advisers) extended across a broad range of reaction and such a range is in line with the data from clients and from the perceptions of lobbyists about themselves in relation to decision-makers. Lobbyists have to reckon that they will meet both encouraging and distancing reactions from decision-makers.

But it is clear from the data that overall commercial lobbyists are an accepted presence in the public policy-making process. No respondent said they were vital and none was totally dismissive. There was concern about their public sector clients and what that implied about access to Whitehall; about opportunities for the complacent acceptance of excessive hospitality, and about their claims to effectiveness. In general, however, hired lobbyists were tolerated with varying degrees of enthusiasm, according to the degree of perceived advantage they brought to the decision-making process and the actors in it.

It is also clear from the data that lobbyists were points of first contact with decision-makers and that their role as face-to-face spokespersons for the interests they served was limited. This is in agreement with the data from lobbyists themselves and fits the **backgrounder** type developed in Chapter Five. But any role they had for clients as active policy advisers and constructors of the good case - **foregrounder** characteristics - would not be visible to the decision-makers. Such a role could be inferred by them but not observed firsthand and it could be argued from this that decision-makers have a particular and partial locus from which to make judgements about the role of lobbyists.

This **backgrounder** behaviour (Chapter Five) can be further described. Respondents noted that personal approaches to them over the telephone backed up by lunch was the most common contact method used by lobbyists. The client was invariably present at lunch and meetings and the visible role of the lobbyist was passive, limited to a support role. It was the same role as that of civil servants vis-à-vis Ministers: 'don't speak unless spoken to.' There were sometimes working meetings but they were less frequent than lunches. Only one decision-maker claimed to know lobbyists well socially. There was no sense from the majority of respondents that lobbyists were intrusive (the exceptions were two of the MPs). If lobbyists were persistent, they were not so to the point of producing widespread disgruntlement. They were generally tolerated because in particular they could offer a relationship of some advantage.

All the decision-makers saw some benefit in relationships with commercial lobbyists. Even Kenneth Carlisle MP, who was generally contemptuous, admitted that they 'probably play a useful role in that they do get the issues out'. Liz Symons of the FDA admitted that interests with an 'attenuated' relationship with Whitehall could benefit from hiring. Benefit was conceived by respondents as mutual in the sense that operational information from outside Government was traded off against access to

Government information and personnel, i. e. access to themselves and Ministers. This theme of mutual benefit as a strong tie between lobbyist and decision-maker was also reflected in the previous data from lobbyists. Decision-makers allowed access to themselves as the price to be paid for information. Indeed, where they thought that the relationship with the lobbyist regularly yielded valuable information, civil servants were ready to cement the relationship by facilitating access to Ministers for the client of the lobbyist in order to impress the former, even if it did not advance his case. Where the decision-maker was a special adviser, contact with lobbyists could yield information to challenge the civil service case for a decision. Mutual benefit claims were also made about lobbyists in their 'escort agency' role of introducing interests ignorant of the policy process to Government: in this way it was argued that public policy was enchanced by wider access and better information flows.

Heinz et al. (1993; 61) have commented on an aspect of mutuality in their work on commercial lobbyists in Washington: lobbyists have to accommodate the needs of decision-makers as well as those of clients. In terms of the hyphen metaphor, hired lobbyists need their Government knowledge and contacts as a condition of gaining and holding clients: the hyphen needs to be secured on both sides for it to work. Relationships with decision-makers, therefore, have to be sensitively handled in ways which respect their culture and expectations. This need for good relations by commercial lobbyists on the Government side of the hyphen was evident in the data. For example, a public interest aspect must be contained in the case advanced if it is to make headway; contact should yield new information and perspectives for decision-makers; lobbyists should appreciate the systemic constraints on public policy.

No decision-maker attributed major influence or effectiveness to commercial lobbyists in the area of core policy: but the latter, as corporate agents working for powerful principals, could have major influence on decisions at the margins of policy, defined as non-core areas of policy design and implementation. It is possible that their influence could be significant in two particular sets of circumstance: when the policy was the subject of a free vote in the House and when the Government was subject to conflicting pressures and sought relief in a new policy initiative. Although decision-makers perceived hired lobbyists as a minor influence, it is important to note that the outcomes they facilitate are regarded as major by the clients who hire them. Clients do not hire for matters they regard as minor.

The analysis above of weak influence by lobbyists in core decision-making is in line with the conclusion of the Heinz et al. thesis (378) about the American Federal Government: 'government officials are now more independent from the constraints of the interest group environment than in the past.'

Even though decision-makers regard commercial lobbyists as minor players in the policy process, they still have expectations about the individual behaviour of the effective lobbyist, whatever its influence on decisions. See Appendix Two.

Notes

1. Source is note of a telephone conversation with Jeremy Mayhew, on Thursday, 23 September, 1993.
2. Source is note of a discussion with Cliff Grantham in his office at the DfE, on Monday, 22 November, 1993.
3. Source is note of a discussion with Kay Dixon in her office at the DfE, on Monday, 20 December, 1993.
4. The programme, transmitted at 8.30 pm, was a general review of the relationship between lobbyists and MPs, with its major focus on the latter.
5. Letter to the author on Monday, 21 March, 1994.
6. A survey of 100 MPs' attitudes to lobbying entitled *Effective Lobbying* and conducted by Access Opinions Ltd for The Market Access Group found that only 4% were happy to meet a professional lobbyist alone while 28% were happy to see the company representative only. 33% of the sample were happy to meet both together with the company representative as the advocate: it was 19% when the lobbyist was the advocate.

   The survey also concluded: 'the most valued method for a company or organisation to influence MPs is to meet those who have a special interest - with research-based lobbyists behind them to ensure the right messages reach the appropriate political ears.' The most favoured locations for a meeting were the House of Commons ranked first and then, the company's London office; a Westminster restaurant; an out-of-London location; and last, a reception.
7. The BBC Radio Four programme *File on Four* of 9 February, 1993 gave an insight into the scale of US lobbying when a staff officer to Senator Bob Dole reported that on important legislation, he received up to 75 phone calls a day.
8. Angela Rumbold MP, former PPS to Secretary of State Nicholas Ridley and a former Education Minister, said on the Radio 4 programme *Selling Your Soul,* 17 July, 1993 about lobbying on legislation: 'there is also negotiation on individual points; never negotiation on fundamental principles. But at the edges, there is always room for negotiations. That is the critical point.'

7 Lobbyists for hire: corporate accessories

'What we need in the study of commercial lobbying is light, more light and still more light'.

(*Austen Mitchell MP in the Introduction to Jordan, 1991*)

Focus on the hiring

Lobbying for hire (commercial lobbying) is incompletely mapped territory. Some aspects of the terrain have been better recorded than others; for example, the relationship of hired lobbyists to Parliament. Some aspects have been more drawn in self-interest than mapped; for example, claims by these lobbyists that they have changed public policy.

But there has been no mapping of other parts of the terrain. What services clients want from their hired lobbyists; how these lobbyists interact with their paymasters, and how decision-makers react to these hirings are examples of new ground which this work has sought to throw light on.

The primary focus here has been the 'for hire' feature of these lobbyists. In that, this work differs from previous texts where the focus has been on the lobbyists as political actors in the public policy-making process. It has looked at commercial lobbyists from the viewpoint of their being an extra lobbying resource and it has looked through three sets of eyes - the hirer, the hired and the decision-makers. Its stance is not, therefore, inside the policy process looking out at its subject: rather it is above the process examining how an extra resource fits in.

This 'for hire' characteristic is the most differentiating feature of commercial lobbyists and so marks them off from in-house and voluntary cause lobbyists serving only one interest. It is not apparent that there are other differentiating features: for example, there is very little evidence that *how* commercial lobbyists work is different from their employed peers.

Previous analysis has least covered this 'for hire' feature. New data has been brought into the public domain as follows: clients (Chapter Three) and decision-makers (Chapter Six) have been surveyed in depth for the first time on their attitudes and behaviour towards the subject. Contact with the lobbyists themselves (Chapters Four and Five) has also presented a more richly detailed and comprehensive portrayal of what they do for clients and how they interact with decision-makers than had been presented in the UK before.

The 'for hire' feature makes business people of commercial lobbyists: they need clients; they have to satisfy them that they give value for money (1n). To locate commercial lobbyists in a market place of changing demand and supply is to put them in a new, dynamic perspective. Commercial lobbyists have established competitors, such as lawyers, and others are lining up. *PR Week* reported (Jan 27, 1995; 10-15) that corporate boardrooms 'seem keen to embrace the advice of management consultants . . .'. But it can still be assumed that, in the UK as in the US, 'the lion's share of representational work' for interests is done by full-time employees, where the ratio is four to one (Heinz et al., 1993; 66, 372). Commercial lobbyists, therefore, have to seek out clients and they always need an eye for business development because clients come and go. They negotiate fees which the market for their services will bear. They are seen by many clients as a distress purchase and this perception limits their marketing opportunities. They have to manage a multiplicity of clients in terms of their own time and energy and in terms of avoiding conflicts of interest; activities which they generally do to the satisfaction of clients.

Once hired, commercial lobbyists are professional advisers to mainly large and powerful private sector interests: they are accessories to these corporate interests, hired for services used to defend and strengthen those interests. They are not prime movers on the political scene: they wait to be moved by those who need them. They could not exist outside of the competition of interests: outside of what *The Government Report* has pictured as the lobbying battle. They have to be a well connected hyphen but they are not an independent hyphen: their clients call them into existence if and when they want links made with the public policy-making process.

Heinz et al. (1993; 11) make a related point about American hired lobbyists: that the US literature has seen them as part of the organisations they represent 'with the individual representatives having no separate existence or automony'.

Commercial lobbying is a business. This is not to state a hitherto unknown fact. No previous research has denied it. There are no public statements by commercial lobbyists denying it. Rather the perspective has not been activated in any UK research beforehand. It is a perspective which has to be activated once the 'for hire' feature is the primary focus. Their business form of organisation flows directly from that feature. Their work is not capital intensive. They get a brief from clients and advise them on how to progress it, with their public role then either more or less visible. They work through contacts, using interpersonal skills and their knowledge of the policy-making system and of current issues. They are mostly grouped together like other corporate advisers into partnerships or private companies and less frequently into divisions of public companies.

Focus on the 'for hire' aspect of lobbying (which Sir Bernard Ingham has called an honourable trade [*PR Week*; 27 January, 1995; 3]) does not imply a moral ferment against commercial lobbyists. The focus was identified for two reasons: no work had been done using it in the UK and it is a common and well established feature of professional advisers. Nor does the focus imply that hired lobbyists always work for the highest bidder: the market is much too imperfect for that. During the interviews, one respondent replied that 'the business-like aspect is not really remarkable; it is the same commercial motivation that operates in any consultancy firm in that you try and get business; people ask you to work - you charge them a fee'.

This work concurs with the commonplace that professional advisers work for fees: it is the unexplored consequences of a commonplace, not previously noted about these lobbyists, which have been set out here.

The sections below review the major conclusions of clients, decision-makers and lobbyists themselves about their work, make a historical comparison and draw conclusions.

Commercial lobbyists as corporate advisers

The 'for hire' feature is not a unique one among professional advisers to corporate bodies - lawyers, bankers, accountants, architects, advertising and public relations agencies all share in it. Making this point of commonality is a reminder that the demand for their services ebbs and flows according to the imperatives of the larger environment. If lawyers supply advice on the law, bankers and accountants on capital and money flows, architects on the built environment, what do hired lobbyists offer? Advice about persuasive techniques to influence public policy.

Contact with clients (Chapter Three) shows that the hirers had varying opinions about individual lobbyists. Like any group of corporate advisers, the lobbyists were ranked in terms of overall reputation and competence.

The data from clients and lobbyists (Chapters Three, Four and Five) demonstrates that what lobbyists do can be categorised as the supply of services under the following heads: the supply of access for clients to decision-makers; of representation to decision-makers; of policy advice to clients, and of administrative support to clients. How many and how much of these services are hired in by the clients can be conceptualised as a propensity to hire lobbyists (Chapter Three) with clients at different positions on a scale. Propensity to hire is a reminder of the great variation in what any particular hire lobbyist does for a client. Commercial lobbying is what clients want it to be.

There is no common set of operational circumstances facing clients which could explain all or most of the hiring of services. Nor is there a positive correlation between the companies' levels of hiring and externalities, such as inclusion in a particular business sector, their position in big company tables of turnover or perceived degrees of government interest in their businesses. Moloney and Jordan (1994) have built on client interviews in this work to suggest a tentative explanation. Large business plcs have a contingency-based approach to lobbying and will augment their large, existing lobbying capacity, including hiring in extra capacity, if this increases the probability of success.

What is demonstrable is that commercial lobbyists work for 'the big battalions in society' - a phrase used unattributably by one lobbyist interviewed. The political perspective of neo-pluralism (Chapter Two) which *privileges in a challenged and fractured way* the general business interest above others in a market economy provides a theoretical explanation of this relationship. A small proportion of commercial lobbyists' work is for *pro bono* clients but that proportion has been squeezed by the post-1989 recession. This research has shown that these 'battalions' are drawn currently from the public sector in more significant numbers than they were. This amends previous findings that the clients of commercial lobbyists were 'overwhelmingly' the big businesses of the private sector.

Rather, clients are those organisations from whatever sector who are subject to changing operating environments by market or government activity; or clients who seek to initiate changes in their operating environments, *and* who can afford the fees charged by lobbyists for hire. The composition of client lists reflects the market and political developments of the day affecting the public and private sectors.

The theoretical political perspective taken in this work is the neo-pluralist perspective. But, as argued in Chapter Two, that does not imply that each business or any one business sector is dominant in its relationships. Businesses are in a constant, competitive struggle for advantage inside the single most influential interest bloc. They lobby government in order that the public policy environment is most sympathetically arranged to aid their competitive struggle. The above argument is consistent with the empirical findings set out here about the public sector hirings of lobbyists. These hirings fall into two categories. Some are about the terms of the ejection of the hirer into the business sector and out of the diminished public sector. Some are about new internal arrangements inside the diminished public sector which Government wants run on more business-like lines.

Hired lobbyists as political advocates

Being like barristers - high status corporate advisers - is one comparison some commercial lobbyists like to make. They see themselves as political advocates, especially so when they sense that the large London-based legal firms are a growing threat to their professional niche. The language used by the lobbyists themselves was 'they advocate a case on a client's behalf' (Miller); 'you're presenting a case, preparing a client's argument . . . '(Jeger); 'I very much think of myself as being a political advocate' (Rycroft). UK lobbyists of this bent look approvingly and apprehensively to the US where Heinz et al. (1993; 60) have argued that 'The most pervasive professional group among representatives . . . is the legal profession'.

The lawyer comparison made by UK commercial lobbyists is often - but not always - associated with an anti-public relations stance. Looked at from this angle, it is powered by a search for a well established and prestigious professional status; by a longing to escape from the negative connotations of lobbying and into a functional category of high social status such as the legal profession. The **foregrounder** and **backgrounder** typology developed in Chapter Five accommodates a barrister and solicitor distinction and could be helpful in further research with analysing the nature of the market share threat posed by legal firms and how it could be countered.

But there are limits to the comparison with lawyers, especially the more the role of the hired lobbyist is understood beyond the level of slogan and inter-professional rivalry. Michael Burrell of Westminster Strategy (Chapter Four) has pointed out that barristers accept that everybody has a right to legal representation, 'however dastardly they may be'. But hired lobbyists need to empathise with clients because '. . . in practice you can't really give good advice to clients to whom you feel hostile'. Berry (1991) further argued that there are no recognised exams or declared standards of behaviour for lobbyists. Douglas Smith argued two more limitations. Firstly that the legal system is highly established, visible and legitimated and that there is no comparable system of lobbying. Secondly, that cogency of case may be a necessary condition for lobbying success but it is not sufficient: '. . . you need the contacts to translate cogency into the desired political behaviour'.

Overall, the comparison with barristers is a reminder that commercial lobbyists are aware of the competitive nature of their position: they are competing with other types of corporate adviser, most of whom are more established and more prestigious. Lawyers and management consultants already do their work but it is under-researched to what extent. Equally the comparison is a reminder that commercial lobbyists operate in a world which calls for a range of skills: and which ones are used depends on circumstance. Where the matter lobbied is much technical and little political, case advocacy will be to the fore: where the matter lobbied is much political and little technical, influencing personal contacts and creating public pressures will be to the fore. Douglas Smith of Westminster Advisers summed up:

> You talk to people about the case for ten minutes and then about, say, Oldham football for fifty minutes. The case and the human pressure created by contacts is the right combination.

Commercial lobbyists are client-led

The focus on hiring reveals how the hiring principle and lobbying services offered to the hirer are inter-related. Hired lobbyists are business sensitive and are active in seeking out more work. They see their peers in a competitive way. They have a market pricing approach to fees as opposed to a cost plus one: they will charge what their clients will stand. Their fee structure is entirely responsive: it is a vehicle designed principally to maximise their revenue and the vehicle is made out of components designed for that purpose. They like retainers because it guarantees a cash flow; but they have to do specific project work. Timesheets are widely used for monthly billing: one lobbyist told that 'all our thinking is done by the hour or by quarter of an hour units'. Fees related to pre-defined lobbying outcomes - success fees - are probably more commonly charged than lobbyists are ready to admit. Few think such fees raise an issue of propriety. Sometimes they will do work on a loss-leader basis to encourage more work later. When clients are in straitened circumstances as when market regulators appear, fees rise exponentially.

Hired lobbyists do not work on behalf of issues: they work for clients. They are client-led. They offer a range of services to clients and within it, they will do what clients want. They let clients 'pick 'n mix' their services.

But commercial lobbyists do have work preferences. Their pattern of preferences suggests (Chapter Five) two conceptually ideal types of lobbyist: the **backgrounder** and the **foregrounder**. These types can be useful in categorising and analysing the work of lobbyists but no lobbyist can be, by definition, a **backgrounder** or a **foregrounder.** The balance of data in this research is that **backgrounder** characteristics are more common in lobbyists. For business reasons, they more frequently do the process work of advising about whom to contact and about how a case should be presented: they prefer not to represent clients alone before decision-makers; and they work for too many different clients to be policy experts of any depth. They are content to be more silent or unseen in public than voluble and visible. This conclusion was confirmed in conversation with a civil servant servicing the Nolan Committee. He had been seconded to the public affairs section of a large British Bank and noted the inability of hired lobbyists to handle the intricacies of the brief after headline issues had been dealt with. Lobbyists would also prefer not to run public media campaigns but will do so if the client instructs. Hired lobbyists are more unsighted advisers than public actors. They are temporary civil servants to their client principals.

Varied relationships with decision-makers

To satisfy clients, hired lobbyists need at least the acquiescence of the decision-makers so that they can be role players in the policy-making process. To embellish the hyphen metaphor of Norton and Grantham (1986), they need to be well connected on both the business and political sides of their decision-making. In fact, they have a range of relationships with decision-makers, the latter being anything from suspicious or envious to supportive (Chapter 6). Some decision-makers see them as unwelcome interlopers in a bilateral relationship between interests and policy-makers. But in general lobbyists have enough of the neutral opinion and of the passive co-operation of decision-makers in order to operate. (There is mounting evidence from the hearings of the Nolan Committee that the good opinion of some MPs is being strained.)

Commercial lobbyists believe that they are offering a mutual benefit to decision-makers in the form of an information exchange about how policies do or would work. They most commonly say that decision-makers see this benefit but they also note the presence of distorting filters, such as personal chemistry, political partisanship and their own reputation. The 'for hire' feature works assymetrically in this instance both for and against their interests. It can mean that with many clients, they do not concentrate their contacts on small numbers of decision-makers and so fray relationships; but they can be seen by some decision-makers as dilettantes or as seekers of public policy information for profit.

On the other side of the relationship, evidence from decision-makers indicates that the latter accept commercial lobbyists in the sense of tolerating an extant feature of the policy process to which they have occasional recourse. Some of the toleration edges towards enthusiasm: some borders on contempt. Decision-makers see new information as the benefit of their relationship with the lobbyists. In fact, it is the major - if not the only - benefit in their perception of the relationship. (York [1986] argued that lobbying could be seen as a social good because it supplies information on policy costs and benefits).

Hired lobbyists are not seen by decision-makers as central role players: rather they are viewed as not very visible and as passive aides to a principal. Although decision-makers identify cases of effectiveness involving individual lobbyists, the latters' role as influencers of policy is, except in unusual circumstances, put at the margin. The data on this point suggests the potency of the **backgrounder** category of lobbying behaviour. But this picture of lobbyist as passive support is from a specific social location - that of the decision-maker. From the client's location, the lobbyist he has hired may be much more active and initiating and in line with the **foregrounder** category of behaviour. Decision-makers see hired lobbyists from the constitutional and macro political point of view. Clients see things differently: they see the matters about which they hire lobbyists as major influences on their affairs. What is minor to Government may be major to an interest.

1950 to 1994: a long perspective

It is illuminating to contrast commercial lobbyists today with their equivalents or near-equivalents in the late 1940s for what the comparison reveals by way of similarities and differences.

The Report of the Committee on Intermediaries was presented to Prime Minister Attlee in March, 1950. Its terms of reference were 'to inquire how far persons are making a business of acting as specialists in the submission of applications for licences and permits, or otherwise as intermediaries between Government Departments and the public; and to report whether the activities of such persons are liable to give rise to abuses . . .' (2n).

The Committee gave examples of the work of these hired lobbyists of the 1940s: income tax disputes and claims; Admiralty contracts; import/export licences; marketing help for a 'firm with a synthetic substitute for a natural material . . . '; patent claims; pension claims; making supplementary petrol applications, getting building licences and seeking departmental purchasing contracts. It is apparent that much of the work was about representing individuals as well as companies and many of the intermediaries had been civil servants in wartime: references to accountants were frequent. 'Big firms' were not found to need intermediaries but some 'smaller firms' did. Overall Whitehall Departments reported a stream of intermediaries coming and going before them: it was understood that one 'has now taken up a fried fish shop and grocery business'.

The examples above reflect the policies of Government of the day - 'the working of a widespread system of controls' left over from the wartime planned economy. Over the last 40 years, Government involvement in the economy has moved away from direct, physical control and rationing but the policy of involvement is still intact: it now takes the form of market regulation. (3n) Thus, in an ironic contrast between Attlee's and Thatcherite politics, Government policy itself continues to create the demand for lobbying.

The report concluded that 'there are persons making a business' out of this access-building and representation-making work but that 'they are few in number and do not occupy an important part in the field in which scope for intermediary activities exists'. It also found 'that the activities of such persons are clearly liable to give rise to abuse but we are not satisfied that these activities are on such a scale as would justify the attempt to apply any general restriction on them'.

The Committee did not want to hinder the hyphen function. It said: '. . . without some form of intermediary activity, using the term in its widest sense, it is difficult to see how some of the controls could be effectively operated'. Transferred to 1995, this one sentence, written 40 years ago in a climate of disdain and complacency for intermediaries, concedes the conceptual case for contemporary commercial lobbyists.

The Committee offered the following reasons why intermediaries would stay few in number. The administrative machine of the day, still running elements of the wartime command economy with many bureaucratic controls, was complex and this would discourage numbers. Further, in an early appearance of the legal comparison, it noted that the intermediary 'is in much the same position as a lawyer would be in if there were no books or methods of instruction both in the substance of the law and the procedure of its administration'. Hence the tools for lobbying were not available. Thirdly, the intermediary's contacts in the civil service would be perodically moving posts through job changes and promotions and the report called the personal contacts of lobbyists 'a wasting asset'. It also noted the need the intermediary has of a good reputation with decision-makers: to be regarded as a 'responsible and reliable person'. Reputation would be risked by taking up bad cases.

The Committee also noted that the need for intermediaries diminishes 'in proportion to the extent to which a Department succeeds in making itself accessible to, and its procedure understood by, the public'. Intermediaries are needed when Departments are 'remote and incomprehensible'. The need for simple and understandable administrative procedures was stressed in the Committee's recommendations: as was that for private intermediaries to declare whom they were acting for. If the declaration did not satisfy the Department, it should deal directly with the 'applicant'.

The similarities and differences between 1950 and 1995 are striking. The most noticeable difference is the existence of the contemporary intermediaries - commercial lobbyists - as a broadly accepted set of role players in the public policy-making process, a group with an estimated, current £25m fee turnover. The Report, looked at historically, was therefore wrong in its basic judgement that there was little scope for intermediaries. Doig (1990) noted this, saying that it was not foreseen how former politicans and civil servants could exploit their knowledge as intermediaries. Also different is the absence today of any widespread sense that the intermediaries exist because of inadequate public administration or that Government holds the key to the future of commercial lobbyists in its own administrative reform. The view that efficient public administration can largely remove the need for intermediaries permeates the 1950 Report. Today one strong political theme in debate about the existence of lobbying firms would be that private business provides services which public administration cannot or should not.

But some civil servants contest that view, arguing that Whitehall could reduce demand by interests for hired lobbyists. Departments could do this through procedural devices of openness and direct contact with the external world. This would reduce the nurturing conditions of ignorance, alienation and dazzlement about Westminster and Whitehall amongst interests which encourage the growth of commercial lobbyists. This was noted 40 years ago.

> We have been much impressed by the fact that the usefulness of an intermediary diminishes in proportion to the extent to which a Department succeeds in making itself accessible to and its procedure understood by the public (205).

In developing this argument of departmental openness, it is useful to remember that intermediaries (third parties in a relationship) can take many forms, including the collective and individual. One such collective form was suggested by an Under-secretary who talked of conferences, seminars, meetings organised under the auspices of his Department. It is also possible to reduce the need for intermediaries through personal access: departments could nominate individual officials as 'easy entry points' for groups. Another Under-secretary talked about the need for these forms of direct contact in an actively critical sense when he said that Departments were 'at fault' when public sector bodies used hired lobbyists in their relationship with Whitehall and Westminster.

Direct contact can also be a potential sanction in any regulatory regime against commercial lobbyists. The 1950 Committee saw this when it recommended that departments should by-pass intermediaries if relationships were not satisfactory. One intermediary said that 'the Ministry had put him out of business'.

Today commercial lobbyists are needed by 'big firms' in a way unknown in the late 1940s while the representation of individuals is now rarely done by them: today's intermediaries are corporate representatives. The 1940s pattern of work with its emphasis on individual interests was a response to a widespread command economy including retail rationing. The same responsiveness can be seen today, albeit in areas affected by the contemporary pattern of Government activity. For example, it can be seen in the large number of local authorities which have hired lobbyists to deal with the review of local government; and also in private and public sector bodies who have hired lobbyists as they cope with regulatory regimes.

The well connected hyphen

Commercial lobbyists need corporate clients to survive as a business: equally they need Government in the sense that the Government's policies of regulation and reform create circumstances where there is a demand from large plcs for lobbyists. They also need Government in a narrower, operational sense: they supply access and representational services to clients and they could not deliver these to clients if the Government refused to deal with them. There can be tension in these linkages. In their contemporary study of hired lobbyists in Washington, Heinz et al. (1993; 61) argued:

> The ability of private representatives [hired lobbyists] to trade on their knowledge and contacts at an agency where they were previously employed gives Washington insiders a large stake in their relationships with the agencies. They may thus be as concerned to accommodate government officials as to satisfy their clients. Because Washington representatives are pulled toward both the client and the government, they may play one against the other and attempt to please both.

Hyphens can be seen as pulling elements together or separating them. The data is in support of the connecting function. The 1950 Committee spoke of the need by Government for 'intermediary activity, using the term in its widest sense' and this is a continuing need noted by lobbyists (Chapters Four and Five) and by decision-makers (Chapter Six). Government needs contact, information and ideas from outside itself. If commercial lobbyists in the UK today were faced with a hostile regulatory regime against them, this argument of beneficial information flows to the Government for an efficient public policy-making process would be a powerful counter to their critics.

Potential threats about - but never actual introduction of - regulation of lobbyists is another similarity with the latter 1940s. The scale of abuse was then judged too small to justify a general regulation: the recommendation was different behaviour by the Departments. Today, there is hardly any attention to this Departmental/hired lobbyist relationship: even the Nolan Committee heard little about it from witnesses. The Commons in 1992 decided not to press ahead with a partial restriction in the form of a Parliamentary Register of hired lobbyists and referred the matter back to the Select Committee for Members' Interests.

But Nolan may yet be a turning point for the public reputation and role of lobbyists for hire. Up to the the formation of the Committee, the latter excited a low level, non-specific concern in observers outside Parliament but that concern was never translated into any persistent, politically powerful call for their direct regulation. Illustrating the weak nature of concern is the provenance of these pre-Nolan proposals for regulation. The source of one proposal is the PRCA (Public Relations Consultants' Association), a private trade association which has stepped in following the refusal of Parliament to start a lobbyists' register (4n). The PRCA's jurisdiction, and even presence, in the field of commercial lobbying is strongly disputed by some major lobbying firms and the latter have come together in the APPC (The Association of Professional Political Consultants) to form another self-regulatory body. To the larger public, these are unknown bodies. The first Nolan report of May 1995 opted for a ban on MPs working for lobbying firms but the July vote in the Commons rejected this or, more optimistically, held it over for more consideration in the autumn.

But the matter of regulating commercial lobbyists is dependent on an answer to the earlier question of whether their role in public policy-making can be evaluated and judgements made about their effectiveness in influencing lobbying outcomes. If they are not effective or influential, there is no case for regulating them.

Hired lobbyists and effectiveness

It can be argued that the more academic work done on lobbying, the less the ability of the observer to predict or even accurately describe the activity. It is as though the fabric under hand cannot bear too heavy a stitch. The certainty of the 'iron triangle' (where lobbyists could be placed as reinforcing bolts at the interest group corner) has been replaced by the more delicate and diffuse images of 'policy networks' and 'policy communities'. Richardson (1993; 7) comments on this loss of predictability.

This progression of image towards the diaphanous continues. Heinz et al. write about the 'hollow core': that is the title of their decade-long study of interest group activity in Washington with particular reference to the representative (commercial) lobbyist. They have dispelled any image of 'capture' of the policy-making process by private interests or their agents. They write that:

> A part of the reason for the uncertainty in outcomes that we observed . . . is that power countervailed power. In any real contest, it is problematic to predict outcomes with certainty. (391)

In their preface (xvi), they explain that the preferred meaning of their title was that:

> . . . it might mean that the networks of policy-makers lack central actors who stand in the middle of the system and have the ability to shape winning coalitions. That is, the hollow core might be an image that is something like the opposite of the power elite.

Furthermore, they doubt (369) the effectiveness of interest group activity generally:

> Although greater numbers of organisations of all types . . . actively monitor and participate in the making of national policy, and although the scope and intensity of their efforts has [sic] increased significantly, the returns on these efforts are not at all clear.

They add (407) that the 'absence of strong effects here [private interest representation] is not a methodological failing so much as a reflection of the uncertain and situational nature of influence in national policy-making systems'.

Their final judgement is that increased interest group activity does not change the balance of power amongst policy-making players and that the policy-making system is stable: 'thus the policy system may move very little despite escalating effort' (412).

The Heinz et al. study had a wider purview than this research in that it broadened out into the general aspects of (American) interest group politics. But this work has reached similar conclusions about evaluation and about effectiveness. The literature review here suggests that the problems of evaluating the effectiveness of interest group activity in the UK is unresolved: and that the problems extend to the agents of groups, such as hired lobbyists. This research confirms Grant's judgement (1989) that it is the methodological problems facing the whole field of group activity which prevents evaluation of effectiveness. But if effectiveness cannot be demonstrated via a coherent and explicit methodology, can it be inferred intuitively and judgementally? The data suggests that commercial lobbyists achieve low levels of effectiveness, defined as the ability to achieve pre-stated and measurable goals by their own behaviours. The statement by the former Secretary for Transport John MacGregor to the Nolan Committee (*The Independent*, 25 January, 1995, p. 5) that '. . . lobbying played no part in influencing him' presents another empiricial challenge to lobbyists' effectiveness. Overall, the general inference is that, in most cases, they are minor role-players of low effectiveness in the public policy-making process.

This research shows that clients do not hire lobbyists on the assumption that they are per se *the* crucial, extra resource which will win the battle for advantage for their employers. Rather clients are hiring an extra resource, an aide, an auxiliary. They hire in a range of services - basic document monitoring upwards - from commercial lobbyists as a support for their pre-existing lobbying activities. These hirings are reinforcements: large plcs invariably have their own political network of contacts and also the capacity to articulate their case. Commercial lobbyists are wanted for what extra they bring to a scene already supplied with lobbying capacity. In that sense they are a *corporate accessory* and when hired, a needed and valued one. They are part of somebody else's team; they usually follow somebody else's game plan, and they play on a pitch not of their choosing.

Hired lobbyists themselves invariably hesitate to claim a clear, causal relationship between their efforts and lobbying outcomes. They do not claim a formula for successful lobbying; they accept that evaluation of their effectiveness is difficult. Typically their promotional literature talks about advising clients on 'how to influence events in the political arena'; that political contacts can reveal 'commercial opportunities and provide protection from potentially harmful legislation' and 'advice and assistance in preparing, presenting and assessing cases made to Government'.

Commercial lobbyists are sensitive about the evaluation of their outcomes as a group and as individuals and it is, in part, because of their 'for hire' feature. Faced towards decision-makers, they can accept with constitutional propriety and professional equanimity both the general case that group effectiveness is difficult to evaluate and that their own effectiveness as a supporting service to groups is also difficult to evaluate.

But they cannot be so relaxed when they face their clients. Their first task is to please the client paying their fees: to provide their clients with value for money, a phrase which is effectiveness looked at from the point of view of the hirer-hired relationship. They do not have to provide - unless asked - a definition of their own effectiveness. In this, they are like all corporate advisers. They are client-led in everything that they do. For them, therefore, the key question is not how they themselves evaluate effectiveness; rather it is how do clients evaluate it.

In their relationship with clients, commercial lobbyists benefit from these difficulties of evaluation. Empirically, clients show considerable diversity in their evaluation benchmarks: from being better understood by policy-makers; via a 'feel good' factor from having set foot in the inner sanctum of policy-making, to a demand that a fixed legislative outcome happens. There is no universal benchmark.

In their client relationships, therefore, commercial lobbyists firstly listen and usually then suggest a simultaneous, twin-track approach to evaluating effectiveness. The first track is to make judgements about observable activities which are agreed as - or are implied to be - goals; e.g. seeing an important Minister, civil servant, special adviser or MP; or winning a tax concession. The second track is to agree or imply as goals less observable activities, e.g. gaining higher personal profile among decision-makers or creating greater awareness about the client. In this way, the measurable and imponderable aspects of evaluating effectiveness are incorporated into clients' judgements about value for money and are inextricably mixed together. The corporate adviser can survive for another hiring.

The research showed this process at work. Measurable effectiveness was claimed for a Private Members' Bill on bingo advertising; for aspects of the Broadcasting Act in relation to the ITV Association; for aspects of the Water Act in relation to the Water Services Association and for the contents of EU directives on packaging. More imponderable were claims such as 'you've positioned the client as an adviser to Government' and the impact on 'opinion forming and in moving a particular policy issue forward'.

The analysis above has been about evaluating the effectiveness of commercial lobbyists as agents of interests. The literature showed that effectiveness could also be approached at a more micro level of activity: namely the operational behaviour of individual lobbyists. This is the attribute-listing, the good practice approach to the work of professionals, with its focus on individual behaviours rather than group outcomes. This work further developed this approach in Appendix 2 when clients, lobbyists and decision-makers were asked about individual attributes of lobbyists. But this research can find no consistent positive correlations between good practice by individual UK commercial lobbyists and outcomes they sought for their hirers. It can describe desirable behaviour noted by other policy players: it cannot describe effective behaviour needed for desired outcomes.

This is in line with the finding of Heinz et al. (408) who concluded that there was no clear connection between the hiring of 'Washington heavyweights' as lobbyists and desired policy outcomes: 'we doubt that the search for individual influence is likely to produce many theoretical insights into the nature of the national policy-making process'. The individual attributes of commercial lobbyists, therefore, have not been identified as a determinant of - or as a significant pre-disposing factor making for - desired lobbying outcomes. The lobbyists who display the attributes of good practice may get hired more frequently but it is not clear that their lobbying achieves more.

Claims of individual, good, lobbying practice were made by the lobbyists themselves, by clients and decision-makers in the interviews and they were of the type already cited in the literature. But there was one noticeable difference from the American literature. The most commonly reported attribute of American good practice was a good ethical opinion about the lobbyist: the ethical attribute did not emerge from the UK interviews.

Theoretical perspectives on commercial lobbying

Chapter Two on theoretical perspectives argued that neo-pluralism, as elaborated by Lindblom (1977), offered the best 'fit' explanation of commercial lobbying as portrayed in the literature. The same conclusion was confirmed by research undertaken for this work but in an attenuated way.

Perspectives other than the neo-pluralist (the classical pluralist and the neo-Marxist from the standpoints of public relations and of group behaviour) were first used to filter the data but found relatively lacking in explanatory power. Instead, the interviews confirmed the strong links between large companies and hired lobbyists suggested in the literature. It is argued that the classical pluralist perspective could not persuasively explain why business provides the majority of clients for hired lobbyists or the issues lobbied. The data provided little demonstration of the validity of the critical, neo-Marxist perspective. The classical was too weak and too thinly elaborated a perspective to accommodate the richness of the data; the critical perspective too elusive to be operationalised. But the exploration of these two rejected perspectives was not a waste of effort. The classical reminded the research that the business/hired lobbyist link happened in a context of general lobbying by a great range of interests and that there was a complicated 'balance wheel' (Truman's phrase) keeping this general competition of interests stable - a finding in line with Heinz et al. above. The critical perspective was a reminder that an analytically powerful tool such as *information subsidy* could provide conceptual insights even if the interviews did not yield empirical support for the validity of the tool.

The research design of this work also produced confirmation of the explanatory power of neo-pluralism. The same topics were covered with the three sub-populations involved in commercial lobbying - clients, lobbyists and decision-makers. This triangulation confirmed the salience of business/businesses as clients; the perceived importance of these businesses to the UK economy and to Government as market regulator; the struggle for competitive advantage by sectors and single entities inside the business bloc; the success and failure of individual lobbies; the large lobbying resources available to big companies and a varying propensity to hire lobbyists. Overall, these findings are supportive of a neo-pluralist, Lindblomite perspective: hiring lobbyists is an expression of *the privileged but challenged and fractured position* of business/businesses in a market economy.

The above analysis assumes commercial lobbying is an accessory to group activity and it is an attempt to answer the question why businesses lobby using hired lobbyists. In this formulation, the role of commercial lobbyists is predicated on the independent and undifferentiated activity of business lobbying; commercial lobbying is a subordinate variable. The neo-pluralist perspective therefore allows an explicit conclusion that business will use all appropriate resources to lobby effectively: but it provides only a strong, implied answer to the particular question 'why hire lobbyists'. It cannot very specifically handle the centrality of the hired lobbyist.

The Nolan Committee and light

The 1950 Committee on Intermediaries conluded that hired lobbyists were too small a subject to turn a light onto: to be the subject of continuing, independent scrutiny. Finer ended his examination of lobbying in 1966 with the ringing call for light, more light. The significance of the Nolan Committee set up twenty eight years later is that *it is that light: an independent scrutineer.* Its light has sweeped more broadly and deeply than just the relationship of decision-makers to lobbyists: it has looked also at industry and quango relationships as well as the ethical and cultural values surrounding all the policy-players. But in this investigative *son et lumiere*, its shafts of light aimed at lobbyists were still the most powerful since 1950. The Committee published its first report on 11 May, 1995 and, under its current remit, stands for another two and a half years, with further reports planned.

Until the Nolan hearings in February and March 1995, there had been very few sustained, sceptical public voices about commercial lobbyists in the UK. Doig's substantial, critical academic work about them (1986, 1990, 1991) has not been echoed by other scholarly writers. Hollingsworth's more popular approach (1991) which looked at MPs and all their outside interests had not been taken up in sustained newspaper or public campaigns. *The Observer, The Guardian* and *The Independent* newspapers have periodically published critical pieces but this did not lead to a public outcry and to popular calls for the regulation of lobbyists or MPs outside interests until the end of 1994. Berry (1993) sought to re-assure the centre-left that commercial lobbyists were not a matter for concern. *PR Week* periodically urged them to self-regulate before they are regulated.

What does exist - and the literature shows has existed immemorially - is a popular suspicion that hired lobbyists are helping the already powerful to become more powerful. This suspicion surfaces in unflattering epithets such as 'corridor creeps' and 'influence peddlers' if the speaker is basically antipathetic; and in 'naughty and nice', 'escort agency' and 'access brokers' imagery if the speaker is more forgiving. Suspicion is also increased when commercial lobbyists charge success fees where they gain financially from the achievement of a pre-defined outcome. This practice is potentially a corrosive influence on standards of public propriety for it makes a direct linkage between the individual behaviour of players in policy-making and their monetary reward and so raises questions about motivation. Commercial lobbyists react to these overall concerns by talking generically about lobbying and lobbyists but by hardly ever using the terms as self-descriptors.

Commercial lobbyists are a small, distinct, *accepted but minor* addition to the *dramatis personae* of UK public policy-making. They cannot be avoided in the policy process because the general right to lobby is admitted and that right is much demanded by the powerful interests in UK society. The interviews demonstrate that both the hirers of lobbyists and the decision-makers who are lobbied accept a role for commercial lobbyists. In 1994, they are too well established to be excluded from the policy-making process for they live off the opportunities and threats generated by active Government in the UK. Ironically, there is work for them when regulation is being created and when regulation is being abolished.

Their contribution to the effectiveness of their clients' lobbying cannot be isolated with any precision. They, therefore, cannot be isolated enough from their clients to identify them as an 'unethical' or 'undemocratic' distortion of the public policy-making process. The agent can hardly be castigated if the liberty of the principal to lobby is constitutionally enshrined and politically unstoppable. And in a sense, this inability to separate out the hired lobbyists works in their favour, given that they are an extra resource for their clients. Like the advertising agency, they *may* be the marginal addition which makes the favourable difference for the client but usually it cannot be demonstrated.

But even after the conclusion above, a residue of concern remains and a conjunction of events in late 1994 led to that popular concern becoming more active, leading to the establishment of the Nolan Committee. The thin stream of concern about hired lobbyists became conflated with broader concerns (appointments to quangos; Ministers taking up jobs in industries they had privatised; the personal behaviours of MPs, their outside interests, the nature of public service today) and together they created an atmosphere of generalised concern about 'sleaze" and standards in public life. Hired lobbyists are too much minor players in public policy-making to ignite this generalised concern: but concern about them within the tinder of the broader concerns above has added critical mass to public unease.

Commercial lobbyists could thank Nolan for confirming their minor status. In a tactical sense of distracting attention, it has suited MPs and Ministers if the public gazed on agents and minors rather than on the principals in policy-making. But Nolan has shifted the spotlight to principals, with its five weeks of hearings in February and March and its first report of 55 recommendations in May 1995 covering MPs, Ministers, civil servants and quango members.

The exact loci of concern about hired lobbyists is to be found in relationships with some MPs and Ministers; and in relationships with some publicly funded bodies and with senior departmental civil servants. This research agrees with Berry (1993; 344), who wrote as lobbyist turned academic, that 'there is no evidence to support the general view that commercial lobbyists have in some way set out to corrupt Parliament or to buy special favours in Whitehall and Westminster'. Earlier, he had found (1991; 248) that 'the level and scale of abuse appears to be minimal'. That is an informal and indirect finding of this research too, although it was not a purpose of this work to investigate such evidence. The evidence given to the Nolan Committee in its early 1995 hearings also tends to support a localised and isolated diagnosis of dubious behaviour by hired lobbyists in particular and all lobbyists in general.

But what mainly encourages the populist and negative view of lobbying and engenders the conditions for occasional Parliamentary abuse (5n) is the lack of sufficient transparency and openness concerning the outside interests of MPs. Progress is slowly being made through clarification and tightening up of the rules of disclosure of the Register of Members' Interests. But the overall impression created since the first Register in 1974 is that Parliament has slowly, partially and unwillingly taken to the public disclosure of its Members' interests. This incremental creep to openness continued for The Register required since March 1994 (6n) MPs to declare the names of any final end client of a lobbying company to which they are linked and whose affairs they actively represent. Nolan recommended, inter alia, that MPs should declare any reward, pecuniary or otherwise, they receive for lobbying on behalf of clients. The Select Committee looking at Nolan could not agree on this requirement (nor on the recommended ban on MPs working for commercial lobbyists) and split on party lines, as did the House itself in the July 20 debate (*The Times*, 20 July; pp 1, 9). The anti-Nolanite MPs argued that disclosure was an invasion of their privacy: to which the most politically potent reply is Doig's argument that MPs should not be paid for this lobbying work as they are already paid to represent interests. The only standard of behaviour to completely allay concerns (e.g. that Members have something to hide from constituents) about the lobbyist link is that MPs should openly represent whatever interest they like but they should take no fees.

The 40 or so MPs (7n) who worked in March 1994 for lobbying firms were doing so in accordance with current House rules on disclosure of Members' outside interests but the rules are inadequate in regard to transparency and openness. These rules do Parliament a disservice and lower its reputation: they also mire the reputation of commercial lobbyists. (8n) Not only can it be argued that MPs are being double paid to represent interests but they are blurring the distinction between MP and paid lobbyist; between their constitutional freedom to represent any interest in the public interest and their political freedom to represent any interest for a fee.

Berry wrote (1993; 345) that 'lobbyists after all must deal with the system as they find it'. He is right to emphasise the passive and secondary position of commercial lobbyists. Their activity is a symptom of and a response to systemic needs, not the cause of those needs. They are in themselves minor role players in policy-making but because they are lobbyists, they can - because of that very designation - be used as a ready-made and convenient smokescreen to distract criticism from more important players and more important relationships. This is the case with the external interests of MPs. It is therefore argued that systemic reform of aspects of MPs relationships with outside interests will benefit the reputation of commercial lobbyists. What is publicly known and publicly acceptable should not tarnish their reputations and may reduce the unfocused concern felt about them.

Lobbyists can also be brought on stage to divert attention away from Ministers, special advisers and civil servants. The research among the latter two suggests another, and possibly more important, area for systemic change. In Whitehall, openness and direct contact by Departments with interests would diminish the demand by those interests for hired lobbyists. In consequence, the interests could in many cases lobby on their own behalf. In a sense, civil servants and commercial lobbyists are in competition for access to interests. The officials want information and the lobbyists want fees. Officials have it in their own power to change their behaviour enough to overcome much of that competition. One Under-secretary wrote that his colleagues were not in contact with lobbyists and he put this down to 'our success in making ourselves so accessible as to ruin the lobbyists' sales pitch' (9n).

The response of Departments is never likely to be co-ordinated enough and their information needs never likely to be simple enough, for the complete ruin of the 'sales pitch' of lobbyists but it could be reduced in its attraction to clients. Again, the point is that commercial lobbyists are a symptom of other more important relationships, i.e. the relationship of principals: the relationship between Government and interest group.

Intermediaries can be justified when the interest is in the private sector but the justification is not obvious when the interest is in the public sector. It is surely a misuse of public money that one part of the public sector has to buy the services of private companies to introduce and represent itself to another part of the same sector.

This research began with the simile of commercial lobbyists as mercenary soldiers for Finer's *Anonymous Empire* of lobbying interests. The Empire still needs them today but invariably as junior officers. Full light on the Empire will show more clearly what these mercenaries do for their hirers and what they want from the politicians and senior civil servants who are the Empire's general staff. And when that light has been shone, they can be looked upon as a small, lightly armed regiment of the Transparent Empire.

Nolan and the future

The Nolan first report and recommendations of 11 May, 1995 and the Government's acceptance within days of their 'broad thrust" appeared to mark the definite end of a period of lobbying which could be characterised as laissez-faire and market-led, done in a foggy confusion of Parliamentary culture and rules about MPs holding paid employment from outside interests. If implemented, the report would usher in a period of explicit regulation about hired lobbyists in particular: MPs should not do paid work for them. It would raise the possibility of a future ban about Members undertaking paid work directly without intermediaries for single interests.

Nolan's first report puts the need to re-assure the public about the probity of public office-holders above concerns about tampering with Parliamentary sovereignty and is the base reason for its proposed regulation. It noted (15, par. 4): "There is no precedent in this century for so many allegations of wrongdoing, on so many different subjects, in so short a period of time." The Committee set itself the task (16, 7) "to rebuild this public confidence" and a major means of doing so, apart from overturning a "culture of moral vagueness" is the recommendation (8) of "procedures and institutions that will deter and detect wrong-doing."

The precise locus of that regulatory regime is - at the moment - the MP/lobbyist relationship looked at from the viewpoint of the MP in relation to the most controversial sub-set of lobbyists, namely firms of commercial lobbyists. This locus is too narrow and insignificant a one for a sturdy regime to be built on and should be regarded as only the first foundation as regulation is extended to the more important Minister/ lobbyist and civil servant/lobbyist relationhips. But Nolan has another two years in which to shine more light on the Anonymous Empire.

Nolan avoided in their first report the one regulation of MPs' behaviour which would have obviated the need for extra regulation of the House. It did not recommend a ban on all paid outside employment by MPs: instead it has recommended (page 7, par. 1) that MPs "should remain free to have paid employment unrelated to their role as MPs." The Committee has made the judgement that a total ban on all paid employment outside the House may not be ahead of public opinion (23, 17 and 29, 51). But it would be disruptive to the business of the House and politically impracticable in terms of being voted for, given that (29, 52) three-fifths of MPs have paid employment or receive funds from sponsors. Instead their first recommendation amounts to a partial ban: it amounts to a ban on paid employment *related to their role as MPs* and is given clear expression in the Committee's third recommendation, the one cutting MPs' links with commercial lobbyists and public relations firms. But this partial ban does not cover two other employment categories for MPs -paid work for single bodies, such as single firms or trade associations and directorships of companies.

The Committee's hesitancy on banning these two employment categories may be seen in their fourth recommendation which calls the House "to set in hand without delay a broader consideration of the merits of Parliamentary consultancies generally . . . " (7,4) and their fourth and fifth recommendations (7, 5 & 6) which calls for a code of conduct and ethics officer for MPs and for more comprehensive and detailed disclosure of interests. Nolan's thinking - viewed from this analysis - is that some paid outside employment for MPs is unacceptable now (working for lobbyists) and that some other categories may become unacceptable subject to public opinion and to carrying a majority of MPs. By summer 1995, it was clear that Parliament would accept certain aspects of Nolan regulation (a code of conduct; a Commissioner for public standards; a more powerful House committee to judge their behaviour; declaration of interests when asking questions) but that a majority could not be found for earnings disclosure and for a ban on working for lobbyists. It appears that the House returns to these issues in autumn 1995 when the reformers will have to press their case that changes are wanted by public opinion and that they do not improperly interfere with the privacy of Members or with Parliamentary Soverneignty, and that they should not be voted for on party lines.

The majority of public debate on Nolan's first report concentrated very substantially on the MP/lobbying link. For lobbyists, relationships with civil servants (for example, Mark Bowler of the Mortgage Lenders' Council said on Today, Radio 4, 17 May, 1995 that he spent "95%" of his time with civil servants) and with Ministers are more important. It is important that public debate widens its focus to include these relationships because they touch on the central issues of access and transparent dealings with public policy players more influential than MPs. From this viewpoint it is reassuring that the Government has accepted that any proposed business careers for recent former Ministers be referred to the extant Advisory Committee on Business Appointments chaired by Lord Carlisle.

Notes

1. The *PR Week* editorial of 17 February, 1994 urged commercial lobbyists to regulate themselves before someone else did. It noted that Parliament has an interest '. . . but lobbyists should remember they are not part of some quasi-statutory organisation or club. They are commercial operators, offering their services for profit'. This is one of the very few public print references to the commercial lobbyists as businesses. Two self-regulatory bodies were set up in autumn 1994: the Association of Professional Political Consultants (letter from the APPC to the author 19 September, 1994) and 'a rival initiative launched jointly by the PRCA and the Institute of Public Relations . . . ' (*PR Week*, 30 September, 1994). The same article also reported a new code of conduct for lobbyists in Brussels.
2. But the terms of references excluded the following class of intermediary: 'The inquiry is not intended to cover the activities on behalf of their clients by members of recognised professions'.
3. *The Independent* p 1 of 20 January, 1994 reported that President of the Board of Trade Michael Heseltine had set up seven deregulation task forces which had recommended 8 regulations to be repealed out of a total of 3, 500 reviewed. Heinz et al. (385) provide an American perspective on the size of regulatory regimes: 'The size of the Federal Register, a rough measure of the degree of regulatory change, almost tripled from about 30,000 pages in 1970 to just under 90,000 in 1980, although the de-regulation of the Reagan era reduced this bureaucratic output to 50,000 by 1985'.
4. The PRCA was reported in *PR Week* 17 February, 1994 to be launching a Register of Professional Parliamentary Advisers, open to its members and non-members. It would list clients and MPs with a pecuniary interest in the lobbyist and be lodged at the House of Commons.
5. The *Observer* carried a report on 9 April, 1989, alleging 'venal MPs' and the payment to MPs of £200 for a written Parliamentary Question. This research did not come across any declared or implied improprieties by lobbyists in relation to MPs. John Cole, then BBC political editor, said on BBC 2 *Newsnight*, 7 March, 1990 that the rules on Members' interests were 'shady at

the edges': a judgement confirmed by embarrassed and angry reaction in the House and broadsheet press to the the Riddick/Tredinnick 'questions for a £1,000' allegations of 10 July, 1994.

6. Information confirmed in a telephone conversation with the Office of the Registrar in the Commons at 12. 30 pm on 4 March, 1994.
7. *PR Week* of 10 March, 1994 listed 43 MPs, all but six Conservatives, with links to PR consultancies and lobbying firms. The source was reported to be the latest edition of the Register of Members' Interests.
8. One of the new self-regulatory body the APPC (see 1 above) has in its code of conduct for members the following: 'Not to place themselves in a position of potential conflict by appointing any MP to their main or any subsidiary or associated board or by paying any retainer or commission to an MP or person acting on their account'. (letter to the author of 19 September, 1994.)
9. Letter from the Department of the Environment to the author, dated 18 February, 1994.

Appendix 1
A note on commercial lobbying and Parliamentary representation

Individual v functional representation?

Lobbyists represent the collectivity of a group interest while MPs represent the individuals in a territory defined as a Parliamentary constituency. Thus Parliament is a formal political institution representing electors and is the focus of attention from group interests. It is relevant therefore to examine the role of commercial lobbyists as an element in the tension between theories of individual representation and functional representation. Judge (1993; 106 -132) has reviewed theories of pluralism, corporatism and policy communities and networks in the light of Parliamentary representation. In that review, commercial lobbyists made an explicit entrance in the form of Ian Greer Associates when the latter were hired by Thames Water Authority (127) 'in order to amplify its opposition within Westminster to the regulatory authority . . .'. The theoretical explanation is the concept of 'issue escape' where there is a breakdown in a policy community/network and there is an exceptional transfer of the issue to Parliament for resolution. Judge also notes the likelihood of backbench revolt in relation to 'issue escape'.

In the light of Judge, it is possible to elaborate the hyphen metaphor of commercial lobbyists. That hyphen operates within theories of functional representation and there is therefore a tension between the hyphen and liberal theories of individual representation. Functional representation draws policy-making away from formal political institutions into policy communities/networks and commercial lobbyists are part of the latter as when they make direct linkages between their client interests and civil servants. But equally they can be part of the apparatus of shifting policy-making back to formal institutions (part of the 'issue escape' team) as when commercial lobbyists organise briefings for MPs (see references to the Sunday trading issue in Chapter Four, 82-83).

Commercial lobbyists in their hyphen role are a business and it is theoretically likely that they will be attracted to interests which can pay and those interests are likely to be the more powerful in society. It is therefore likely that most commercial lobbying will be for business interests and will strengthen the 'special advantages' of business in government decision-making noted by Truman (1951; 259).

Many UK commercial lobbyists - but not all - are discreet about their clients and thus their hyphens are very often invisible ones. This opaqueness mirrors Judge's argument (1993; 113) that British pluralism is different to American in this aspect of openness. To those who still would echo today Finer's famous cry in 1958 and 1965 for 'Light! More Light!' on interest group politics, the torch of transparency should be able to shine on the hyphens.

Theorists such as Judge who argue for the centrality of Parliament in decision-making have to attempt a fusion of Liberal theories of representation which focus on the individual citizen as the object to be represented and functional representation theories such as Whig theory - especially as articulated by Burke - which make a corporate interest the object to be represented. Clearly the individual elector-MP relationship and the lobbyist-MP relationship have a resonance in both Liberal and Whig theories in that the voter and the lobbyist can be one and the same person and Judge (1990; 19-28) has set out some of the similarities and differences. Yet it is possible to argue that the rise of the commercial lobbyist represents - under certain circumstances - a strengthening of interest groups in the politics of Parliament and that the modern role of the MP has to account for the tensions created by these competing theories of representation in Parliament.

A complex reconciliation

For example, historically as MPs have been subjected to more lobbying by interests, they may find themselves overworked and like Hamlet's 'a man to double business bound', they could have their overall effectiveness reduced by both overload and internal contradictory pressures. Increasing volumes of lobbying make the process of reconciling the constituency interests of individual electors, group interests espoused by the MP and the national interest - a reconciliation required by Whig theory - correspondingly more complex in the terms of a coherent role for the MP-as-decision-maker.

Reconciliation becomes more difficult also for another reason: interests can no longer be so exclusively identified with regions and therefore constituencies. For example, MPs in South Wales and Lancashire no longer represent the coal industry in the same way today as they did in the 1950s: then constituency and group interests corresponded. But today, the number of pits in these regions has severely declined.

Now the interests these MPs may be asked to represent could be associated with the whole national territory, e.g. food safety or water pollution. A non-exclusive link between a MP's constituency and the interest represented leads on to a new problematic for the Whig theory to digest. MPs are offered choice about the interests they take up in a way that Burke himself did not have when he sat for the great seaport of Bristol. Modern characteristics of interests - their number, their increasingly pan-national nature, the character of their physical distribution, their transience in a fast changing society - suggests questions about the ability of MPs to adequately brief themselves about interests they represent: choosing interests to represent, developing knowledge and expertise to do so effectively may become harder.

Some empirical light has been shed on these matters by *The Government Report* (1987) which carried out its aforementioned survey among 120 MPs, 28 ministers and 43 current or former officials. Eighty per cent of these MPs complained about the volume of representation they receive and 79% said they have very little time to read and assimilate detailed information. The survey also showed that without exception the MPs sampled are committed to their role of constituency representative and that a third were not interested in representations from outside their constituency and just under half the remainder did not wish to consider national lobbies unless they were represented in their constituency.

Despite the growth in lobbying, the survey found that the majority of MPs wanted lobbyists to pay regard to their (i. e. that of MPs) specialist interests - interests that the majority of the MPs surveyed thought that they should develop. The authors of *The Government Report* are commercial lobbyists themselves and they report the reaction to this type of lobbying as tolerant but with the proviso that government generally expected lobbying to be done directly by clients themselves.

Lobbyists and constituencies

Another limiting factor for the commercial lobbyist is the constituency focus of MPs mentioned above: the implication is that unless the lobbyist can show a substantial link in policy or people with the constituency, then the lobbyist's role is severely hampered. Michael Burrell, managing director of lobbyists Westminster Strategy, (1991; 5), noted this constituency orientation and responded by suggesting that lobbyists should provide opportunities for MPs to meet voters from their constituencies. Former minister Jock Bruce-Gardyne (1986) also noted the power of the constituency link:

> Far more effective for the lobbyists, if more expensive and time-consuming, is pressure through the grass roots. For no MP can safely ignore representations from his voters, however these voters may have been motivated. Nor can the opinions of an MP be discounted when they reflect views pressed upon him by his voters (154).

This constituency constraint on lobbying puts in some doubt the claims of lobbyists, especially commercial ones, that one of their functional strengths is better access to MPs than that enjoyed by non-professionally represented interests. Such a constraint half closes the door to interests and issues which cannot be constituency linked and makes way for the unmediated voice of local electors. Commercial lobbyists perhaps now need to qualify their claims of superior access in the face of the reported strong preference of MPs for constituency-related interests and issues.

In summary, commercial lobbying, representing corporate interests, challenges the liberal theory of Parliamentary representation where the focus is on the individual voter. But it also poses questions for the Whig theory of representation when the sheer number and geographical spread of interests raise questions about the effectiveness of any representation by MPs.

Appendix 2
Attributes of the 'perfect' lobbyist for hire

Introduction

American literature on contract lobbyists (commercial lobbyists) contains several attempts at an attribute-listing analysis of the behaviour of the effective lobbyist (see Milbrath, 1963; Dexter, 1969; Berry, 1984; Drew, 1985) with considerable emphasis on ethical behaviour. Cigler and Loomis (1991; 25) also refer to this literature. A review of the American literature (Jordon and Moloney 1993) has shown that the single most mentioned attribute in the USA was the personal ethics of the lobbyist but this feature did not surface in the meetings for this project. For the decision-makers interviewed here, the focus for ethical concern was themselves in the ways shown in Chapter Seven, rather than the behaviour of lobbyists.

The attributes listed below by decision-maker (some unattributable) were in reply to the question 'describe the behaviour of the perfect hired lobbyist':

Personableness

'He's aware; he knows the system... he's the sort of person with whom you can feel reasonably at ease and that sort of chemistry is very important' (John Mills).

'. . . they need an extensive network of contacts in the political world' (Bill Robinson).

Representations are eased with lobbyists who are known beforehand.

Lobbyists should not press for information which decision-makers are reluctant to give.

'Personal chemistry' with lobbyists was a key to access with the anonymous Under-secretary.

'. . . you need to be personable and friendly and not a bore to have a lunch with because I think a lot of it depends on that and getting the people over a lunch table' (Bill Robinson).

Policy knowledge

'He's someone who . . . knows his patch quite well; who knows that he shouldn't phone you up constantly for trivial information' (John Mills).

'. . . being in a position to tell you something you may not be aware of' (Cliff Grantham).

Avoiding the 'superficial and the presentational' and exhibiting policy knowledge (the anonymous Under-secretary).

'They have looked at an issue from the perspective of Government and not just from their client's interest. They are sensitive to the decision-making process and know what is the right time to raise an issue and with whom' (ex-special adviser).

'The good ones combine that [personableness] with the ability to master the brief of the client . . . ' (Bill Robinson).

'Genuinely deliver access . . . and help point up an argument' (Liz Symons).

Recognition of mutuality

'. . . he recognises that you're quite busy and that if he wants to use you in an effective way, it's got to be two-way and he's got to offer you meetings or visits or conferences which provide a value to the civil servant' (John Mills).

Don't waste time, especially with lunches: have focused, half-hour business meetings instead.

Don't ask decision-makers to meet clients when there is no substantial benefit forthcoming for the former.

A good lunch and the company of beautiful women in exchange for information already available or easily accessible (the anonymous Under-secretary).

Timing

'. . . a firm that approaches you early on is optimising advantage' (Cliff Grantham).

'. . . the bad lobbyist is somebody who elevates an issue too high, too early and ends up just creating . . . aggravation' (ex-special adviser).

'. . . trying to get something on the agenda or off the agenda at the last minute never works' (ex-special adviser).

Contact with client

'. . it's important after the initial contact has been made, to facilitate meetings with clients themselves, possibly with the attendance of consultants there if necessary. And a good follow-up to that meeting' (Cliff Grantham).

'. . . a good lobbyist is somebody whose main involvement is restricted to providing advice, intelligence and analysis and who isn't up front . . . lets the interest they are representing do the talking . . . ' (ex-special adviser).

'. . . to identify who in the client organisation understands the arguments, actually has the personal and other skills to deploy over a lunch table, in a meeting or whatever' (Bill Robinson).

Annotated bibliography

Official publications

House of Commons. (1984-5). Select Committee on Members' Interests. *First Report.* HOC 408.

House of Commons. (1987-88). Select Committee on Members' Interests, *Parliamentary Lobbying.* HC 518-1, -2, -3, -4, -6.

House of Commons. (1990-91). Select Committee on Members' Interests, *Third Report, Parliamentary Lobbying.* HC 586.

House of Commons. (1991-92). *Registration and Declaration of Members' Financial Interests.* HC 326.

Local Government Information Unit. (1986). *Lifting The Lid on Lobbying.* London.

The Nolan Committee. (1994). *Committee on Standards in Public Life: Issues and Questions.* HMSO (Dd. 8389342), London.

Public Relations Consultants Association. (1988). *How to lobby in Britain.* London.

Report of the Committee on Intermediaries. (1950). London, HMSO. Cmnd. 7904.

Books and monographs

Abercrombie, N., Hill, S. & Turner, B. (1980). *The Dominant Ideology Thesis.* London, George Allen & Unwin.
The ruling ideology fractured.

Alderman, G. (1984). *Pressure Groups and Government in Great Britain.* London, Longman.
An early commentator on rise of commercial lobbyists: advocate role but fees hinder wider access.

Baskin, O & Aronoff, C. (1988). *Public Relations The Profession and the Practice.* Iowa, USA; Wm. C. Brown.
PR textbook: lobbying as pluralism.

Beer, S. H. (1982). *Britain Against itself*. London, Faber & Faber.

Berry, J. M. (1984). *The Interest Group Society.* Boston, USA; Little Brown.

Bottomore, T. (1984). *The Frankfurt School.* London, Tavistock Publications.

Bruce-Gardyne, J. (1986). *Ministers and Mandarins.* London, Sidgwick and Jackson.

Bryce, A. (1928). *The American Commonwealth.* New York, USA; Macmillan.
Reminds that popular mistrust of lobbying is historical.

Burnard, P. (1991). 'A method of analysing interview transcripts in qualitative research.' In: *Nurse Education Today.* London, Longman. 461-6.

Burrell, G. & Morgan G. (1979). *Sociological Paradigms and Organisational Analysis.* London, Heinemann.
Paradigmatic underpinnings for methodology.

Canfield, B. & Moore, H. (1973). *Public Relations: Principles, Cases and Problems.* Homewood, USA; Richard Irwin.

Cates, P. (1988). 'Realities of Lobbying and Governmental Affairs.' *In:* Heath, R. L. and Assocs. *Strategic Issues Management.* San Francisco, USA; Jossey Bass. 238-57.
Lobbyist's view from an American state.

Choate, P. (1990). *Agents of Influence.* London, Business Books.
Conspiracy view of 'how Japanese lobbyists are manipulating western political and economic system.'

Cigler, A. & Loomis, B. (1983, 1st. ed; 1986, 2nd; 1991, 3rd.). *Interest Group Politics.* Washington, USA; CQ Press.
Outcomes of US group politics more uncertain.

Cockett, R. (1989). *Twilight of Truth* London, Weidenfeld & Nicolson.
In part, history of Downing St. press office in context of 1930s appeasement/ newspaper relations.

Corbin, J. (1986). 'Coding, writing memos and diagramming.' *In:* Chenitz, W. & Swanson, J. *From Practice to Grounded Theory: Qualitative Research in Nursing.* Menlo Park, USA; Addison Wesley Publications. Ch. 9.
Researcher-friendly account of developing conceptual patterns in qualitative data.

Coxall, W. (1985). *Parties and Pressure Groups.* London, Longman.

Crable, R. E. & Vibbert, S. L. (1986). *Public Relations as Communication Management.* Edina, USA; Bellwether.
Systems approach to public relations.

Cutlip, S., Center, A. & Broom, G. (1985). *Effective Public Relations.* London, Prentice-Hall.

Dahl, R. (1956). *A Preface to Democratic Theory.* Chicago, USA; The University of Chicago Press.

Dahl, R. (1961). *Who Governs?* New Haven, USA; Yale University Press.

Dahl, R. (1971). *Polyarchy: participation and opposition.* New Haven, USA; Yale University Press.

Dahl, R. (1982). *Dilemmas of Pluralist Democracy.* New Haven, USA: Yale University Press.

Dahl, R. (1989). *Democracy and its Critics.* New Haven, USA; Yale University Press.

Davies, M. (1985). *Politics of Pressure.* London, BBC Publications.

deKieffer, D. (1981). *How To Lobby Congress: A Guide For The Citizen Lobbyist.* New York, USA; Dood Mead.
A non-business view of lobbying.

Dexter, L. A. (1969). *How Organisations are represented* in *Washington.* Indianapolis, USA; Bobbs-Merrill.

Doig, A. (1990). *Westminster Babylon.* London, Allison & Busby.
In part, statement of the anti MP-as-lobbyist thesis.

Domhoff, G. (1978). *The Powers That Be.* New York, USA; Random House.

Downs, A. (1957). *The Economic Base of Democracy.* New York, USA; Harper & Row.

Drew, E. (1983; 1st. ed.). 'A Portrait of a Lobbyist.' *In:* Cigler, A. & Loomis, B. *Interest Group Politics.* Washington, USA; CQ Press. 217-50.
The Washington contract lobbyist by an investigative journalist.

Dubs, A. (1989). *Lobbying An Insider's Guide to the Parliamentary Process.* London, Pluto Press.
A manual for voluntary sector lobbying.

Dunleavy, P. & O'Leary, B. (1987). *Theories of the State.* Basingstoke, Macmillan Education.
Review of neo-pluralism.

Eagleton T. (1991). *Ideology.* London, Verso.
Views on the underpinning of qualitative research.

Ellis, N. (1990). *Parliamentary Lobbying: Putting The Business Case to Parliament.* London, Heinemann.
DIY guide.

Finer, S. E. (1958; 1966). *Anonymous Empire: A Study of the Lobby in Great Britain.* London, Pall Mall.
Early evidence of emerging commercial lobbyists.

Gandy, O. (1982). *Beyond Agenda Setting. Information subsidies and Public Policy.* Norwood, USA; Ablex.
Develops thesis that lobbying is information subsidised by powerful interests.

Gandy, O. (1992). 'Public relations and Public Policy: The Structuration of Dominance in the Information Age.' *In:* Toth, E. & Heath, R. *Rhetorical and Critical Approaches to Public Relations.* Hove, Lawrence Erlbaum. 131-63.

Gardner, J. (1991). *Effective Lobbying in the European Community.* Deventer, The Netherlands; Kluwer Law & Taxation.

Gill, J. & Johnson, P. (1991). *Research Methods For Managers.* London, Paul Chapman.

Glaser, B. (1978). *Theoretical Sensitivity.* Mill Hill, USA; The Sociology Press.

Glaser, B. & Strauss, A. (1967). *The Discovery of Grounded Theory.* London, Weidenfeld & Nicolson.

Grant, W & Marsh, D. (1977). *The CBI.* London, Hodder and Stoughton.

Grant, W. (1982). *The political economy of industrial policy.* London, Butterworths.

Grant, W. & Nath, S. (1984). *The politics of economic policy making.* Oxford, Basil Blackwell.

Grant, W. (with Sargent, J.). (1987). *Business and Politics in Britain.* Basingstoke, Macmillan Education.

Grant, W. (1989). *Pressure Groups, Politics and Democracy in Britain.* London, Philip Allan.
Reviews, inter alia, methodological problems of evaluating group effectiveness.

Grant, W. (1993). 'Pressure Groups and the European Community.' *In:* Mazey, S. & Richardson, J. *Lobbying in the European Community.* Oxford, OUP. 27-46.
A view on business as a fissiparous interest.

Grant, W. (1994; 2nd ed.) *Business and Politics in Britain.* Basingstoke, The Macmillan Press.

Grantham, C & Seymour-Ure, C. (1990). 'Political Consultants.' *In: Parliament and Pressure Politics.* Oxford, Clarendon Press. 45-84.
Broad analysis of commercial lobbyists in policy-making.

Green, P. (1992). *Reputation Risk Management.* London, Pitman Publishing.

Greer, I. (1985). *Right to be Heard.* London, Ian Greer Associates.
The commercial lobbyist as polemicist.

Grunig, J. (1989). 'Symmetrical Presuppositions as a Framework for Public Relations Theory.' *In:* Botan, C. & Hazleton, V. Jr. (eds.) *Public Relations Theory.* Hove, Lawrence Erlbaum. 17-44.

Grunig, J. & Hunt, T. (1984). *Managing Public Relations.* New York, USA; Holt, Rinehart & Winston.
First statement of current ruling paradigm in public relations practice and theory.

Grunig, J. & White, J. (1992). 'The Effects of Worldviews on Public Relations Theory and Practice.' *In:* Grunig, J. (ed.) *Excellence in Public Relations and Communication Management.* Hove, Lawrence Erlbaum. 31-64.

Haas, E. (1964). *Beyond the Nation-State.* California, Stanford University Press.

Hague, R. & Harrop, M. (1989). *Comparative Government and Politics.* Basingstoke, Macmillan.

Ham, C. & Hill, M. (1993, 2nd ed.). *The Policy Process in the Modern Capitalist State.* Hemel Hempstead, Harvester Wheatsheaf.

Hamilton, D. et al. (1978). *Beyond the Numbers Game.* London, Macmillan Education.

Hammersley, M. (1989). *The Dilemma of Qualitative Method.* London, Routledge.

Hammersley, M. & Atkinson, P. (1983). *Ethnography: Principles in Practice.* London, Tavistock.

Hayes, M. (1981). *Lobbyists and Legislators.* New Brunswick, Canada; Rutgers University Press.

Heath, R. & Nelson, R. (1986). *Issues Management: Corporate Public Policymaking in an Information Society.* London, Sage.
A corporate justification for lobbying.

Heath, R. and Assocs. (1988). *Strategic Issues Management.* San Fransico, USA; Jossey Bass.
A management theory setting for lobbying.

Heinz, J., Laumann, E., Nelson, R. & Salisbury, R. (1993). *The Hollow Core.* Cambridge, USA; Harvard University Press.
Comprehensive analysis of contract lobbyists in Washington.

Hennessy, P. (1989). *Whitehall.* London, Seeker & Warburg.

Hiebert, R. (1966). *Courtier to the crowd: The story of Ivy Lee and the development of public relations.* Ames, USA; Iowa State University Press.

Hoffman, J. E. (1980). 'Problems of Access in the Study of Social Elites and Boards of Directors.' *In:* Shafer, W. B., Stebbins, R. A., & Turowetz, A. (ed.) *Experiencing Fieldwork.* New York, USA; St. Martins Press. 45-56.

Hollingsworth, M. (1991). *MPs For Hire.* London, Bloomsbury.
Some MPs' connections with commercial lobbyists.

Holtzman, A. (1966). *Interest groups and Lobbying.* New York, USA; Macmillan.

Hughes, J. (1990). *The Philosophy of Social Science.* Harlow, Longman.
Researcher-friendly account of methodological underpinnings.

Jorgensen, D. L. (1989). *Participant Observation.* London, Sage.

Jones, B. et al. (1991). *Politics UK.* Hemel Hempstead, Philip Allan.
Contemporary UK pressure group analysis.

Jordan, G. & Richardson, J. (1987). *Government and Pressure Groups in Britain.* Oxford, OUP.
Early use and review of term commercial lobbyists.

Jordan, G. (ed.) (1991). *The Commercial Lobbyists.* Aberdeen, Aberdeen University Press.
Only dedicated UK text on subject .

Judge, D. (1990). 'Parliament and Interest Representation.' *In:* Rush, M. (ed.) *Parliament and Pressure Politics.* Oxford, Clarendon Press. 18-42.

Judge, D. (1993). *The Parliamentary State.* London, Sage.
In part on how hired lobbyists affect Parliamentary representation.

Key, V. (1968). *Politics, Parties and Pressure Groups.* New York, USA; Crowell.

Kimber, R. & Richardson, J. (eds.) (1974). *Pressure Groups in Britain.* London, Dent.

Kuzel, A. (1992). 'Sampling in Qualitative Inquiry.' *In:* Crabtree, B. & Miller, W. (ed.) *Doing Qualitative Research in Primary Care: Multiple Strategies.* Newbury Park, USA; Sage. 31-44.
Defence of small scale sampling.

Lattimer, M. (1994). *The Campaigning Handbook.* London, Directory of Social Change.

Lesly, P. (ed.) (1991). *The Handbook of Public Relations and Communications.* London, McGraw-Hill.

Lewis, N. 'Corporatism and Accountability: The Democratic Dilemma.' *In:* Crouch, C. & Dore, R. (editors) (1990). *Corporatism and Accountability: Organised Interests in British Public Life.* Oxford, Clarendon Press. 63-101.

Lindblom, C. (1977). *Politics and Markets.* New York, USA; Basic Books.

Marsh, D. & Locksley, G. (1983). 'Capital: The Neglected Face of Power?' *In:* Marsh, D. (ed.) *Pressure Politics.* 53-83. London, Junction Books.
Supportive of Lindblom.

Marquand, D. (1988). *The Unprincipled Society.* London, Jonathan Cape.

McConnell, G. (1966). *Private Power and American Democracy.* New York, USA; Knopf.

McFarland, A. (1976). *Public Interest Lobbies.* Washington, USA; American Enterprise Institute for Public Policy Research.

Milbrath, L. (1963). *The Washington Lobbyists.* Westport, USA; Greenwood Press.

Miller, C. (1987). *Lobbying Government.* Oxford, Blackwell.
Best DIY account of how to be a lobbyist by a practitioner.

Mitchell, A. (1991). 'The View from the Lobbied: A Consumer's Guide.' *In:* Grant, J. (ed.) *The Commercial Lobbyists.* Aberdeen, AUP. 3-12.

Morse J. (1991). 'Strategies for Sampling.' *In:* Morse, J. *Qualitative Nursing Research: A Contemporary Dialogue.* Newbury Park, USA; Sage. 127-45.

Nelson, J. (1989). *Sultans of Sleaze: Public Relations and the Media.* Maine, USA; Common Courage Press.

Norton, P. (1991). 'The Changing Face of Parliament and its Consequences.' *In:* Norton, P. (ed.) *New Directions in Britsh Politics.* Aldershot, Edward Elgar. 58-82.

Olasky, M. (1987). *Corporate Public Relations A New Historical Perspective.* Hove, Lawrence Erlbaum.
Critique of public relations (and lobbying) as free market distortion.

Olsen, M. E. (1970). *Power in Societies.* New York, USA; Macmillan.

Olson, M, Jr. (1965). *The Logic of Collective Action.* Washington, USA; Harvard University Press.

Olson, M, Jr. (1982). *The Rise and Decline of Nations.* New Haven, USA; Yale University Press.

Patton, M. (1980). *Qualitative Evaluation Methods.* London, Sage.

Patton, M. (1990). *Qualitative Evaluation and Research Methods.* London, Sage.
Detailed account of naturalistic interview techniques.

Pearson, R. (1992). 'Perspectives on Public Relations History.' *In:* Toth, E. & Heath, R. (ed.) *Rhetorical and Critical Approaches to Public Relations.* Hove, Lawrence Erlbaum. 111-30.

Perry, K. (1994). *Business and the European Community.* London, Made Simple.
Euro-lobbying channels reviewed.

Pimlott, J. (1951). *Public Relations and American Democracy.* Princeton, USA; Princeton University Press.
Early and superior critique of public relations practice.

Potter, A. (1961). *Organised Groups in British National Politics.* London, Faber.

Pross, A. (1992). *Group Policy and Public Policy.* Don Mills, Ontario; Oxford University Press.
Sympathetic Canadian view of lobbying.

Ricci, D. (1984). *The Tragedy of Political Science.* New Haven, USA; Yale University Press.

Richardson, J. & Jordan, G. (1979). *Governing Under Pressure; The Policy Process in a Post-Parliamentary Democracy.* Oxford, Blackwell.

Richardson, J. (ed.) (1993) *Pressure Groups.* Oxford, Oxford University Press.
Marginal on commercial lobbyists.

Riley, J. (1990). *Getting the Most from Your Data.* Bristol, Technical and Educational Services.

Rivers, P. (1974). *Politics by Pressure.* London, Harrap.

Roberts, G. (1970). *Political parties and pressure-groups in Britain.* London, Weidenfeld and Nicolson.

Ross, R. (1977). *The Management of Public Relations.* New York, USA; John Wiley.
Textbook.

Rush, M. (ed.) (1990). *Parliament and Pressure Groups.* Clarendon Press, Oxford.
Chapter on commercial lobbyists.

Sawatsky, J. (1987). *The Insiders.* Toronto; McClelland & Stewart.
Journalistic account of Ottawa lobbying.

Schatzman, L & Strauss, A. (1973). *Field Research, Strategies for a Natural Sociology.* New York, USA; Prentice Hall.

Schlozman, K. & Tierney, J. T. (1986). *Organised Interests and American Democracy.* New York, USA; Harper Row.

Shaw, M. (1990). 'Members of Parliament.' *In:* Rush, M. (editor) *Parliament and Pressure Politics.* Oxford, Clarendon Press. 85-116.

Silverman, D. (1985). *Qualitative Methodology.* London, Gower.
Researcher-friendly introduction to research methods.

Simons, H. (1981). 'Conversation Piece: the Practice of Interviewing in Case Study Research.' *In:* Adelman, C. (ed.) *Uttering, Muttering.* Oxford, Grant McIntyre (now Blackwell Scientific). 27-50.

Smith, H. (1988). *Power Game.* New York, USA; Random House.

Smythe, D. (1981). *Dependency Road: Communications, Capitalism, Consciousness and Canada.* Norwood, USA; Ablex.

Stewart, J. (1958). *British Pressure Groups.* London, Martin Robertson.

Strauss, A, & Corbin, J. (1990). *Basics of Qualitative Research.* London, Sage.

Truman, D. (1951). *The Governmental Process.* New York, USA; Alfred Knopf.

Van Schendelen, M. (editor) (1993). *National Public and Private EC Lobbying.* Aldershot, Dartmouth.
Marginal on commercial lobbying.

Vogel, D. (1989). *Fluctuating Fortunes.* New York, USA; Basic Books.
'. . . business does make its own political history, but . . . in circumstances that are largely beyond its control.' (292)

Wenner, L. (1990). *US Energy and Environmental Groups: Institutional Profiles.* New York, USA; Greenwood Press.
Business dominance 'due to the belief in free enterprise embraced by most Americans.'

White, J. (1991). *How to Understand and Manage Public Relations.* London, Business Books.

Whiteley, P. F. and Winyard, S. J. (1987). *Pressure for the Poor.* London, Metheun.

Willis, D. & Grant, W. (1987). 'The United Kingdom: Still a Company State.' *In:* Van Schendelen, M & Jackson, R. (eds) *The Politicisation of Business in Western Europe.* London; Croom Helm. 158-83.
Government/business relations surveyed where business is responsible for economic management - 'the company state'.

Wilson, G. (1991). 'Contract Lobbying in the USA.' *In:* Jordan, G. (ed.) *The Commercial Lobbyists.* Aberdeen, Aberdeen University Press. 65-75.
Critique that cost makes US contract lobbyists an asymmetrical influence in decision-making.

Wilson, G. K. (1985). *Business and Politics.* Basingstoke, Macmillan.

Wilson, G. K. (1990). *Interest Groups.* Oxford, Basil Blackwell.
Notes emergence of American contract lobbyists as separate industry.

Wilson, M. (1979). 'Variety in Social Science Research.' *In: DE 304, Block1.* Milton Keynes, Open University Press. 3-25; 80-127.

Wiseman, J. & Aron, M. (1972). *Field Projects in Sociology.* London, Transworld Publishers.

Wittenberg, E. & Lesly, P. (1991). 'Working with Federal Government.' *In:* Lesly, P. (ed.) *The Handbook of Public Relations and Communications.* Hemel Hempstead, McGraw-Hill. 74-85.
Lobbying as free market lubrication.

Wittenberg, E. & Wittenberg, E. (1989). *How to Win in Washington.* Oxford, Blackwell.

Wolpe, B. (1990). *Lobbying Congress How the System Works.* Washington, USA; Congressional Quarterly Inc.

Wootton, G. (1970). *Interest-Groups.* New Jersey, USA; Prentice Hall.
Short history of PR development in US and UK. Ambiguous on influence of business.

Wootton, G. (1975). *Pressure Groups in Britain, 1720-1970: An Essay in Interpretation with Original Documents.* London, Allen Lane.

Worsley, P. (1970). *Introducing Sociology.* London, Penguin Press.

Unpublished theses

Berry, S. P. (1991). *The growth and development of the commercial lobbying industry in Britain during the 1980s.* PhD thesis, London University. London.
A portrait good on systemic concerns raised about hired lobbyists.

York, K. (1986). *Lobbying, Information and Welfare.* PhD thesis, University of Michigan. Ann Arbor, USA.
Information from lobbyists can be social good.

Journal articles, papers and booklets

Berry, S. P. (1992). 'Lobbyists and Their Techniques.' *In: Parliamentary Affairs.* 45 (2), 220 - 32.
Includes insights from a former lobbyist turned academic.

Berry, S. P. (1993). 'The rise of the professional lobbyist: a cause for concern?' *In: Political Quarterly.* July, 344-51.
The case for reforming MPs' relationships; not lobbyists'.

British Interest Group Project. (1992). *What is studied when pressure groups are studied?* Aberdeen, Aberdeen University Press.

Bruce, A. (1994). 'Public Affairs in "Tomorrow's Company".' *For: The Management of Public Affairs* seminar. Oxford, Templeton College. 9 September.
Quotes survey that medium-size companies lobby via trade associations.

Burrell, M. (1991). 'Lobbying the Regions.' *Public Relations.* 5 January. London, Institute of Public Relations.
The case for the constituency route for lobbyists.

Butler, A, & Smith, D. (1986). *Lobbying in the British Parliament.* London, Public Relations Consultants' Association.

Casey, M. (1991). *The Power of the Lobbyist: Regulation and Vested Interest.* Edinburgh, The David Hume Institute.
A view from a former Under-Secretary turned lobbyist.

The Communication Group plc (1994). *Your Guide to Westminster and Whitehall.* London, The Communication Group.

Doig, A. (1986). 'Access to Parliament and the Rise of the Professional Lobbyist.' *Public Money* March. 39-43.

Doig, A. (1986 a). 'Influencing Westminster: Registering the Lobbyists.' *Parliamentary Affairs.* Vol. 39, 517 - 35.
Two critical views from the persistent critic.

Doig, A. (1994) 'Full Circle or Dead End? What Next for The Select Committee on Members' Interests?' *Parliamentary Affairs.* July, 356-73.

Elkin, S. (1989). 'The Political Theory of American Business.' *In: Business In The Contemporary World.* Spring, 25-37.
A statist view: business and government in mutual control create the 'commercial republic.'

Galle, M. (1992). 'Soaring Growth of Lobbying Dangerous.' *Newsletter European Association of Public Relations Education and Research.* Vol. 1, 2; 25-6. Ghent, Belgium; CERP Education.
An early, if not the first, proposal to regulate EU lobbying.

Gibbs, D., et al. (1994). 'Taking the State Back Out: Reflections on a Tautology.' *In: Contentions.* Vol. 3; 3; 115-37.

The Government Report. (1987). The Public Policy Consultants. London.
A rare survey of how Government sees commercial lobbyists from the viewpoint of process.

Grant, W. (1984). 'Pressure Groups and the Policy Process.' *Social Studies Review.* March, 156-9.

Grant, W. (1990). 'Insider and Outsider Pressure Groups.' *Social Studies Review.* January, 107-11.

Grantham, C. (1989). 'Parliament and Political Consultants.' *Parliamentary Affairs.* Vol. 42, 503-18.
Useful views from a lobbyist turned special adviser.

The Harris Research Centre. (1995). *Parliamentary Perceptions of the Lobbying Industry.* June. London.

Haug, M. & Koppang, H. (1993). *Lobbying and PR From a research project on the PR Department's role in company lobbying. At:* CERP Autumn Conference. Nov. 6. France, Strasbourg.
In part, a parallel project from a Norwegian stance.

Holbeche, B. (1986). 'Policy and Influence: MAFF and the NFU.' *In: Public Policy and Administration.* Vol. 1, 3; 40-7.

Howell, K. (1995). *A Neo-functionalist Analysis of the European Life Insurance Industry.* Bournemouth University, Financial Services Research Centre.

Hull, R. (1991). *Presentation to the Seminar on Pressure Groups and Policy Making in the European Community.* May 17. Oxford, Nuffield College.
Insights from former EU official.

Hunt, J & Nash, T. (1986). 'Lobbying: Art, Craft or Profession.' *Chief Executive.* Feb, 14-6.

Jordan, G. (1989). 'Inside Lobbying: the British Version.' *Political Studies.* Vol. 37; 1, 107-13.

Jordan, G. & Moloney, K. (1993). 'Why are Lobbyists Successful: God, Background or Training?' *For: Symposium at LSE, March 24, organised by Politics Department, Newcastle University and by Hansard Society.*

Laptev, M. (1993). *Background Note to the EC Institutions.* London, Charles Barker.
A lobbyist's view.

Loveridge, R. (1990). 'Triangulation - or how to survive your choice of business school PhD course.' *Graduate Management Research.* Winter, 18-25.

Mackey, S. (1994). *Controversy in Town Hall Public Relations.* Arts Faculty, Deakin University, Warrnambool, Victoria, Australia.
Introduction to public relations paradigms.

MacMillan, K. (1991). *The Management of European Public Affairs.* European Centre for Public Affairs. Oxford, Templeton College. Occasional Paper No. 1, July.
Commercial lobbyists as gap-fillers in company campaigns.

Mancuso, M. (1993). 'The Ethical Attitudes of British MPs: A Typology.' *In: Parliamentary Affairs.* Vol. 46, 2; 179-91.

Manley, J. (1983). 'Neopluralism - a class analysis of pluralism I and pluralism II.' *American Political Science Review.* Vol. 77, 371-83.

Marsh, I. (1988). 'Interest Groups and Policy Making.' *In: Parliamentary Affairs.* Vol. 41, 4; 469-89.

Mazey, S. & Richardson, J. (1992). 'British Pressure Groups in the European Community: The Challenge of Brussels.' *In: Parliamentary Affairs.* Vol. 45, 1; 92-107.

Mazey, S. & Richardson, J. (1992). 'Environmental Groups and the EC: Challenges and Opportunities. *In: Environmental Politics.* Vol. 1, 4; 109-28.

McLaughlin, A., Jordan, G., & Maloney, W. (1993). 'Corporate Lobbying in the European Community.' *In: Journal of Common Market Studies.* June. Vol. 31. 2.

Miller, C. (1987). 'Lobbying: New Trends in the UK.' *In: Contemporary Record.* Spring, 13-15.

Miller, C. & Hayes, R. (1984). *Lobbyists: Public Service or Expensive Sham.* London, Bow Group.

Moloney, K. & Jordan, G. (1994). 'Why Companies Hire Lobbyists.' Unpublished paper, *Department of Marketing, Advertising and Public Relations,* Bournemouth University.

Moore, P. (1991). *A Market in Influence? A Study of the Personnel, Clientele, Methodology and Effectivenesss in a Leading UK Government Relations Consultancy.* London, Brunel, University of West London, Government Dept.
Informative analysis of business aspects of one lobbying firm.

Norton, P. & Grantham, C. (1986). 'The Hyphen in British Politics? Parliament and Professional Lobbying.' *British Politics Group Newsletter.* no. 45, 4-8.
The hyphen function.

Pedler, R. (1994). *The Management of Public Affairs.* Oxford, Templeton College.
Survey evidence - widespread hirings of lobbyists for diverse support roles.

Post, J. (1982). 'The Public Affairs Function in American Corporations.' *Long Range Planning.* April. Vol. 15, 12-21.

Presthus, R. (1974). 'Interest Groups and Lobbying: Canada and the US.' *Annals of the American Academy of Political and Social Science.* 44-57.
Cultural variation and effectiveness perceptions.

Richardson, J. (1990). 'Government and Groups in Britain: Changing Styles.' *Strathclyde Papers on Government and Politics.* Glasgow.

Rush, M. (1990). 'Lobbying Parliament.' *Parliamentary Affairs.* April. Vol. 43; 2, 141-48.

Rush, M. (1993). 'Registering the Lobbyists: Canadian Experience and a British Proposal.' *For: Symposium at LSE, March 24, organised by Politics Department, Newcastle University and by Hansard Society.*
Detailed review of one Parliament's experience of lobbyist regulation.

Sargent, J. (1991). 'In Defence of a Commercial Approach to Lobbying.' *For: Pressure Groups and Policy Making in the European Workshop.* 17-19 May. Nuffield College, Oxford.

Smith, M. (1986). 'The lobbyist's business.' *Government and Industry.* Issue 18; 3.1, 01-19.

Smith, M. (1992). *Lobbying.* London, Government Policy Consultants.

Smith, M. J. (1990). 'Pluralism, Reformed Pluralism and Neopluralism: the Role of Pressure Groups in Policy-Making.' *Political Studies.* Vol. 38, 302-22.

Thomas, C. & Hrebenar, R. (1990). 'A New Look at Lobbyists and the Lobbying Community in The American States.' *For: American Political Science Association Annual Meeting,* 30 August-2 September. Hilton Hotel, San Franciso, USA.
Commercial lobbyists in the US states.

Thomas, C. & Hrebenar, R. (1991a). 'The Regulation of Interest Groups and the Lobbying Community in the Fifty States: Some Preliminary Findings.' *For: Midwest Political Science Association Annual Meeting.* The Palmer House Hotel, Chicago, USA. 18-20 April.

Thomas, C. & Hrebenar, R. (1991b). 'Lobbyists in the Fifty States: The Results of Recent Research.' *For: Western Political Science Association.*

Turk, J. (1985). 'Information Subsidies and Influence.' *In: Public Relations Review.* Vol. 11, 3; 10-25. Maryland, USA; University of Maryland.
Fieldwork on the Gandy thesis.

Van Der Straten Waillet, C. (1989). 'Lobbying the European Community. *In: International Public Relations Review.* Vol. 12, No. 3; 10-15.

Wedgewood, D. (1987). 'Dialogue with Whitehall and Westminster.' *For: Conference on Corporate Communications*, London International Press Centre, 15 October. Organised by Tolloy Conferences.
A lobbying definition and insights from a lobbyist.

Whiteley, P. & Winyard, S. (1983). 'Influencing Social Policy: The Effectiveness of the Poverty Lobby in Britain.' *In: Journal of Social Policy,* January, Vol. 12, 1; 1-26.

Whiteley, P. & Winyard, S. (1988). 'The Poverty Lobby in British Politics.' *In: Parliamentary Affairs.* April, Vol. 41, 2; 195-208.
Both above reviews of non-business lobbying.

Windsor, D. (1989). 'The Theory of Business Politics.' *For: American Political Science Association Annual Meeting,* Atlanta, USA, 31 August-3 September. Section 32.
A review of business politics models.

Newspapers, Magazines, Yearbooks and Directories

Cabinet Office (1993, 1994). *The Civil Service Year Book.* London, HMSO.

Dod's Parliamentary Companion. (1987, 1989, 1993). Hurst Green, Dod's Parliamentary Companion.

The Economist. (1989). 'Corporate eyes, ears and mouths.' 10 March: 105-6.

Greatorex, W. (1989). ' Is Your MP in Somebody's Pocket.' *The Reader's Digest.* January, 34, 31-6.

Helm, S. (1991). 'Private Words on Public Matters.' *The Independent* . London. 18 November, 23.
Lobbyists as private sector diplomats.

Howard, A. (1989). 'The Unsavoury Enemies of Democracy.' *The Independent.* 23 September, 19.

The Independent. (1993). 'Clampdown on Senators' gifts.' 8 May, 10.

Marr, A. (1992). 'A giant U-turn to get the party back on track.' *The Independent* 19 November, 25.

Marketing (1984). 'The Keys to the House.' 10 May, 30.

Observer. (1989). 'A £10m Trade in Influence.' 9 April.

Observer Magazine. (1990). 'Something To Declare: The Inside Guide To MPs Outside Interests.' 14 October.

PR Week. (1989). 'The Lobby falls foul of its "booze and bribes" image.' 20 April.

PR Week (1990). 'Lobbying begins to lose out.' 7 September.

PR Week (1990). 'Weeding out Whitehall Waste.' 18 October.

PR Week (1993). 'Calling the House to order.' 28 January.

PR Week (1993). 'CERP proposes EC lobby controls.' 18 February.

PR Week (1993). 'Darkness before the Dawn.' 29 April.

PR Week (1993). 'Out of the shadows.' 29 April.

PR Week (1993). Letters. 13 May.

PR Week (1993). Special Report Lobbying. 7 October.

PR Week (1994). 'No reason to hide.' 17 February.

PR Week (1994). 'PRCA Registers Concern.' 17 February.

PR Week (1994). 'Vote of Confidence for MPs.' 10 March.

PR Week. (1994). 'High demand for lobbying skills.' 26 May .

PR Week. (1994). 'Brussels lobbyist code of conduct launched.' 30 September.

PR Week. (1995). 'Lobbying is too important to leave to the "pros"'. 30 March.

PR Week. (1995). 'The nasty face of pressure groups.' 7 April.

PR Week. (1995). 'Seven lobbyists to join APCO UK start-up.' 14 April.

The PRCA Public Relations Year Book. (1989). London, Financial Times Business Information.

Russell, L. & Atack, S. (editors). (1991). *The Directory of Public Affairs and Government Relations.* London, Berkeley Press.

Shipley, P. (1979, 2nd ed.) *Directory of Pressure Groups and Representative Organisations.* London, Bowker.

Soames, E. in Faulder, C. (1984). The politics of persuasion. *Good Housekeeping.* April.

The Times 1000 1992-3. Times Books.

The Times. (1993). Obituaries. 11 June,17.